Doing Critical
Management Research

SAGE SERIES IN MANAGEMENT RESEARCH

SERIES EDITORS

RICHARD THORPE
Department of Management
Manchester Metropolitan University

MARK EASTERBY-SMITH
Centre for the Study of Management Learning
The Management School, Lancaster University

The *Sage Series in Management Research* contains concise and accessible texts, written by internationally respected authors, on the theory and practice of management and organizational research. Each volume addresses a particular methodological approach or set of issues, providing the reader with more detailed discussion and analysis than can be found in most general management research texts. These books will be indispensable for academics, research students and managers undertaking research.

Doing Critical Management Research

Mats Alvesson and Stanley Deetz

SAGE Publications
London • Thousand Oaks • New Delhi

SAGE Publications Ltd
6 Bonhill Street
London EC2A 4PU

SAGE Publications Inc
2455 Teller Road
Thousand Oaks, California 91320

SAGE Publications India Pvt Ltd
32, M-Block Market
Greater Kailash – I
New Delhi 110 048

British Library Cataloguing in Publication data

A catalogue record for this book is available from the British Library

ISBN 0 7619 5332 9
ISBN 0 7619 5333 7 (pbk)

Library of Congress catalog card number available

Typeset by SIVA Math Setters, Chennai, India
Printed in Great Britain by Redwood Books, Trowbridge, Wiltshire

Contents

Acknowledgements

Some parts of Chapters 2 and 4 have appeared in an earlier version in M. Alvesson and S. Deetz 'Postmodernism and critical theory approaches to organization studies' in Clegg, S. et al. (eds) *Handbook of Organization Studies*, London: Sage 1996. Parts of Chapters 3 and 5 draw upon M. Alvesson 'Leadership studies: from procedure and abstraction to reflexivity and situation', *Leadership Quarterly*, 1995, vol. 7, no. 4, pp. 455–85. We are grateful to the publishers for the right to use these materials.

List of figures and tables

Figures

Tables

1

An introduction to critical research

Critical research methods articulate a relationship between two quite diverse intellectual streams. One is a critical tradition actualized today in both critical theory and postmodernist work. Both critical theory and postmodernism are oriented, in albeit different ways, to questioning established social orders, dominating practices, ideologies, discourses, and institutions. The other is qualitative or what might more appropriately be called 'interpretive' research that aims at understanding the micro-practices of everyday life.

Critical research generally aims to disrupt ongoing social reality for the sake of providing impulses to the liberation from or resistance to what dominates and leads to constraints in human decision making. Typically critical studies put a particular object of study in a wider cultural, economic and political context, relating a focused phenomenon to sources of broader asymmetrical relations in society, for example class, late capitalism, affluent/post scarcity society. Recently more micro-oriented forms of critical study have been developed; while these still consider the wider social context, more emphasis is placed on the specific practices that reproduce asymmetry in will formation, decision making, and – more broadly – the construction of social reality.

Qualitative research has become associated with many different theoretical perspectives, but is typically oriented to the inductive study of socially constructed reality, focusing on meanings, ideas and practices, taking the native's point of view seriously without questioning either the wider context of it or the processes forming it. Here the empirical description and understanding of a delimited part of existing social reality is the prime objective, sometimes supplemented with ambitions to stimulate modest social change, through moderate questioning of current practices and/or providing a knowledge basis for social engineering.

Neither of these streams are homogeneous but include a number of diverse orientations, some of which are to be discussed later in this book. Here it is of interest to emphasize the difference between (a) a critical scholarly orientation typically being inspired by philosophical ideas and theoretical ambitions to develop basic ways of understanding the world somewhat distanced from the variation and low-abstract nature typically encountered in empirical settings, and (b) qualitative research normally downplaying theory as a crucial point of departure for the benefit of the careful and nuanced empirical study of local phenomena. Many of the most influential critical theorists, such as Habermas and Giddens, are known for their lack of interest in conducting empirical work. One intention of this book is to show what can be gained by doing interpretive studies grounded in a critical social philosophy and what critical theory can gain through more careful empirical work.

Little is present in critical theory that encourages a move from in-depth questioning orientations and somewhat distant theoretical debates to enter empirical work in 'the field'. As will be reviewed in greater detail, works on critical method generally tend either to express quite general critical theory methodological principles that have a general relevance for but rather little specific bearing on fieldwork (for example, Morrow, 1994), or to follow mainly conventional ideas about qualitative method and then add specific elements from critical theory without the latter making a strong impact on the full project (for example, Thomas, 1993). What is needed, we think, is a more ambitious rethinking of how the basic ideas of critical theory, postmodernism and related critical orientations – such as poststructuralism and feminism – may inspire qualitative research. Or, to start with the latter, how methodology may benefit from an ambitious incorporation of critical-philosophical insights.

This book aims to go some way along this line. We say some way because there is never any particularly tight relationship between a certain theoretical orientation and ideas on methodology (nor is the latter, as is sometimes claimed, independent of the former). Flexibility and open-mindedness are necessary virtues when playing with this relationship, considering when to loosen and when to tighten it. Rather than a fully fledged and distinct critical methodology for management/social research, we are proposing a relatively loose framework characterized by a set of comments, reflections and possible guidelines for qualitative management research with a critical edge.

The book is about how one may think creatively, reflectively and critically in management (and other social) research; it is not a 'cookbook' on how to dress properly to gain access and make interviewees feel relaxed, manage the tape recorder, take notes or code interview transcripts. This is not to say that the latter issues are insignificant. On the contrary, mastering the technicalities and developing practical skills in conducting interviews and observations are important parts of any successful research project. Many of these issues are, however, of a general character and not specific to critical research. They are well treated in the available literature (for example, Easterby-Smith et al., 1991). The development of an intellectual position regarding research activities and the researcher's place in organizational development and wider social needs is a necessary precursor to these more technical issues.

While often implicit, kept in the background, marginalized or even denied, in all research philosophical, theoretical and political assumptions and issues are central. At one time, proponents of qualitative research claimed that they developed theory and results on a stable empirical ground, that social reality was mirrored in the research project's empirical and conceptual outcome (for example, Glaser and Strauss, 1967). Aided by the careful hand of the researcher, data are seen as speaking for themselves or showing the way to theoretical results. But few today would make such a claim. Theoretical assumptions are central, as a careful critical scrutiny of any research project will show. Such assumptions enter into research in ways different from how they enter into more normative and quantitative forms of research, but they are no less important. Political and ethical questions are impossible to avoid in any type of research. Our primary choice is not whether theory and values, but whose and which. Critical research puts these issues in the forefront and sees them as central for both reflection and creativity (Alvesson and Sköldberg, 1999).

The nature of this volume

This book is a moderately advanced work. While we intend it as an introduction to critical research methods, it is not an introductory text for the novice; we presuppose some familiarity with qualitative research methods. We do not provide comprehensive overviews of available methods, nor do we explain or give advice about how they can be skilfully applied. A useful introductory text is Easterby-Smith et al. (1991). A comprehensive, slightly more advanced coverage of the entire field of qualitative methods can be found in Denzin and Lincoln (1994). We intend to begin where these texts leave off. We hope to provide students and professionals who already have a basic knowledge about critical social science and qualitative methods a way to practice these understandings together. This work thus not only complements more typical treatments of qualitative methods but also more conceptual works on critical management theory (for example, Alvesson and Willmott, 1992, 1996; Deetz, 1995a).

The book, however, is not intended to be of interest only to critically oriented individuals concerned with management or related areas such as organizational sociology or corporate communication. Also people seeing themselves as more simply qualitative or interpretive than distinctly critical or postmodernist may find most of the book to be relevant as ways to think through their own theoretical commitments and research practices. In addition, people interested in topics other than management and organizations – for example, social interactions in other formal institutional settings such as education, social work, prisons, hospitals/health care – should find most of what is said here of great relevance. In other words, neither 'critical' nor 'management' are highly exclusive concerns warranting a cutting off from more general concerns in interpretive work or in studying a broad range of social phenomena.

What is method?

The question may be answered in many ways. We spare the reader a review of all the possible answers, ranging from detailed techniques to gather data to broad strategies for doing research projects. Thinking of 'method' in highly rational terms – design, control, procedure, validity, reliability – where the research results are produced in a neat and orderly manner is less common today, especially among qualitative researchers. Increasingly most researchers are aware of the complexities involved. For example, Fontana and Frey argued that:

> no matter how organized the researcher may be, he or she slowly becomes buried under a growing mountain of field notes, transcripts, newspaper clippings, and tape recordings. Traditionally, readers were presented with the researcher's interpretation of data, cleaned and streamlined and collapsed in rational, noncontradictory accounts. More recently, sociologists have come to grips with the reflexive, problematic, and, at times, contradictory nature of data and with the tremendous, if unspoken, influence of the researcher as an author. (1994: 372)

We view method broadly and see it as a mode and a framework for engaging with empirical material. Less significant than the particular techniques or procedures are the ways in which the researcher approaches the subject matter, the questions asked and the answers sought, the lines of interpretations followed and the kind of descriptions and insights produced. Method is how one develops research questions, how one attends to social reality, what vocabularies are used in clarifying and reinterpreting what emerges in the voices of the members of the site community. Method is also how one achieves a level of systematicity and logic in the way empirical material is treated, for example principles for how to cope with the ambiguities and contradictions in interview statements, observations and other empirical material. Method connects theoretical frameworks with the production and productive use of empirical material. It involves careful and systematic consideration of what empirical material may tell us. Method is thus not primarily a matter of 'data management' or the mechanics and logistics of data production/processing, but is a reflexive activity where empirical material calls for careful interpretation – a process in which the theoretical, political and ethical issues are central.

Our specific interest in organizational management

Management can be defined as a function, a set of activities or a profession. It is about coordinating and controlling work and operations in a formal organizational setting. Management means having responsibility for the accomplishment of certain results. Sometimes management and the persons who primarily are working with such tasks, that is managers, are seen as being the opposite of operations (meaning the direct production of goods or services) and the people who actually do these things. Management is sometimes defined as the carrying out of tasks through other people.

Upon closer reflection, the relationship between managers and non-managers is less clear-cut. Managers also 'work', they do things; and workers 'manage' in the sense that they plan, decide, solve problems, coordinate, take initiatives, exercise influence, and so on. Especially in knowledge-intensive work and in modern 'flat' organizations, a rigid division of labour between brain and control work and manual and operative work is not very illuminating. Management may be seen as comprising activities that shape the overall orientation of an organization and exercise influence on people in the organization and the organizational environment – more specifically consisting of nature, animals, customers, tax payers, competitors and other parts of the public.

Management as a concept and category is a social construction filled with history and political motives. What management is and what managers do cannot be answered very well in the abstract; there are both historical and organizational variations and the concept itself is a social resource put to many practical uses. There is considerable agreement that conventional, universal statements of what management is about and what managers do – planning, organizing, coordinating and controlling – do not tell us very much about organizational reality, which is often messy, ambiguous, fragmented and political in character (Mintzberg, 1975; Weick, 1979; Jackall, 1988; Watson, 1994).

Management research aims to develop knowledge about the management of organizations. Sometimes management is defined very broadly, also including aspects of the operations of companies that have little to do with organization and people, for example finance, logistics and parts of strategic management, marketing and accounting. In the present book, we limit the definition to include those parts of management oriented to organizational aspects – though relatively broadly defined. This means that the process aspects of strategies, the customer–employee interaction aspects of marketing and the behavioural dimensions of accounting are included in the management concept.

One may ask what is distinctive about management research? Are there methodological principles specific to the field or could one use any general or sociological methodology for studying managerial and organizational phenomena? In principle, one could do the latter. Actually, there are very few fields in social science which call for a unique and exclusive methodology. Ideas on questionnaires, interviewing, experimental design, archive studies, use of tests or scales, and making observations typically transgress academic divisions of labour. So do management studies, for that matter. It is not a very well-integrated field, but typically draws upon theories and includes the study of topics with origins in other areas: psychology, sociology, political science, communication, anthropology, economics, etc. These other areas may often be divided up in other ways. Sociology could, for example, vanish if one chooses to see organizational sociology as organization theory, social psychology as a subfield to psychology or a field of its own, stressed cultural studies and gender studies as specific disciplines, etc. There may be bureaucratic, political and identity reasons for emphasizing division of labour – and professional associations and group belongingness – but intellectually it is clear that progress is typically achieved by people not easy to fit into well-established academic structures and boundaries: Marx, Freud, Weber, the Frankfurt School and Foucault come to mind.

Nevertheless, there are some specific circumstances worth considering when studying management phenomena. Easterby-Smith et al. (1991) mention the eclecticism of managerial work – working across boundaries and including technical, economic, political, psychological, cultural and communicative types of work. They also stress the work situation of managers – they are powerful and busy, which may mean that they do not want to fill in long questionnaires or spend time on long in-depth interviews; the concentrated interview may be the only technique available. A perhaps more significant reason for considering the specifics of management research is the manager's capacity or desire to utilize research projects for their own purposes – either by communicating favourable impressions and images through the researcher and his or her publication or through utilizing the research results for accomplishing changes. The researcher may function as a PR agent or a consultant irrespective of whether he or she is aware of it or wants it. Thus we encounter the political nature of management research. Studying management means studying asymmetrical relations of power, including dependencies. A study typically concentrates on or at least involves actors having formal and symbolic resources for the exercise of non-democratic, systematic forms of control over organizational participants, and indirectly over other groups and non-human objects (animals, nature).

Another issue is that management typically is about the running of organizations that are exposed to market competition and that issues of economic performance are important. So is the case for companies in capitalist countries as well as for many other organizations, in particular public ones exposed to 'market-like' mechanisms. Management studies must appreciate the specific features of the company as an institution and the kind of constraints following from this.

Of course, management research is not entirely unique, even in this last respect – competition and the possibility of discontinuation also characterize other social institutions – and most of what we are saying in this book is of general relevance in social research. Nevertheless, there are some issues of particular interest to this field of inquiry and we devote much attention to how one may reflect upon the study of core management phenomena, such as leadership and organizational culture.

Some management researchers think that this field of inquiry should develop knowledge for managers so that they can improve organizational performance. This would make management research distinct in two senses: (a) being governed by a specific interest and externally anchored criteria of what is valuable and relevant knowledge, and (b) restricting critical reflection on appropriate goals and considerations for research and subordinating the enterprise to that which is believed to be appealing to a specific interest group in society. We certainly see managers – a most heterogeneous group – as a category with a legitimate interest in management knowledge, but there are other interests and groups of people which may have an interest in such knowledge. Management and organizational functioning deserve to be studied from a wide range of angles, including those drawing attention to the less rosy aspects of such activities and reporting outcomes of a mixed nature for those directly and indirectly affected (Alvesson and Willmott, 1992, 1996; Deetz, 1992, 1995a). This brings us to the task of critical research.

Critical social science

All research is, in a sense, critical. The rule is that one does not accept any claims without careful monitoring of the reasons and other kinds of support for them. Critical checking of flaws and errors are a vital part of any research project and the evaluations done within the research community. Before a Ph.D. is granted or a text published, representatives of the research community critically scrutinize drafts and give feedback. The researcher is helped to minimize problems. This kind of critical checking is vital in all research.

Critical social science goes, however, far beyond fault-finding in this sense. Critical social science develops a specific form of critical thinking akin to that summarized by Brookfield (1987). Brookfield suggests four components:

1 identifying and challenging assumptions behind ordinary ways of perceiving, conceiving, and acting;
2 recognizing the influence of history, culture, and social positioning on beliefs and actions;
3 imaging and exploring extraordinary alternatives, ones that may disrupt routines and established orders;
4 being appropriately sceptical about any knowledge or solution that claims to be the only truth or alternative.

According to this view, critical social science engages more in critique than criticism; it aims beneath the ordinary complaints and usual oppositions to explore and discuss assumptions and deeper social formations. Critique here refers to the examination of social institutions, ideologies, discourses (ways of constructing and reasoning about the world through the use of a particular language) and forms of consciousness in terms of representation and domination. Critique explores if and how these constrain human imagination, autonomy, and decision making. Attention is paid to asymmetrical relations of power, taken for granted assumptions and beliefs.

Critical social science also investigates arbitrary and rigid ways of dividing up and understanding social reality that follow cultural and linguistic convention. Such mental and linguistic maps are seen as natural and unavoidable by people, who therefore subordinate themselves to them and limit their conceivable ways of living their lives. Critical social science thus addresses how cultural traditions and the acts of powerful agents contribute to freezing social reality for the benefit of certain sectional interests at the expense of others. A frozen social reality is thus opened up and made accessible for political reconsideration and decision making.

Critical social research is thus oriented towards challenging rather than confirming that which is established, disrupting rather than reproducing cultural traditions and conventions, opening up and showing tensions in language use rather than continuing its domination, encouraging productive dissension rather than taking surface consensus as a point of departure. The intention is thereby to contribute to emancipation, for example, to encourage rethinking and the emotional as well as cognitive working through of ideas and identities which are repressive. Alternatively, and less optimistically, the enterprise may be seen as one of fueling resistance to those powers defining who we are, what we should be and aspire to, and how we should live our lives as normal and well-adjusted persons.

The trick with critical social empirical research is to create a balance between a critical basic orientation, being informed with theoretical ideas and a political agenda, and an open, empirically sensitive interest in discovering themes of repression. Too much of the former means a risk of elitism and insensitivity for the rich variety of empirical material and different people's choices and needs; too much of the latter easily leads to a narrow focus, the researcher being caught up in surface phenomena, conventional understandings and/or overstimulation of a mass of data (sense impressions), thus the critical edge is lost.

Critical orientations to organizational studies

As we have indicated, several theoretical orientations could be followed in developing critical management research. We have found the various works organized by the terms 'critical theory' and 'postmodernism' to provide a complex and conflictual but productive point of departure. Anyone who has followed the writings in critical theory and postmodernism during the last decade or so understands the difficulties we face in trying to provide a short, understandable and useful overview of this work to use in grounding our methods discussion. As we show in Chapter 4, the two (themselves complex) labels refer to massive bodies of literature – most of which are difficult to read. Compared to most other research perspectives, the majority of the various critical theory and postmodernist positions are still relatively new to management studies. Texts in the field cross many traditional disciplinary divisions. Many researchers draw on both traditions; others argue for irreconcilable differences between them. The differences and conflicts both within and between these two general headings have filled many pages, both within and outside of organization studies. It may well be argued that nothing fair, coherent and brief can be written on them. But understanding these theoretical literatures in a general way provides important guidance to research methods.

The general projects of critical theory and postmodernism do not represent a fad or simple fascination. Certainly some popular accounts on postmodernism invite such a critique, and we do not believe that this label is necessarily the best or will last. We do not believe that postmodernism and critical theory should be studied because they are new and different, but because they provide unique and important ways to understand organizations and their management.

Researchers in organization and management studies came to critical theory and postmodern writings relatively late, with critical theory emerging in the late 1970s and the beginning of the 1980s (for example, Benson, 1977; Burrell and Morgan, 1979; Frost, 1980; Deetz and Kersten, 1983; Fischer and Sirianni, 1984) and postmodernist writings in the late 1980s (for example, Smircich and Calás, 1987; Cooper and Burrell, 1988). This is no surprise given the 'modernist' assumptions embedded in organizations and the rather dogmatic and exclusionary character of dominant research traditions of either a positivist or Marxist bent. Part of the reason both critical theory and postmodern writings have now found fertile ground in management studies is the decline of and disillusionment with what is broadly referred to as 'modernist assumptions' by both organizational theorists and practitioners.

The increased size of organizations, rapid implementation of communication/information technologies, globalization, the changing nature of work, reduction of the working class, less salient class conflicts, professionalization of the workforce, stagnant economies, widespread ecological problems and turbulent markets are all parts of the contemporary context demanding a research response. Many of these developments provided a growing crisis in the heart of the modernist discourse with its instrumental rationality and connection to state democracies. Management in a modernist discourse works on the basis of control, the progressive rationalization and colonization of nature and people – whether workers, potential consumers or society as a whole. But there are structural limits to control. The costs of integration and control systems often exceed the value added by management within the corporation.

The shift from manufacturing to service industries as the most typical economic form in the post-industrial Western world also has implications for control forms (Alvesson, 1987). As the cost of control grows and the means–end chains grow longer, strategy and instrumental reasoning are strained. Themes like corporate culture, identity, quality management, service management and the renewed call for leadership, soul and charisma during the late 1980s and early 1990s illustrate this. Objects for management control in post-industrial settings are decreasingly labour power and behaviour and increasingly the mind-power and subjectivities of employees. These new social conditions provide a new urgency and new areas of application for postmodern and critical theory work in organization studies – consider the amount of critical theory work on organizational culture (see Alvesson, 1993a and Willmott, 1993 for overviews) – but have little to do with their formation. These rather indicate the new social conditions to which critical theory and postmodern writing have provided innovative and instructive analyses.

While these new conditions have provided opportunities for organizational change, we think little is gained by proclaiming a new postmodern period, or talking about postmodern organizations (Alvesson, 1995). Empirical indications are highly selective and weak (Thompson, 1993). The portrayal of one's own time as unique and a time of great transition is an unfortunate tendency of many periods in Western thought (Foucault, 1983). Theoretically, this enterprise is equally unconvincing. The talk about postmodern organizations often means a relabelling of what are also called organic, or post-Fordist organizations, with little or no conceptual gains and quite a lot of confusion (Parker, 1993; Thompson, 1993). For example, the work of Peters (1987), or even Clegg (1990), talks about significant changes in organizations that we think can be usefully explored using postmodern and critical theory discourses, but they do not. We are only interested in these theoretical approaches and what they offer to organization studies not in claims of organizations as postmodern.

What is then included under the umbrella concepts of critical theory and postmodernism? Sometimes critical theory is given a broad meaning and includes all works taking a basically critical or radical stance on contemporary society, and with an orientation towards investigating exploitation, repression, unfairness, asymmetrical power relations (generated from class, gender or position), distorted communication, and false consciousness. We, however, use the term here with a more restricted meaning, referring to organization studies drawing concepts primarily, though not exclusively, from the Frankfurt School (Adorno, Horkheimer, Marcuse and Habermas). Much of the foundation for this work is summarized, though not without some conceptual confusions, in Burrell and Morgan's (1979) radical humanism paradigm and in Morgan's (1986) images of domination and neuroses.

Postmodernism is in many ways much harder to delimit. In the social sciences, the term has been used to describe a social mood, a historical period filled with major social and organizational changes, and a set of philosophical approaches to organizational and other studies (Featherstone, 1988; Kellner, 1988; Parker, M., 1992; Hassard and Parker, 1993). We will focus on this last designation, emphasizing the more socially and politically relevant writings and the use of conceptions of fragmentation, textuality, and resistance in organization studies. These philosophically based approaches to organization studies have emerged out of the works of Derrida and Foucault in particular, and to a lesser degree Baudrillard, Deleuze and Guattari, and Laclau and Mouffe. Much more so than with critical theory, this is a wide group of writers and positions with quite different research agendas. Still their work shares features and moves that can be highlighted in treating them together.

Their themes include focusing on the constructed nature of people and reality, emphasizing language as a system of distinctions which are central to the construction process, arguing against grand narratives and large-scale theoretical systems such as Marxism or functionalism, emphasizing the power–knowledge connection and the role of claims of expertise in systems of domination, emphasizing the fluid and hyper-real nature of the contemporary world and the role of the mass media and information technologies, and stressing narrative/fiction/rhetoric as central to the research process.

We emphasize the critical edge of postmodernism. We see it as part of a broader critical tradition which challenges the status quo and supports silenced or marginalized voices. This is a common emphasis, but by no means the only one. Many postmodernists' ideas have been utilized for different political purposes. The critique of foundations and Utopian ideals has been understood by some as leaving a distinctly apolitical, socially irrelevant, or even neo-conservative stance (Habermas, 1983; Margolis, 1989; Sarup, 1988). The absence of a political stance grounded in a systematic philosophy has been a source of complaint, but this does not mean that a different, more 'local' and 'responsive', political stance is absent (see Waltzer, 1986). Sometimes people distinguish between 'reactionary postmodernism' and a 'postmodernism of resistance' (Foster, 1983; Smircich and Calás, 1987). Like the majority of authors in social science and organization theory, we have chosen the latter route in our account. Most applications in social science have taken postmodern conceptions in a radical/critical direction – although an unconventional one.

Both postmodernism and critical theory writings are filled with attempts to distinguish themselves in comparison to the modernist project. This contrast is central to their views of research methods. Much of mainstream management research is built on a modernist science and hope growing out of the Western Enlightenment. Kant described the Enlightenment as the escape from self-inflicted tutelage. In pre-Enlightenment communities, personal identities, knowledge, social order, and dominant historical narratives were carried and legitimized by tradition, though individuals actively 'inflicted' the tradition upon themselves. The Enlightenment promised an autonomous subject progressively emancipated by knowledge acquired through scientific methods. It noted the rise of reason over authority and traditional values. Its science, as developed over time, proclaimed a transparent language (freed from the baggage of traditional ideology) and representational truth, a positivity and optimism in acquisition of cumulative understanding which would lead to the progressive enhancement of the quality of life. The Enlightenment's enemies were darkness, tradition, ideology, irrationality, ignorance, and positional authority. Each of these themes of the Enlightenment are deeply embedded in modernist management theory and research.

In the organizational context, we use the term 'modernist' to draw attention to the instrumentalization of people and nature through the use of scientific-technical knowledge (modelled after positivism and other 'rational' ways of developing safe, robust knowledge) to accomplish predictable results, measured by productivity, and technical problem-solving leading to the 'good' economic and social life, primarily defined by accumulation of wealth by production investors and consumption by consumers.

Modernism initially represented emancipation over myth, authority and traditional values through knowledge, reason, and opportunities based on heightened capacity. Early twentieth-century organization studies were organized around the development of modernist over traditional discourses. Taylor's and Weber's treatment of rationalization and bureaucratization showed from the start the corporation as a site of the development of modernist logic and instrumental reasoning. The traditional was marginalized and placed off in the private realm. While writings in human relations, quality of work life, and later cultural studies would continue to claim a place for traditional values and norms with their particular logics, each would be 'strategized' and brought to aid further rationalization of work for the sake of convenience, efficiency, and direction of the work effort.

'Performativity' would come to be valued over any earlier Enlightenment narrative of emancipation or human values (Lyotard, 1984). In fact in the new age embellishment, one could even be emancipated from the body's needs, desires and emotions and bring the body's spirit, soul and faith under rational control. Foucault's (1977, 1980b, 1988) demonstrations and critical treatment of the rise of self-surveillance and bio-power as control systems described the furthest development of self-rationalization in modernity.

Critical theory and postmodernism open new discussions. In particular, critical theory showed how modernism itself was based on myths, had acquired an arbitrary authority, subordinated social life to technological rationality, and protected a new dominant group's interests (Adorno and Horkheimer, 1979 [1947]). The old conflict between a modern and a traditional discourse, where the modern laid claim to all the positive terms, is suddenly displaced by a new set of conflicts – those arising from the problems of modernity itself.

Both critical theory and postmodernism see their work as responses to specific social conditions. Contemporary society, as a result of science, industrialization and communication/information technologies, has developed positive capacities but also dangerous forms of domination. Both critical theory and postmodernism describe Western development as one where a progressive, instrumental modernism gradually eclipsed traditional society with fairly clear payoffs but also great costs. They agree that something fundamental has gone awry and that more technical, instrumental 'solutions' will not fix it. While their diagnoses are similar (to use a less than totally adequate medical metaphor), they differ in their pronouncement and response. Critical theorists see the modernist's project as sick and see hope for reconstruction in recovering good aspects and redirecting the future; postmodernists pronounce its death and proclaim the absence of a thinkable future.

The critical theorists, especially Habermas (1984, 1987), focus on the incompletion of the positive potentialities of the Enlightenment. Different forces have utilized their power and advantages to force new forms of tutelage, often *consentful* in character. As we will discuss in regard to organizational studies, critical theorists have focused on the skewing and closure of the historical discourse through reification, universalization of sectional interests, domination of instrumental reasoning, and hegemony. In different ways they hope to recover a rational process through understanding social/historical/political constructionism, a broader conception of rationality, inclusion of more groups in social determination, and overcoming systematically distorted communication. Central to this is the critique of domination and the ways those subjugated actively participate in their own subjugation. The political and astute intellectual is given an active role in the production of an enlightened understanding. The hope is to provide forums so that different segments of the society and different human interests can be part of a better, more moral, historical dialogue, so that each may contribute equally to the choices in producing a future for all.

The postmodernists also focus on the dark side of the Enlightenment, its destruction of the environment and native peoples, its exclusions, and the concealed effects of reason and progress; but postmodernists see the entire project as being wrong. The problem is not who or what participates in it; the project is inherently problematic. They seek to find the 'non-enlightened' voices, the human possibilities that the Enlightenment itself suppresses. This discourse is filled with the pronouncement of the end of the historical discourse of progress and emancipation and its endless deferral of social promise: that more technology, more knowledge and increased rationality will somehow accomplish the promise.

Man (the humanist subject as a coherent entity with natural rights and potential autonomy) is pronounced dead and in his place is the decentered, fragmented, gendered, classed subject; the grand narratives of theory and history are replaced by disjoined and fragmented local narratives, potentially articulated and sutured; and metaphysics with its philosophies of presence and essence has lost terrain to the celebration of multiple perspectives and a carnival of positions and structurings. The future is endlessly deferred and without positive direction, but life can be made more interesting through deconstruction and the recovery of suppressed conflicts and marginalized groups. The intellectual has no privileged position or special knowledge, but can act only in situational, local ways like all others, that is he or she cannot offer external or even broadly valid truth. Since there can be no theory of history or projection into the future, resistance and alternative readings rather than reform or revolution become the primary political posture.

The tasks of critical management research

Critical management research follows the general spirit of critical social science as developed in these theoretical orientations, but focuses on management phenomena. Given that an elite is to a considerable degree studied, the more egalitarian and democratic perspective of critical social science must be complemented with an appreciation of how organizations function and the various constraints following from the economic purposes central in most organizations. Unfortunately, sometimes critical researchers disregard this aspect of companies and other organizations. The balance of managerial and non-managerial perspectives are important. We do not hold the negative view of management and managers which characterizes many radical schools. Organizational structures, routines and other social processes often constrain the management function in ways that lead to less successful organizational functioning and less mutually satisfying decisions. If critical management research is to be a distinct field of inquiry and contribute positively to human development, its issues cannot be swept away by a broad-brushed approach and anti-capitalism position or a general critique of disciplinary power (Alvesson and Willmott, 1996). Important here is a feeling for organizational context, the nature of managerial work, and a careful investigation of how social processes reproduce suboptimal performance and social harms. We wish to be careful that ideas present in existing hierarchies and undemocratic social relations are not simply replaced by equally naïve, Utopian ideals. No new organizational form or process can accomplish all the good things at the same time. And all contain their own seeds of destruction and contradictions.

Many 'progressive' organizational researchers spent the early part of their careers working toward decentralization, debureaucratization and employee participation only to discover, as many corporations moved in these directions, that new, more powerful and insidious forms of control and domination came along with them (see Barker, 1993; Deetz, 1998). Organizations cannot simply be changed by proclaiming new progressive ideologies and different preferred forms. Unnecessarily dominant controls and constraints which distort organizational decisions and lead to less satisfactory fulfillment of the full variety of human needs and desires must be the focus for change.

Critical research has an important and complex role to play. The contemporary critical researcher lacks any basis for a 'universal' role as the conscience of the collectivity or as a 'specialist' engaging in privileging systems of expertise growing out of conceptions of universal or objective truth. The researcher's role today is more appropriately one of enabling more open discourse among the various members of organizations, and between them and external social groups and the larger societies in which they operate. We believe that this is best achieved if critical studies offer counter-pictures to dominant ideals and understandings. The attempt is to initiate open discussion of images widely spread by dominant groups and mainstream management thinking through drawing attention to hidden aspects and offering alternative readings. To accomplish this, the research process itself should be openly par-ticipative and involve the same qualities that are important for organizations themselves. As such, our type of critical manage-ment studies include three overall, overlapping kinds of tasks. We refer to these as 'insight', 'critique' and 'transformative redefini-tions'. While we address these in detail in Chapter 6, a brief intro-duction is useful here.

The insight task demonstrates our commitment to the herme-neutic, interpretive and ethnographic goals of local understand-ings closely connected to and appreciative of the lives of real people in real situations. The critique task demonstrates our com-mitment to the analytical aspects of critical traditions which recog-nize the possibility of domination in local formations and to reconnect local forms and meanings to larger social, historical and political processes. The transformative redefinition task demon-strates our commitment to the more pragmatic aspects of critical thought, recognizing that insight and critique without support for social action leaves research detached and sterile.

Insight

Everyday knowledge and scientific research are produced out of a set of interrelated structures which are both present in them and extend outward in an implicative web. Most of the time social members as well as traditional researchers take for granted this knowledge and the formed nature of objects and events. 'Insight' denotes the process of seeing into the various ways in which this knowledge and the objective character of objects and events are formed and sustained. Insight can properly be called the leading edge of human thought; it is structured along the lines of the powerful exemplar rather than a mass of data. Insight is both the process of producing a unity of interest in the data – of knowing what data to collect and how it fits together – and understanding the conditions for such a unity.

The first task is, therefore, to investigate local forms of phenomena. Critical studies relate empirical themes at hand to the wider historical, economic, cultural and political context, but domination and decisional constraints are often local in form and the connection between levels is complex and less than obvious. Organization-specific, micro-level aspects are an important dimension of study. Actor-induced or institution-level forms of social domination may be explored. Corporate culture and other forms of workplace level control, norms for the regulation of moral life among managers, the use of strategic marketing techniques and practices for the control of customers' identities and responses, for example, may all be targets of critical study. Exploring the operations of power, especially micro-power, in the empirical site of a company always says something of broader ideologies and discourses, but a focused effort may also point to local variations and lead to the development of a more specific theoretical understanding of the local context.

Critique
The second task – critique – is to counteract the dominance of taken-for-granted goals, ideas, ideologies and discourses which put their imprints on management and organization phenomena. The interest is less on local variation than on more general characteristics of management and organizations. Ecology, consumerism, careerism, technocracy, organizational society and its pressure for conformity and adaptability, and ideologies of managerialism may be relevant themes to investigate. They may impact on each organization differently, but are general social concerns that relate to every organization within the society and, often, the larger global community. To focus solely on a particular organization may lead us to contribute to parochialism, that is we can become caught up in the grip of a particular culture with them and inadequately reflect on other ways of understanding and living. We may fail to see how cultural blindness is simultaneously the outcome of, as well as a force behind, the development of consumerist orientations and dependencies on the steady flow of goods and services to sustain consumerist identities in affluent (Galbraith, 1958) or post-scarcity society (Carter and Jackson, 1987). The task is thus the critical study of macro-cultural conventions and (self-) constraints.

This may appear to be a macro-level approach and of less relevance for management studies. But management and organizational functioning is the central, researchable site in the production/reproduction of these cultural and economical orientations (Deetz, 1992). In addition, these constraints stamp their imprints on organizational life. Understanding a company calls for an understanding of how a specific view on nature dominates – or is challenged and/or reconceptualized among managers and other actors. Tracking traces of totality in the local empirical site is, consequently, an important task for critical management studies relating macro- and micro-issues.

Political, economic and community forces are inscribed in organizational arrangements, social relations, and in every perception. It is not sufficient to describe these as naturally occurring, they arise historically and arbitrarily advantage certain groups. The critical researcher does not so much give a norm or criteria for evaluation of organizational systems as provides a set of interests and analytical foci for acting upon them – a way of thinking about these systems. Grossberg (1987) referred to the task as one to 'describe (and intervene in) the way messages are produced by, inserted into, and function within the everyday lives of concrete human beings so as to reproduce and transform structures of power and domination' (p. 393).

Critique thus is directed at the conventions and structures of social orders and the forms of knowledge and privileged understanding which are complicit with such orders. Critique itself operates as part of the relationship between the researcher and the researched; it opens the possibility of a conversation that exceeds the partialities of each.

Transformative redefinition
A third task is the development of critical, managerially relevant knowledge and practical understandings that enable change and provide skills for new ways of operating. The practical and educational ideals of our form of critical research lead to a pragmatic view of management. Instead of simply critically investigating the contradictions and forms of domination coming from profit and efficiency goals, an effort is made to integrate these with more democratic and non-repressive forms. This is difficult and the risk of co-optation significant (Alvesson, 1987). Marrying different ideals can easily lead to a rather rosy picture of a contradiction-free organizational reality, where all the good things in life – autonomy, democracy, creativity, productivity, profit and environmental protection – are seen as being fully supportive of each other. Nevertheless, the investigation of

different organizations and types of management principles, practices and processes may well lead to critical insights that may encourage more progressive and mutually satisfying – although hardly contradiction-free – forms of management.

Co-optation is best avoided, not by simple reiteration of ideals but through careful involvement in the developmental life of the organization. Transformative redefinition is the natural counterpart to insight and critique. It can easily be claimed that critical writings in both the Enlightenment and post-Enlightenment traditions have placed too much attention on awareness and understanding and not enough on enabling alternative responses. The implicit faith – that if people knew what they wanted and the system of constraints limiting them, they would know how to act differently – has little basis. Those who hold out for significant change often miss the implications of modern forms of control. Meaningful change is in the micro-practices at the innumerable sites of power relations (Foucault, 1980b). New social relations are not instant but develop in an ongoing struggle including much practice and frequent false starts.

Critical transformative redefinition involves the production and distribution of a kind of political competence. Following Simons, political competence in modern society means, 'not just access to information but access to the entire range of skills required to decode, encode, interpret, reflect upon, appraise, contextualize, integrate, and arrive at decisions respecting that information' (1989: 198).

Finally, the three tasks function together. The first task directs us to avoid totalizing thinking through the paying of careful attention to local processes; the second guides us to avoid myopia through looking at the totality; and the third task directs us to avoid hypercritique and negativity through taking the notion of critical pragmatism and positive action seriously. Most critical research concentrates on one or another of the tasks, but a sound ambition would be to include at least a modest contribution to all three tasks of critical management research.

The logic and structure of the book

Chapter 2 initially provides an overview of the differences between the various orientations to management research, showing how critical orientations deviate from 'mainstream', functional–normative and interpretive orientations. The chapter concludes with a discussion of the role of theory in research, arguing that with the constructionist assumption of critical orientations the relationship of language and representation to research practices and reports changes greatly. We discuss some possible values guiding critical research: creative empirical grounding, reorganizing attention, encouraging self-transformation, breaking closure, etc.

Chapter 3 offers a critique of conventional ideas in methodology, in particular those shared by neo-positivistists, quantitative and qualitative researchers. The critique is partly contingent upon the insights of the critical theoretical orientations, but draws upon other sources. Substantial parts of it centre on and around the over-reliance on the robustness of 'data' and the denial of the constructive, interpretive nature of all empirical material. In short, we do not collect data that we then interpret. Data is an outcome of interpretation and construction, for example, we must actively use knowledge, intellect and intuition in order to give some sense impressions a meaning and we must also actively intervene – ask questions, negotiate and check meaning with interviewees, prevent them from addressing at length themes of little relevance for the research project, we must steer our presence into and around a particular site, make notes/decide not to make notes/decide what to write down. We construct data to interpret.

Chapter 4 more fully develops the critical tradition developed in critical theory and postmodernism as possible responses to difficulties in conventional quantitative and qualitative research. We show what types of concerns and research grow out of each theoretical orientation and how these impact on research. The focus will be on both differences between these theoretical positions and how they can productively complement each other.

In Chapter 5 we develop a set of new general rules for method. These are, like the entire book, on the level of reflection and a guiding framework rather than on the level of procedure, protocol and technique. The general rules are in line with, facilitated by, and supportive of critical research, but do not apply exclusively to this branch of inquiry.

Chapter 6 sharpens the edge of the book's message, providing more detail on the actual process of critical research. We identify three elements in critical research: *insight* through interpretation pointing at non-obvious aspects of a social phenomenon; *critique* through exploring issues of domination and the freezing of social reality in a certain ideological and institutionalized order; and *transformative redefinition*, the indication of alternative ways of thinking, relating and acting within and against this order. These three elements are illustrated at some length in a case study on social relations and hierarchy in an industrial company.

Chapter 7 explores two interpretive tactics in critical research: de-familiarization and dissensus reading. De-familiarization aims to turn the well known into something unfamiliar and strange, thus making it less self-evident, natural and unavoidable. Dissensus readings break up established meanings and closure in how we reason through exploring language. In this chapter we also investigate some of the difficulties within critical management and social research, including the problem of 'hypercritique', involving unfair descriptions and other problems associated with a biased negativity. The chapter discusses the possibilities of making critical research less anti-management and more relevant for organizational practitioners. We have here an ambition of overcoming the closure of disclosure-seeking critical management research. Modes of engagement in critical studies are also discussed, as are the possibilities and problems of multiple interpretations.

In Chapter 8 we address the practice of critical management research. Many of the ideas and discussions here, as in other parts of the book, are relevant for less critical research but are calibrated against the specifics of critical studies. We address problems of access; reflective approaches to interviewing; how one (perhaps) may go beyond moral storytelling and impression management and norm-guided talk in interviews; the possibilities and pitfalls of ethnographies, as well as a more concentrated form of ethnographic work labelled a partial ethnography.

2

Alternative social science research perspectives

As Burrell and Morgan (1979) developed at length, all social research takes place out of a background set of ontological, epistemological and axiological assumptions. These provide taken-for-granted understandings of the nature of the world and the people in it, preferred methods for discovering what is true or worth knowing, and basic moral and aesthetic judgements about appropriate conduct and quality of life. Unfortunately, as developed at length elsewhere (Deetz, 1996), Burrell and Morgan's analysis of these is in some ways misleading. Their conceptual distinctions among research perspectives favour dominant traditions of the past; and their claim of paradigmatic incommensurability discourages the investigation of similarities and collaborative possibilities and cross paradigm critique.

In this chapter we show a way of thinking about research positions that we think better highlights their assumptions and relationships. To do this we will use a grid stimulated by and similar to the popular one by Burrell and Morgan (1979) but with changes that highlight similarities and differences more usefully and better direct our attention to concerns in developing research methods (see also Deetz, 1994a, 1996). Our primary intent is to show how the critical orientations we use here differ from traditional normative research and much of the interpretive research conducted by social scientists. In doing this, we will also initiate an investigation of the problems with more typical contrasting of varieties of social science research based on quantitative/qualitative, objective/subjective, or science/humanism distinctions. These issues are taken up in Chapter 3. Additionally, we begin to explore some of the alternative conceptions available within the critical traditions. These are developed in Chapter 4. Finally, we end the chapter with a discussion of the role of theory in social science research.

Dimensions of difference in research programmes

Here we will use two dimensions for our analytic distinctions: 'consensus–dissensus seeking' and 'local/emergent–elite/a priori conceptions'. The consensus–dissensus dimension focuses on the relation of research practices to the dominant social discourses. Research perspectives can be contrasted based on the extent to which they work within a dominant set of structurings of knowledge, social relations, and identities, called here a 'consensus' discourse, and the extent to which they work to disrupt these structurings, called here 'dissensus' discourse. This dimension is used to show a significant way that we can think about what makes postmodernism and critical theory different from other current research programmes. The second dimension focuses on the origin of concepts and problem statements as part of the constitutive process in research. Differences among research perspectives can be shown by contrasting 'local/emergent' conceptions with 'elite/a priori' ones. This dimension will be used to show one interesting way to think about the differences in postmodernism and critical theory discourses; see Figure 2.1.

The two dimensions together attempt to show what is negotiable and what is not in research practice, how research reports are

**Relation to dominant
social discourse**

Dissensus

(dialogic studies)	(critical studies)
(postmodern,	(late modern,
deconstructionist)	reformist)

**Origin of concepts
and problems**   Local/emergent _____ Elite/a priori

(interpretive studies)	(normative studies)
(premodern,	(modern,
traditional)	progressive)

Consensus

Figure 2.1 *Contrasting dimensions from the metatheory of representational practices (Adapted from Deetz (1994a).*
© *Sage Publications)*

organized, and the anticipated political outcome of the research activity (the direction in which it points, whether or not it has that particular practical effect). Unlike Burrell and Morgan (1979) we do not wish to suggest that the grid identifies paradigms but rather particular lines of assumptions and understandings which develop mobile but specifiable relations to each other and position particular types of conflicts and contradictions internal to them. Each of these issues is taken up briefly below.

We recognize that in naming these positions and bodies of work exemplifying them, some things are pulled together that are still different in many now hidden ways and bipolar contrasts are created that change a continuous world to a discontinuous one. We hope the reader will work with us to see the various conceptualizations as interesting ways to call attention to similarities and differences that matter rather than as devices for division and classification. The differences between critical theory and postmodernism are often contested and many researchers draw on both traditions. Still it is useful to give some account of what makes these different traditions, traditions that do not easily collapse into each other but which can each contribute to our consideration of research methods.

Consensus–dissensus
The consensus–dissensus dimension draws attention to the relationship of research to existing social orders. Consensus or dissensus should not be understood as agreement and disagreement but rather as presentation of unity or of difference, the continuation or disruption of any prevailing discourse. See Table 2.1 for a conceptualization of this dimension. This dimension is similar to Burrell and Morgan's use of the traditional sociological distinctions between an interest in 'change' or 'regulation', but enables some advantages. Principally, the change–regulation distinction tended, in most usages, to assume the presence of a coherent dominant group or orders and the primary conflict initiating change was class conflict. While many researchers do use a similar analysis of managerial or company domination, the more pressing 'critical' concerns of the day are the ways dominant discourses (though often disorganized and disjunctive) place limitations on people in general, including managers, and limit the successful functioning of organizations in meeting human needs. The problem is not group against group, but rather the suppression of parts of the human being and the presence of destructive control processes, technocracy, consumerism, careerism, environmental destruction, and exclusive concern with economic growth (see Abercrombie et al., 1980; Mumby

Table 2.1 *Characterizations of the consensus–dissensus dimension*

Consensus	Dissensus
Trust	Suspicion
Hegemonic order as natural state	Conflicts over order as natural state
Naturalization of present	Present order is historicized and politicized
Integration and harmony are possible	Order indicates domination and suppressed conflicts
Research focuses on representation	Research focused on challenge and reconsideration (re-presentation)
Mirror (reflecting) dominant metaphor	Lens (seeing/reading as) dominant metaphor
Validity central concern	Insight and praxis central concern
Theory as abstraction	Theory as opening
Unified science and triangulation	Positional complementarity
Science is neutral	Science is political
Life is discovery	Life is struggle and creation
Researcher anonymous and out of time and space	Researcher named and positioned
Autonomous/free agent	Historically/socially situated agent

Source: adapted from Deetz (1996)

and Putnam, 1992; Alvesson and Willmott, 1995). And further, the processes of domination are less often seen today as macro-sociological and more often as routine micro-practices in the work site itself (Knights and Willmott, 1989; Deetz, 1994a, 1994d). Thus our research methods need to be directed toward these processes. The focus on discursive rather than group relationships aids the understanding of domination and its reproduction.

The consensus pole draws attention to the way some research programmes both seek order and treat order production as the dominant feature of natural and social systems. With such a conception, the primary goal of the research is to display a discovered order with a high degree of fidelity or verisimilitude. The descriptions hope to 'mirror' entities and relationships that exist in the external world in a relative fixed state reflecting their 'real' character. Language within the research process is treated as a system of representations, to be neutralized and made transparent, used only to display the presumed shared world. Existing orders are largely treated as natural and unproblematic. To a large extent, through the highlighting of ordering principles, such existing orders are perpetuated.

The significance of random events and deviance are down-played when looking at norms and the normal, and attention is usually given to processes reducing deviance, uncertainty, and dissonance. In most cases where deviance is the centre of attention it tends to be normalized through looking at the production of deviant groups (that is, other orders). Conflict and fragmentation are usually treated as system problems and research often aids attempts at conflict reduction and system maintenance. While different in other respects most traditional quantitative and quali-tative research programmes share these assumptions and under-standing of science.

The dissensus pole draws attention to research programmes which consider struggle, conflict, and tensions to be the natural state – the key element in both critical theory and postmodernist work. Research itself is seen as inevitably being a move in a con-flictual site. The existing orders indicate the suppression of basic conflicts and, along with that suppression, the domination of people and their full variety of interests. Research aims to challenge mechanisms of order maintenance to reclaim conflicts and tension. The non-normative aspects of human conduct and extraordinary responses are emphasized along with the importance of largely ran-dom and chance events. As will be developed in greater detail later, rather than language naming and describing, researcher concep-tions are seen as striking a difference, de- and re-differentiating experience (Martin, 1990b; Cooper and Burrell, 1988; Cooper, 1989; Weedon, 1987; Deetz, 1992). The 'mirror' metaphor gives way to that of the 'lens', noting the shifting analytical attempt to see what could not be seen before and showing the researcher as positioned and active. For dissensus-style research, the generative capacity (the ability to challenge guiding assumptions, values, social practices and routines) of an observation is more important than representa-tional validity (Gergen, 1978; Rorty, 1989). The research is, in Knights' (1992) sense, 'anti-positive'.

Dissensus work does not deny the significance of an ordered observed world, rather it takes it as a powerful (and power-filled) product and works to break objectifications to show fuller potential and variety than is immediately apparent. For example, consensus orientations in cultural studies seek to discover the organizational culture or cultures. Dissensus orientations show the fragmentation inherent in any claim of culture and the work required for site subjects to maintain coherence in the face of this as well as subjects' own forms of resistance (Martin 1990b, 1992; Smircich and Calás, 1987; Calás and Smircich, 1991). Consensus orientations apply role and identity classifications and relate them to other vari-ables; dissensus orientations see identity as multiple, conflictual, and in process.

While these differences can be characterized clearly in abstrac-tion, in real time every consensus arises out of and falls to dissensus, and every dissensus gives away to emerging (if temporary) consensus. The issue is not the ultimate outcome – desired or likely – but rather which part of this flow through time is claimed in the research process. For example, while critical theorists clearly seek a social consensus which is more rational, their research tries to produce this through the creation of dissensus in place of dominant orders; for instance, ideological critique in the critical theory conception of the negative dialectic is to reclaim conflict and destroy a false order rather than produce a new one. Thus, we place critical theorists on the dissensus end. Critical theories differ from many dialogic or 'postmodern' positions primarily in whether dissensus is produced by the use of elite understandings and procedures (as in Habermas, 1984, 1987; Mumby, 1987; Kunda, 1992; or several essays in Alvesson and Willmott, 1992) or in a deconstructive process whereby elite conceptions are unmasked to allow organizational activities to be given multiple and conflicting descriptions within particular sites (Laclau and Mouffe, 1985; Martin, 1990b; Calás and Smircich, 1991; Linstead, 1993; Kilduff, 1993). The dialogic outcome requires a constant de-differentiation and re-differentiation for the sake of demythologizing and enriching natural language, and consequently opening to reconsideration the most basic and certain experiences of everyday life.

Local/emergent–elite/a priori

The key questions this dimension addresses concern where and how research concepts arise. At the two extremes of this dimension, concepts are either developed in relation with organizational members and transformed in the research process or brought to the research 'interaction' by the researcher and held static throughout the research process – that is, concepts may be developed *with* or applied *to* the organizational members being studied. This dimension can be characterized by a set of paired conceptions which flesh out contrasts embedded in the two poles; Table 2.2 presents an array of these contrasts. The choice of language system and its stability are of central importance since the linguistic/conceptual system directs: the statement of problems; the observational process itself in producing objects, and highlighting and hiding potential experiences; the type of claims made; and the report to external groups.

The elite/a priori pole draws attention to the tendency of some types of research programmes to privilege the particular language system of the researcher and the expertise of the research community, as well as tending to hold that language system constant throughout the research process.[1] Such research tends to be

Table 2.2 *Characterizations of the local/emergent–elite/a priori dimension*

Local/emergent	Elite/a priori
Comparative communities	Privileged community
Multiple language games	Fixed language game
Particularistic	Universalistic
Systematic philosophy as ethnocentric	Grounded in hoped for systematic philosophy
Atheoretical/weak theory	Theory driven/strong theory
Situational or structural determinism	Methodological determinism
Nonfoundational	Foundational
Local narratives	Grand narrative of progress and emancipation
Sensuality and meaning as central concerns	Rationality and truth as central concerns
Situated, practical knowledge	Generalizable, theoretical knowledge
Tends to be feminine in attitude	Tends to be masculine in attitude
Sees the strange	Sees the familiar
Proceeds from the other	Proceeds from the self
Ontology of 'otherness' over method	Epistemological and procedural issues rule over substantive assumptions

Source: adapted from Deetz (1996)

heavily theory driven with careful attention being paid to definitions prior to the research process. The experiences of the researched become coded into the researcher's language system. Demands of consistency and/or reliability require changes in the conceptional system to take place outside of rather than in the research process. Whether intentional or not, the conceptual system of the researcher is considered better – or to more clearly represent what 'really' is the case – than that of everyday people and seeks generality beyond the various local systems of meaning. In privileging a language system, there is further a tendency to universalize and justify such moves by appeals to foundations or essentialist assumptions. Research claims, thus, are seen as freed from their local and temporal conditions of production. In most cases these research approaches follow an Enlightenment hope for producing rational knowledge not constrained by traditions or the particular belief systems of the researcher or researched. The produced knowledge is treated as progressive or reformist in conception, leading to increased capacities or well-being. The more functionalist (or what we call 'normative') versions openly proclaim 'objectivity' and value neutrality based on the shared language game and research methods and tend to overlook the positions of their own community or alliances with other groups. The more critical versions quickly note the presence of values and distortions in normative work, and hold out the hope for a better, purer form of knowledge based in processes that include more interests and means of analysis in the work.

The local/emergent pole draws attention to researchers who work with an open language system and produce a form of knowledge with less lofty claims. Central to their work is the situated nature of the research enterprise. Problem statements, the researcher's attention, and descriptions are worked out as a play between communities. The theoretical vocabulary carried into the research activity is often considered by the researcher as a 'first cut' or guide to getting started, and is constantly open to new meanings, translations, and re-differentiation based on interactions in the research process.

The knowledge form is more often one of insight rather than truth. Such insights may be particularistic with regard to both time and place, even though the emerging analytical frame is designed to aid in the deeper understanding of other particular settings. Cumulative understanding happens through providing stories or accounts which may provide insight into other sites rather than by cumulative universal aspiring claims. The research attends to the feelings, intuitions and multiple forms of rationality of both the researched and researcher rather than using a single logic of objectification or purified rationality. The study is guided more by concept formation than concept application. The 'otherness' of the other (the way people and events exceed categories and classifications of them) is sought by the researcher to force reconception and linguistic change. This is considered more valuable than the identification and naming of preconceived traits, attributes, or groupings. Objectivity, to the extent that it is considered at all, arises out of the interplay and the constant ability of the researched to object and correct. The researcher is more a skilled collaborator in knowledge production than an expert observer. Such a position is expressed well by those engaged in various forms of participatory research (Reason, 1994; Whyte, 1991).

Focusing on the origin of concepts and problems using a dimension of 'local/emergent–elite/a priori' allows three advantages. First, it acknowledges linguistic/social constructionism in all research positions and directs attention to whose concepts are used in object production and determination of what is problematic (see Deetz, 1973). Secondly, the focus on the origin of concepts helps distinguish fundamentally different kinds of knowledge. Elite/a priori conceptions lead more to the development of 'theoretical codified' knowledge – a kind of 'book' knowledge or 'knowing about'. Local/emergent conceptions lead more to the development of 'practical' knowledge – a kind of 'street wisdom' or a 'knowing how'. Thirdly, reconceptualizing this dimension allows us more easily to see that both the application and discovery of concepts may demonstrate implicit or explicit political alliances with different groups in society. For example, to the extent that organizational researchers' concepts align with managerial conceptions and problem statements and are applied a priori in studies, the knowledge claims are intrinsically biased toward certain interests as they are applied within the site community (Mumby, 1988). The knowledge claims become part of the same processes that are being studied, reproducing world-views, personal identities, and fostering particular interests within the organization (Knights, 1992).

A sketch of alternative research approaches

The relation of postmodern and critical theory to each other and to normative and interpretive work can be shown by comparing the types of discourse they generate with regard to issues in organization studies; see Table 2.3. Since we use these characterizations to build our brief discussion of alternative research approaches, we will not discuss them here. What we would like to do is sketch the characteristics of four prototypical research directions highlighted by the grid.

Normative studies

The researchers producing this discourse have been described as methodological determinists, functionalists, covering law theorists, or simply practising the variable analytic tradition. This discourse is still largely dominant in North American organizational research and in applied organizational research throughout the world. It is reconstructed and well justified in Donaldson (1985). We describe this discourse as 'normative' to emphasize the centrality of codification, the search for regularity, normalization of experience, and a strategic/directive control orientation (Deetz, 1973; Hollway, 1984).

Conceptions of operationalization, 'objectivity', and law-like relations are merely the most obvious form of practice. The research practices mirror nineteenth-century conceptions of the natural sciences, often involving the most recent advances in operationalization, hypothesization, statistical reduction, and pattern 'recognition' processes. Conventional practices and methodological determinism have, in most cases, replaced any strong allegiance

Table 2.3   *Prototypical discursive features*

Issue	Discourse			
	Normative	Interpretive	Critical	Dialogic
Basic goal	Law-like relations among objects	Display unified culture	Unmask domination	Reclaim conflict
Method	Nomothetic science	Hermeneutics, ethnography	Cultural criticism, ideology critique	Deconstruction, genealogy
Hope	Progressive emancipation	Recovery of integrative values	Reformation of social order	Claim a space for lost voices
Metaphor of social relations	Economic	Social	Political	Mass
Organization metaphor	Marketplace	Community	Polity	Carnival
Problems addressed	Inefficiency, disorder	Meaninglessness, illegitimacy	Domination, consent	Marginalization, conflict suppression
Concern with closure communication	Fidelity, influence, information needs	Social acculturation, group affirmation	Misrecognition, systematic distortion	Discursive
Narrative style	Scientific/ technical, strategic	Romantic, embracing	Therapeutic, directive	Ironic, ambivalent
Time identity	Modern	Pre-modern	Late modern	Postmodern
Organizational benefits	Control, expertise	Commitment, quality work life	Participation, expanded knowledge	Diversity, creativity
Mood	Optimistic	Friendly	Suspicious	Playful
Social fear	Disorder	Depersonalization	Authority	Totalization, normalization

Source: adapted from Deetz (1996)

to the positivist philosophy of science that grounds many of the methods and assumptions. The 'objects' constructed by the practices of this science are given qualities of constancy and permanence as if given specific attributes by nature. The combination of a priori conceptions and a focus on consensus leads the artefacts of these practices to be described as facts.

The discourse is decisively modern in Gergen's (1992) sense and the knowledge is considered positive, cumulative and progressive. A grand narrative of emancipation is shaped by a commitment to make a better world through discovery of fundamental processes and the increase of production (Lyotard, 1984). The organization is usually treated as an existing object produced for instrumental ends, usually making money, though some conception of the invisible hand makes that goal well integrated with other social goals of development and widespread availability of goods and services.

This discourse is most present in classical management theories, theories of leadership, contingency theory, most other systems theories, and other places more completely described by Burrell and Morgan (1979) in their discussion of 'functionalist'. But it is also clearly present in those advocating the management of culture (for example, Schein, 1992; Deal and Kennedy, 1982) through their conception of culture as a variable or object to be strategically deployed (see Barley et al., 1988 on the normative co-optation of cultural research). Many of those working with new conceptions of organizations as 'post-modern' (those seeing organizations as having new chaotic features rather than those who take a theoretical postmodernist approach, see Parker, M., 1992) have a discourse primarily structured in a normative fashion (for example, Bergquist, 1993). Many Marxist studies utilize normative themes. Most academic Marxist works depend on privileging particular social communities and employ economic and structural explanations based on normative conceptions; Lenin's embracing of scientific management was in no way inconsistent. Within managed economies, the managerial elite group giving rise to the concepts was quite different, of course, from the managerial elite accepted by most Western European and North American studies. Elite planning and strategic management are generally highly dependent on this discourse (see Knights and Morgan, 1991; Knights, 1992).

Interpretive studies

For interpretive researchers the organization is a social site, a special type of community which shares important characteristics with other types of communities. The emphasis is on a social rather than an economic view of organizational activities. Traditional methods of studying communities are seen as especially useful. The discourse often draws on traditional and pre-modern themes (Gergen, 1992). This is not to suggest a focus on the past, rather a concern with those aspects of life which have not yet been systematized, instrumentalized and brought under the control of modernist logics and sciences. Interpretive studies accept much of the representational and consenual view of science seen in normative writings, but shift the relationship between theoretical conceptions and the talk of the subjects under study. People are not considered to be objects like other objects, but are active sense makers like the researcher. Theory is given a different conception and different role here. While theory may provide important sensitizing conceptions, it is not a device of classification nor tested in any simple and direct manner. The key conceptions and understandings must be worked out with the subjects under study. Research subjects can collaborate in displaying key features of their world. But, as in normative research, the pressure is to get it right: to display a unified, consensual culture in the way that it 'actually' exists. The report is to display convincingly a unified way of life with all its complexities and contradictions.

Most researchers use ethnography, phenomenology or hermeneutics in a rigorous way as the principal means of grounding their largely qualitative methods. Studies are usually done in the field and are based on a prolonged period of observation and depth interviewing. The interest is in the full person in the organization, thus social and life functions beyond the work process are considered. The workplace is seen as a site of human activity, one of those activities being 'work' proper. The expressed goal of interpretive studies is to show how particular realities are socially produced and maintained through norms, rites, rituals and daily activities. In much of the writings a clear preservationist, communitarian, or naturalist tone exists. It moves to save or record a life form – with its complexity and creativity – that may be lost to modern, instrumental life or overlooked in it. Gergen (1992) describes the romantic sense of this discourse with its depth and connection to the inner life. Cultural studies in organizations are interpretive to the extent that they have not been captured by normative, modernist co-optations (see Barley et al., 1988; Enz, 1992). Most interpretivists have taken culture to be an evocative metaphor for organizational life, rather than a variable or thing that an organization has (Smircich, 1983; Frost et al., 1985, 1991).

Gradually, many researchers doing interpretive work have begun to question the logic of displaying a consensual unified culture and have attended more to its fragmentation, tensions, and processes of conflict suppression (Martin, 1992; Frost et al., 1991). And similarly, much more attention has been paid to the politics of representation and the role of the report author (Clifford and Marcus, 1986; Marcus and Fischer, 1986; Thomas, 1993). It is precisely these moves that aid us in believing that important insights can be gained by actively pursuing a reproachment between critical and interpretive work.

Critical theory studies

Critical researchers see organizations in general as social historical creations, born in conditions of struggle and domination – a domination that often hides and suppresses meaningful conflict. Organizations are largely described as political sites, thus general social theories and especially theories of decision making in the public sphere are seen as appropriate (see Deetz, 1992, 1995a). While commercial organizations could be positive social institutions providing forums for the articulation and resolution of important group conflicts over the use of natural resources, distribution of income, production of desirable goods and services, the development of personal qualities and the direction of society, various forms of power and domination have lead to skewed decision making and fostered social harms and significant waste and inefficiency.

Either explicit or implicit in critical theory work is a goal to demonstrate and critique forms of domination, asymmetry, and distorted communication through showing how social constructions of reality can favour certain interests, and alternative constructions can be obscured and misrecognized. If these can be overcome, conflicts among different interests may be reclaimed, openly discussed, and resolved with fairness and justice. The research aims at producing dissensus and providing forums for, and models of, discussion to aid in the building of more open consensus. Of special concern are forms of false consciousness, consent, systematically distorted communication, routines, and normalizations which produce partial interests and keep people from genuinely understanding, expressing or acting on their own interests (Alvesson and Willmott, 1992, 1996; Mumby, 1988). Of the four orientations, critical theory studies have the most explicit set of value commitments and most direct attention to moral and ethical issues. With this, much of the discourse has a suspicious and therapeutic tone, but also a theory of agency which provides an additional activist tone. People can and should act on these conditions through improved understanding as well as access to communication forums.

Studies have focused both on the external relations of organizations to the wider society – especially the social effects of corporate colonization, rationalization of society, and the domination of the public sphere – and on the internal relations in terms of the domination by instrumental reasoning, discursive closures, and consent processes (Vallas, 1993; Deetz, 1992). Critical studies includes a large group of researchers who are different in theory and conception but who share important discursive features in their writing. They include Frankfurt School critical theorists (Alvesson, 1987; Alvesson and Willmott, 1992; Mumby, 1988), conflict theorists (Dahrendorf, 1959; Lehman and Young, 1974), structurationists (Giddens, 1984, 1991), some versions of feminist work (for example, Harding, 1991; Pringle, 1988), and most doing recent versions of labour process theory (Braverman, 1974; Burawoy, 1979, 1985; Knights and Willmott, 1990). While not necessarily so, in practice researchers working from the later, more explicitly political and moral writings of Foucault engage in a critical discourse (see Knights, 1992).

Dialogic studies

We have chosen the term 'dialogic' as a descriptor rather than the more obvious 'postmodernist' to organize this discourse because it attends to key features of this work and because of the growing commercial use of the term 'postmodern', which makes it increasingly difficult to distinguish between realist assumptions about a changing world (a post-modern world which could as well be described as post-industrial, post-Fordist, or ad hoc) and a postmodern or dialogic discourse which denies realist assumptions (Parker, I., 1992; Alvesson, 1995).[2] The term also makes it easier to include older theories, such as Bahktin's (see Shotter, 1993; Tyler, 1988).

Themes of dialogic studies include focusing on the constructed nature of people and reality, emphasizing language as a system of distinctions which are central to the construction process, arguing against grand narratives and large-scale theoretical systems such as Marxism or functionalism, emphasizing the power/knowledge connection and the role of claims of expertise in systems of domination, emphasizing the fluid and hyper-real nature of the contemporary world and the role of mass media and information technologies, and stressing narrative/fiction/rhetoric as central to the research process. Examples of writings including this discourse include: Burrell (1988), Hawes (1991), Martin (1990b), Calás and Smircich (1991), Knights (1992), Mumby and Putnam (1992), and several of the essays in Hassard and Parker (1993).

Dialogic studies focus on the fragmentation and potential disunity in any discourse. Like critical theory studies the concern is with asymmetry and domination, but unlike the critical theorists' predefinition of groups and types of domination, domination is considered mobile, situational, not done by anyone. Group and personal identity cannot be seen as fixed or unitary. The intention is to reclaim conflicts suppressed in everyday life realities, meaning systems, and self-conceptions and the enhancement of local forms of resistance. Fixed conceptions give way to the appeal of that beyond conception, the 'otherness' of the world and other (Linstead, 1993). Rather than critical theory's reformation of the world, dialogic studies theorists hope to show the partiality (the incompletion and onesidedness) of reality and the hidden points of resistance and complexity (Martin, 1990b; Smircich and Calás, 1987). In place of an active political agenda and the often Utopian ideals therein, attention is given to the space for a continually transforming world by recovery of marginalized and suppressed peoples and aspects of people.

Alternative roles of theory in research

'Theory' is one of many modern contested terms. Theory in the popular parlance is treated as abstract and separated from the real world. The development of 'positivist' science and elaboration of the hypothetical deductive model institutionalizes theory as representational of experience. Normative researchers often lament the lack of theory driven research. Interpretive researchers debate how explicit and active their theories should be. Critical theorists emphasize the importance of theory to adequately understand social phenomena. Clearly each of these groups does not mean the same thing by 'theory' and equally clearly many arguments about more or less theory continue because the conception of theory each has in mind is quite different. Undergirding every conception of theory is a conception of language, for as goes the issue of representation so goes the concept of theory. We wish to be clear here how we see theory relating to research. Contrasting this with the more common views is central both to understanding critical research and to the critiquing of existing research programmes.

Theory as a way of seeing and thinking
In our view, theory is a way of seeing and thinking about the world rather than an abstract representation of it. As such it is better seen as the 'lens' one uses in observation than a 'mirror' of nature (Rorty, 1979). Lest the lens metaphor suggest the possible transparency of theory – as if theory disappears if it is a good clean lens – recall that the clearest microscope gives us radically different observations from those of the telescope. Further, if the metaphor suggests the stability of a world only shown differently through different types of lens, where is the world not seen through some lens? The lens metaphor helps us to think productively about theory choice. What do we want to pay attention to? What will help us attend to that? What are the consequences of attending to that?

The treatment of observation as if it preceded and could be compared to theoretical accounts, hides the theoretical choice (whether through concept or instrumentation or both) implicit in the observation itself. Hanson (1965) captured well for the natural sciences what seems so hard for social scientists and everyday people to accept: that all observations are theory-laden. In his metaphor, theory and the external world are like the warp and woof in the fabric called observation. While the woof may typically be the more visible, the observation cannot exist without the warp. The attempt to talk about one in the absence of the other unravels the total observation leaving neither the theory nor the world as of any interest.

The problem with most theories is not that they are wrong or lacking in confirming experiences but that they are often irrelevant, misdirect observation, or function to aid only dominant groups. They do not help us make the observations that are important to meeting critical goals and the needs of the full variety of community stakeholders. Despite popular mythologies, social science theories – whether by everyday people or scholars – are rarely accepted or dismissed because of the data (Astley, 1985). As Gergen (1982) showed, the major theories that have shaped everyday thinking and definition of social science problems have had very little data. Rather they offered compelling conceptions of core life issues, often challenging both existing assumptions and the supporting dominant values. This should be no surprise as Kuhn demonstrated much the same in the natural sciences. There are reasons why certain theories are accepted and others not, but this is not simply down to facts. Further, the use of certain theories and even the findings from them are often best explained by popularity cycles, boredom, career needs, and social and economic conditions (Wagner and Gooding, 1987). Theory and research are deeply value-laden (Hamnett et al., 1984).

Gergen (1978, 1982) and Rorty (1979), among many, have shown the inadequacy of theories as representational and the hypothetical deductive model as a way of thinking about theory choice. The various assumptions of the pre-eminence of objective facts, the demand for verification, the goal of universal atemporal findings, and the presumption of a dispassionate bystander all hide the nature and evaluation of theories (Gergen, 1978, 1982). 'Facts' imply either a completion or suppression of a conflictual negotiation process involving different interests and stakeholders in the research process. 'Scientific procedures' often suppress negotiation or lead us away from examining its character. Hypothesis testing is largely self-fulfilling over time since the theory shapes what will be attended to and people respond interactively in testing situations. All findings are a historical artefact both because of theory and because people change over time, in part in response to social science reports. The question is only whether we accept the conditions and practices necessary to produce the scientific artefact. Every theory carries the values of a research community. Theory users will often substitute its terms and interpretations for those lived by the subject community (Deetz, 1973).

Modern philosophy of science, particularly as practised in the social sciences, overcompensated for the fear of the medieval authority of the church, rhetoric over reason, and the ideological bases of knowledge; in doing so, it became an arbitrary and at times capricious authority producing an ideology of its own, with its own rhetorical appeal (Schaffer, 1989). The greatest problem with a theory is not being wrong (for that will be discovered) but with misdirecting our collective attention and hindering our assessment of where it takes us. Rather than assuming simplistic conceptions of science as a fixed answer, the relation of knowledge to the human community is the task to be worked out. Such a relationship is acknowledged by every good researcher. Most often, however, it merely gets an 'of course' or a smile and a nod before the return to hypothesis testing. If we take this obvious point seriously, how would we change our theorizing, research and teaching?

The point here is not to reject hypothesis testing or finding careful methodical ways to distinguish reality-based from imaginary relations. Such activities, whether in the field or in the laboratory, however, need to be complemented by a more basic understanding of the relationship between theories and the world, relations of power and knowledge, and the relation of theories to real human communities. To do so we best understand theory as a way of being in the world. Theories are developed and are accepted in human communities based on their ability to provide interesting and useful ways of conceptualizing, thinking and talking about life events. The social science community differs from life world community primarily in regard to what is interesting and useful because of both community standards and the events that are significant (Deetz, 1995b). Most often a philosophy of science attempts to reconstruct the practices of researchers as if they could be freed from the events of their time, as if we wished that they were freed, and as if everyday people's theories in natural languages have more difficulties than social science theories in technical languages. More realistically, both everyday life and social science conceptions are needed. Everyday people respond to many mythologies and we have yet to see a life or a society that is based on a social science theory run well. This partially explains the ambivalence of researchers: the annoyance that no one listens to them and the fear that someone might. Rather than beginning with an elitist view of theory, let us start with a reconstruction of everyday life.

The functions of theory

All creatures develop ways of dealing with practical tasks and problems in their worlds. In that sense they all have theories; they have plans, they make observations, they have an idea of how these observations fit together, and a set of activities that follow. This is all we would expect of any theory. Some of them work, others fail. When they work it is always within certain parameters or domains. Few theories are failures with regard to specific situations; all theories ultimately fail if applied far enough outside of the specific conditions for which they were developed. Theories thus differ more in the size of their domain and the realistic nature of the parameters than in correctness. We all operate day in and day out with flat earth assumptions, it is only on the occasions when we wish to do things that require another model that we increase the complexity of our thought. In this sense all theories will fail in time, not because of falsity, but because human purposes and environments change.

Abstracting theory from this life context is essential for testing and critical reflection, but we can lose this essential connection. In this sense, critical reflection and testing are moments in human theorizing but scientific research and theorizing cannot be reduced to these processes. This may be clearer in an example from Austin (1961) in his analysis of the 'representation' problem in language analysis. As he reasoned, the question 'What is a rat?' differs greatly from the question, 'What is the meaning of the word "rat"?' The former treats conception as part of the human act of seeing the world in a specific interest, from a point of view. The latter question removes us from the life context and poses an abstract and universalizing question stripped of the specific domain and practical parameters. Whether the question, 'What is a rat?' arises as a child's question or as part of a dispute as to whether the creature standing in front of one is a rat, the focus is to the world, to the subject matter. The conception raises new looks, new considerations, further observations, and a relation to the other. The latter question poses the issue of correctness, cleaning up the word, nomenclature committees, and operational definitions.

As an analogue, the latter question is about theory, the former about the world with a theory as the point of view. When thinking about theory these are important complementary questions. Unfortunately we often contextualize the former with regard to the latter rather than vice versa. When this happens theory is abstracted from the world rather than intrinsic to our being directed to it. The variable analytical tradition of sequential hypothesis testing, strings of research reports disconnected from their conditions of production, and 'textbook' style knowledge. Results from such studies have this odd quality of being concrete and specific yet only referencing back to themselves in their logical interdependence rather than leading to understanding the world. Mills (1940) aptly referred to this as 'abstracted empiricism'. Ironically, the more applied and specific such knowledge is made, the further it gets from directing attention to significant features of the outside world and the more self-referential it is to its own imaginary world produced out of itself.

By investigating the function of theory in life, we can arrive at more fruitful ways of thinking about testing theory abstracted from life. Allow us to suggest three basic functions: *directing attention*, *organizing experience*, and *enabling useful responses*. Can we see differences that make a difference? Can we form and recognize patterns that specify what things are and how they relate? Can we make choices that not only enable us to survive and fulfil needs but also to create the future we want?

Directing attention   Attention is largely a trained capacity. While our sense equipment is nature's or more properly our ancient forbearers' theory of what we should be able to detect, our conceptual schemes and sense extensions become the manner of our more immediate history. At the most basic level theories direct our attention, that is, they guide us to see details of importance. Plato was certainly right (but for the wrong reasons) that if you did not know what you are looking for, you would not know when you had found it. Perceptually, this is easy to see. Recall the first time you looked into a microscope in a biology class. The grey mass to the new student was clear cells to the instructor. The eye needed to be trained not so much in seeing but in seeing the differences that mattered, setting the apparatus to be able to make those differences visible. The matter organizable as a 'cell' had to be out there, but it also needed to be 'in here' in both setting the right power and noting the key features. Changing theories is like making a gestalt shift, what is figure and what is background is the issue. Like changing the power of magnification of the microscope, you lose the ability to see certain structures for the sake of seeing others. It is not as if one or the other is the better representation of the 'real' thing; each draws attention to and displays a different structure of potential interest, a different real thing.

Perceptual examples show the basic relation but can be misleading. Let us develop an example which keeps the perceptional experience 'constant', but works with the conceptual relation. Let us use a primary school problem. The teacher presents four boxes. In each there is a picture – a tree, cat, dog, and squirrel respectively. The child is asked which one is different. A child worthy of advancement immediately picks the tree. The child knows not only how to divide plants from animals, but also that the plant/animal distinction is the preferred one to apply. The child has to reproduce a social meaning that is culturally possible *and* one that is culturally preferred. Power relations are deeply embedded in perceptional and meaning relations.

All perception is valuational. We know from the outside, however, that the child's choice is arbitrary and hardly a very interesting way to think about the problem; the choice is made more from the power of the teacher and evaluations embedded in routine classroom choices than from the nature of 'reality'. The squirrel as easily could have been picked if the child had distinguished on the bases of domesticity or things we bought at the store. Or the dog could have been picked since the cat, squirrel and tree relate in a playful interactive way. Or the child could have picked the cat since the other three are found in his or her garden. Or any one of them could have been picked based on having/not having, liking/not liking bases.

The issue is not one of the linguistic/conceptual determination of perception (for example, how many kinds of snow Eskimos have). Rather the issue is the choice of the distinctions to be used, the differences that matter. There is little problem working through the reconception of the dog, cat, squirrel and tree and finding a way to see each of them as the different one. Nature is indifferent to the choice. The question is which is the better frame to use to view the world, rather than the issue of accuracy or truth. Once the system of distinction is 'chosen', then questions arise such as: Should this be classified as an animal? What features distinguish plants and animals? And how should individuals be classified (for example, which is a virus?)? And finally, abstract theories and 'empirical' questions and hypotheses can be raised and tested. For example: How many animals are there? And since this is an animal, what behaviours should we expect? The problem with starting with hypotheses tested against the 'real' world is that the reason for the quotation marks around 'chosen', 'empirical', and 'real' is lost. Qualitative research generally, and critical work especially, has to start with the cultural question of 'what is it?' which naturally precedes any question of 'how many?' or 'what correlates with what?'.

The child who picks out the tree rarely raises the alternative conceptual distinctions to make the choice, nor do we typically when presented with the same problem. The issues do not become empirical after we have 'decided' to utilize the plant/animal rather than domestic/wild point of view, it already was empirical. We would smile at the child who when challenged said, 'yes, we could divide them into categories of domestic and wild, but they're *really* plants and animals.' The child's complaint that we are relativists totally misses the point. The presumed real, empirical and unchosen often misses the value-laden, theory-based observation. Critical researchers can reclaim the contested and contestable quality of experience because they can bring to dialogue alternatives that undermine the cultural presumption of naturalness and rightness. This is not a claim of seeing better or purer or more rightly, but of the possibility of reclaiming human choice against power-based 'realism'.

For critical researchers, human choices, even if unwittingly made, are key to making better decisions together. Human choices cannot be lost to the essentialism of either the humanists or the scientists. Quoting Rorty:

> If we fail to discern the same virtues in Skinner as in Bohr, it is not because Skinner does not understand his pigeons or his people as well as Bohr understands his particles, but because we are, reasonably enough, suspicious of people who make a business of predicting and controlling other people. We think that these virtues are not appropriate for the situation. We think that there are more important things to find out about people than how to predict and control them, even though there be nothing more important to find out about rocks, and perhaps even pigeons. But once we say that what human beings are *in themselves* suits them to be described in terms which are less apt for prediction and control than Skinner's, we are off down the same garden path as when we say that what atoms are *in themselves* suits them to be described in terms which *are* apt for predication and control. In neither case do we have the slightest idea what 'in themselves' means. We are simply expressing a preference for predicting rocks over doing anything else with them, and a preference for doing other things with people over predicting their behavior. (1981: 5; italics in original)

Unfortunately we have acquired a number of bad habits from the old philosophy of science which lead us away from understanding the importance of theory in directing attention and reclaiming dialogue against certainty. The metaphysical position that theory provides words to name characteristics of objects in themselves and mirror fixed relations among objects underestimates the inexhaustible number of things and relations our attention might be directed to see in things and hides the important issues in theory selection. Our simple practices of defining terms operationally or attributionally hides the construct's function in providing or collecting a stable object with presumed fixed attributes. Rather than seeking definitions and moving to categorize, we should ask: what are we able to see or think about if we talk about it in this way rather than that?

Organizing experience   Theory not only directs our attention, it also presents our observation as being part of meaningful patterns. The perception of an individual already pulls together past experience with similar people (the lines of relation following the distinctions being utilized) and reaches to anticipate possible actions. Everyday people, like social scientists, are constantly engaged in the process of trying to explain the past and present and trying to predict the future and possible responses to our own actions. But prediction and control, like spiritual and teleological models, account for only part of the available structurings and human interests displayed in patterning. The nature of patterns and types of patterns experienced is potentially very rich. The observation of continuity rather than discontinuity, pattern simplification rather than pattern complexification are not simply given in nature but arise out of human orientation to the world (Foucault, 1970). Predication and control should properly be seen as one human motive which is at times privileged over competing motives and organizing schemes.

One of the facets of modern social science is the projection of its own motive to enhance control onto the subjects that it studies. This is perhaps clearest in interpersonal interaction studies, especially as applied to supervisor–subordinate relations. In everyday life, interpersonal relations often show the greatest degree of open negotiation and mutual decision making. Ironically the usual research emphasis on uncertainty reduction, compliance gaining and persuasion mirror more closely the philosophy of science used by the researchers than that of people we relate to. Researchers could be focusing on the difference of the other enjoying curiosity, excitement of novelty, and self-change (one wonders whether objectifying the other is the cause or result of the fear of control which seems to fill the research).

Clearly all research is historically situated and filled with the preferences of the dominant groups at its time. This gives it relevance as well as blinders. People and societies concerned with individualism and control organize experience differently to those interested in the community and fate. Each orientation can produce empirically confirmable structures and orders, but all are one-sided. Cognitive theorists have been most sensitive to the relation of social science community orders and everyday orders, and tell us much about the various types of ordering relations people have developed and use. Unfortunately, they tend to glorify rule-following reasoning as a metatext for examining and discussing alternatives. While the orders produced may be quite different, the twin themes of differentiation and organization appear central to theorizing.

Enabling useful responses   Theories in everyday life as well as in social science have a pragmatic motive. While this may often be covered up with claim of universal truth, the choice is always of this truth versus that one, this 'what' versus that one. Kelly (1955) demonstrated this clearly from the individual standpoint in his development of the pragmatic basis of personal constructs. Constructs are developed and elaborated in directions which help people accomplish life goals. Institutionalized social science merely extends this individual process. There appears to be little disagreement with this basic motivational frame, though it can be quite complex in practice.

Theoretical conceptions which are useful to one individual or group can be quite detrimental to others. The social choice of theories, therefore, always has to consider questions such as whose goals will count for how much. Consequently, looked at from the perspective of the society, useful responses have to be considered in terms of some conception of social good as viewed from the positions of multiple stakeholders. Unfortunately the issue of pragmatics is often read too narrowly, both in everyday life and in the social sciences. Pragmatics as a simple instrumental motive overlooks the competing human desires to overcome their initial subjective motives, to make their own histories toward a richer collective life, the goals critical work highlights (see Habermas, 1971). When theories are considered instrumentally, efficient and effective goal accomplishment would appear to be easily agreed upon social goods. But not only do such goals have to be assessed from the standpoint of whose goals are accomplished, but efficiency and effectiveness are not themselves goods (Carter and Jackson, 1987: 73ff.).

Dewey gives us a better lead on making choices regarding alternative theories. Rorty phrased his basic questions as: 'What would it be like to believe that? What would happen if we did? What would we be committing myself to?' (1982: 163) Such a position does not so much give us an answer to the questions of social good, but poses the locus and nature of responsibility. Theories about human beings are different from theories about chemicals; they ultimately influence what people, as the subjects of the research, will become. How we conceptualize and talk about ourselves and others influences what we become. Theories function to produce responses which produce ourselves, our social interaction, our institutions, and our collective future. Theories must be assessed in light of the kind of society we wish to produce. We are concerned with meeting our needs and with doing so in a way which makes us better people. In Rorty's words:

To say that we become different people, that we ('remake') ourselves as we read more, talk more, and write more, is simply a dramatic way of saying that sentences which become true of us by virtue of such activities are often more important to us than sentences which become true of us when we drink more, earn more, and so on . . . getting the facts right . . . is merely propaedeutic to finding new and more interesting ways of expressing ourselves, and thus of coping with the world. (1979: 359)

All current theories will pass in time. It is not as if they are in error, at least little more or less so than those in the past. Older theories were useful in handling different kinds of human problems, problems we might find ill-formed and even silly, as others will ours. What remains is the human attempt to produce theories that are useful in responding to our own issues. We are struggling to find interesting and useful ways of thinking and talking about our current situation and helping us build the future we want. Such hope is intrinsic to theorizing rather than external to it. Careful attention to theoretical choices makes it intrinsic to research practices themselves.

Power and knowledge
At least since Bacon most in the West have believed that knowledge is power, that having or possessing knowledge gives its holder choices and influence. Contemporary thinking has of course totally rearranged such an equation. Foucault (1970, 1980a) in particular has focused attention on the power *in*, rather than the power *of*, knowledge. There is a politics within the production of knowledge. As Hoy (1986: 129) expressed it, 'the relation is such that knowledge is not gained prior to and independent of the use to which it will be put in order to achieve power (whether over nature or over people), but is already a function of human interests and power relations.' In this sense in each society in each age there is a regime of truth generated out of a network of power relations. Certain discourses are accepted and made true and mechanisms are developed which enable the distinction between true and false statements. Experts are produced out of the same system to affirm the knowledge claims (Townley, 1992; Knights, 1992).

Again, this does not suggest that 'truth' is relative in any simple way, for within the constraints of interests and values, competing claims can be compared. But the choice of research questions and the choice of constraints and values are historical choices and are politically charged. For example, the frequent tension between religious and scientific truth exists at the point each tries to extend itself into the other's discourse. When science describes what is and religion describes what one should do, they coexist. In contemporary society, science gets in trouble when it tries empirically to derive oughts and religion when it tries to explain empirical reality. The conditions for making a claim to truth differ in each. Knowledge is not so much to be accepted, then, as to be explained. The concern is to explain the conditions constitutive of leading forms of knowledge in particular communities.

The point here is not to find a way to settle conflicting knowledge claims, not to degrade truth, but to recall the disciplinary power necessary for any knowledge claim (Foucault, 1980a). The knowledge claimed in everyday life – in its institutions of science, commerce and religion – as well as knowledge about knowledge claims in everyday life, is politically loaded. Laying out their driving interests and mechanisms of knowledge production and defence is central to understanding how they work. The central problem in most community-based decisions is not in the lack of adequately distributed information (though that can be a problem), but in processes of information production. Open participation can be advanced at each point in information production through examination of choice of questions, conception, and research practices (Harding, 1991; Whyte, 1991), through publication (Deetz, 1995b), and interpretation. Issues of power are involved at each point, issues that are often obscured by claims of truth and expertise. Critical research tries to engage in the power dynamics of truth in organizations without setting itself up as the final arbitrator of truth claims or new knowledge regime.

Notes

1 The discussion in this section is adapted from Deetz's (1996) discussion of the problems of Burrell and Morgan's (1979) paradigm divisions. Several revisions of Burrell and Morgan are crucial. The term 'normative' is used to describe most of the same research positions that Burrell and Morgan called functionalist. This frees the description from a particular school of sociological thought and draws attention to both their search for the normal – the regularity – and the value-laden nature of their use in 'normalizing' people and the existing social conditions. 'Dialogic' draws attention to the relational aspect of 'postmodernism' and avoids the periodicity issue. Note too that critical work is shown with more affinity to 'normative' work (rather than the total opposition in Burrell and Morgan's 'functionalist/radical humanist' configuration) because of their directive qualities in contrast to the strong 'otherness' guidance in interpretive and dialogic work. The a priori/elite–local/emergent dimension replaces the subjective–objective dimension in Burrell and Morgan. The subject–object dualism on which their dimension was based is problematic. First it tends to reproduce the subject–object dualism that is present in the philosophies underlying 'normative' research but not the other positions. Second, it misplaces normative research overlooking its subjectivity in domination of nature

and in defining people's experience for them. And third, it fails to highlight the constructionist quality of all research programmes.

2 This is then basically a sociological or periodization type of postmodern psychology, and is also to some extent used by authors who neither see themselves as postmodernist nor talk about postmodern, for example, Berger et al. (1973) or Lasch (1978, 1984).

3

Critical overview of quantitative and conventional qualitative methodology

For some time, considerable dissatisfaction has existed with conventional approaches to social research, including management research. Much of this conventional research was dominated by positivistic or neo-positivistic assumptions and methods emphasizing ideals such as objectivity, neutrality, scientific procedure, technique, quantification, replicability, generalization, and discovery of laws. The inadequacies of the dominant quantitative, hypothesis-testing approach has led to an increasing use of qualitative methods (Denzin and Lincoln, 1994; Morgan and Smircich, 1980). Still, the popularity, status and use of qualitative methods varies among different social and behavioural sciences and different countries. For example, in the US quantitative approaches still heavily dominate, whereas in British and Swedish management studies qualitative methods take the upper hand. More generally, anthropology is typically as strongly qualitative as psychology is quantitative. In management studies, the study of organizational cultures has been largely anthropological and qualitative while studies of 'organizational behaviour' – leadership, motivation, stress – frequently draw upon the research ideals dominant in psychology.

In this chapter we provide a critical review of 'mainstream' methodology – quantitative as well as qualitative. Initially we examine some of the key assumptions of neo-positivism. Instead of operating on a general level and using examples from a variety of areas, we concentrate on one specific field of study – leadership research – and supplement it with other illustrations. Leadership studies is one of the central themes in management research and is convenient in illustrating some of the basic shortcomings in mainstream methodologies. We then try to account for the limited success of conventional research, continuing with an argument against the ideal of developing a grand theory for leadership. Next, we focus on the misleading characterization of research alternatives by focusing on traditional qualitative–quantitative difference discussions and the contrived nature of the subjective–objective distinction. Some basic difficulties in qualitative methods are highlighted in the final section. This will prepare us to develop in detail the 'critical' alternative in the remainder of the book.

The sorry state of the art of leadership research

Like many other fields of management studies, research on leadership has been strongly dominated by neo-positivist/normative assumptions, together with an emphasis on rules and procedures for the securing of objectivity in practice and results. Thousands of studies have been conducted, particularly in the US. The enormous resources in terms of money, time, energy and talent spent on leadership research can be seen as a gigantic experiment testing whether neo-positivist methodology works or not and a good place to investigate what 'works' means. Does traditional research on leadership meet its own criteria of knowledge accumulation? This question should be central. Mainstream methodology argues that well-conducted studies should lead to a steady growth in knowledge, greater convergence in verification/falsification of theories, and growing support for more and more accurate theories with expanded explanatory and predictive capacities. If the philosophical assumptions and rules for method were sound, then one or a set of empirically well-supported theories, providing an excellent understanding of leadership phenomena and providing valuable advice for practitioners, would have been produced. For outsiders, such as ourselves, the degree of 'success' in terms of providing an understanding of leadership is not very high. Radical rethinking of both research goals and methods appears more appropriate than calling for five thousand more studies following the same logic.

More importantly, while not all agree, most insiders also see the outcome of these enormous efforts as meager. One review of the research concluded that 'the only point of agreement is that existing approaches have largely lost their usefulness for the further development of the field' (Andriessen and Drenth, 1984: 514). Another reviewer, Yukl, claimed that 'progress continues in developing better understanding of leadership traits, behavior, power, and situational factors' (1989: 254). But he also concluded that the field 'is presently in a state of ferment and confusion. Most of the theories are beset with conceptual weaknesses and lack strong empirical support. Several thousand empirical studies have been conducted on leadership effectiveness, but most of the results are contradictory and inconclusive' (Yukl, 1989: 253). Even for an insider such as Yukl, who is sympathetic to 'mainstream' views about social science, the state of the art includes 'some real progress' at the same time as 'the yield of knowledge is much less than would be expected from the immense literature on leadership' (1989: 279). To be fair, some researchers feel more positively about current research (House and Aditya, 1997).

Several authors have called for a profound reorientation from the elaboration and measurement of abstracted constructs to the analysis of leadership as a practical accomplishment and social process defined through interaction based on a qualitative approach (Bryman, 1996; Hosking, 1988; Knights and Willmott, 1992; Smircich and Morgan, 1982). This book argues along these lines, but goes further than most advocates of a qualitative approach in certain respects. For example, we address problems with the constructive and political nature of the research project, the constitutive, 'positioning' role of language, and suggest an approach that allows more space for reflexivity as well as reader engagement in the sense-making of empirical material. We will come back to this. The goals as well as the methods should be more open to scrutiny.

Of course, leadership studies is not the only field in management in which the growth of research leads to variation and confusion rather than convergence of opinion and development of better, well-supported theories. Without going into detail, similar discouraging outcomes may be found in areas such as motivation (Shamir, 1991) and organizational structures (Veen, 1984). This certainly poses a core problem for normative research. But from our standpoint the problem is actually different to, and bigger than, this. The disdain directed at variation and confusion keeps the varied and confusing results from being embraced and explored for richer and more complex understandings of leadership. Instead new studies attempt to simplify and try to get it right. The studies are neither designed for, nor evaluated by, their capacity to challenge leading assumptions or to provide multiple ways of understanding leadership or other organizational phenomena. The central problem with normative research (and the various qualitative research programmes accepting similar neo-positivist assumptions) arises, as we initially sketched, from their view of the nature of reality and the relation of language, theory and research to it. Core to this is their attempt to fix and mirror organizational phenomena. Let us spend a moment applying our more general consideration of theory to this problem.

The development of general and abstract knowledge aiming to explain and predict social phenomena in a law-like, causal fashion requires the production of a stable object which continues through time. Language can thus name and represent the phenomenon/variable and research can describe its nature and its relation to other variables. But problems arise in both assuming/creating 'leadership' as a stable object in the real world of organizations and difficulties occur in language simply representing it in a neutral way.

As we have shown in our discussion of the role of theory, postmodernists and other language-focusing philosophies, such as Wittgenstein's, have done much to show that language does not work as the mirror of nature but tends to function in a much more complicated way. Language use is metaphorical rather than literal, relies on the repression/denial of alternative meanings, is local and context-related rather than abstract, and so on. However, we will not start in this end, but rather look at the efforts of advocates of mainstream methodology to control the subject matter through definitions and to avoid the ambiguity of language through standardized procedure. We do not start from an approach directly antithetic to the mainstream but proceed from the logic and moves of 'the field' – in this case the researchers – and then inductively show the problems. Later we draw upon a more critical kind of thinking; here we start with a line of reasoning more sympathetic and less alien to conventional assumptions.

Problems in freezing the subject matter

There is a wide spectrum of definitions of leadership. Yukl (1989) says that 'the numerous definitions of leadership that have been proposed appear to have little else in common' than involving an influence process. He seems to attribute part of the lack of progress in the field to its variety. However, we think that a common definition of leadership is not practically possible, would not be very helpful if it was, and may also obstruct new ideas and interesting ways of thinking. We think that the question 'what is leadership?' is misleading. A better question would be 'what can we see, think, or talk about if we think of leadership as this or that?' But a single definition of leadership is essential for building cumulative knowledge in the normative tradition.

In Yukl's view, leadership must refer to a phenomenon that can be delimited and ascribed a relatively specific meaning. It must refer to a core phenomenon that cuts through surface variations. The degree of diversity associated with 'leadership' must be restricted to the benefit of a universal quality. Most academic as well as other kinds of leadership talk has totalizing aspirations. Researchers define the term to capture the universal and either intentionally suppress cultural and historical variation and diversity or treat culture and time as variables influencing the 'unitary' thing called leadership. 'Leadership' is typically defined in general terms. The ambition is to say something of relevance across quite diverse settings. It is often used to pull together categorically the behaviours, styles, and personalities of quite diverse groups, for example university department chairs, SS officers, US presidents, gang leaders, project managers, non-violence civil rights spokespersons, and students in experimental groups that seem to be spontaneously ascribed higher status and/or more influence than others. Informal leadership may well refer to (formal) subordinates influencing/guiding (formal) superiors, not just managers interacting with their (formal) subordinates. This diversity means that a coherent definition with universal aspirations may tell us relatively little in terms of the richness and complexity of the quite varied phenomena it supposedly refers to. It hides this variation and gives a false impression of similarity through the use of abstract labels such as task or personnel orientation, authoritarian or participatory orientation.

Leadership is complex in the ongoing life of people. And the everyday word 'leadership' carries this ambiguity in both definition and usage. The normative researcher evokes the richness and importance of this everyday term but tries to strip it of its full social meaning. However, the definer seldom manages to control meaning particularly well outside the confines of his or her own measurement devices. The impossibility of fixing a concept is partly related to the ways in which words are informed by the root metaphors for the phenomenon being studied. Researchers, like other people, structure our worlds metaphorically (Alvesson, 1993a; Brown, 1977; Morgan, 1980, 1986). Words get their meaning through the metaphorical context in which they are employed. This means that words work in an imaginative and associative rather than analytically clear-cut manner. The same definition may then be informed by different metaphors and thus different meanings.

Leadership as a term/set of meanings is not different in this regard from other terms in management research. Organizational culture researchers may, for example, embrace a similar definition of culture as a set of meanings, ideas, values and symbolism shared by a group. But this may well be accompanied by a high diversity of thinking due to the metaphor for culture perhaps being one of a compass functionally guiding direction, a sacred cow protecting certain basic assumptions and ideals from being questioned or changed, or a frozen reality where the (dominant) meanings, ideas and values fix the current social reality and subordinate the organizational members to it (Alvesson, 1993a). Definition is thus only a limited element in how language and cognition work. The attempt of normative researchers to limit language concerns to definition are not likely to succeed, even if it were to be preferred.

'Leadership' is not likely to be standardized, even if a particular definition may appear to dominate, given the variety of existent 'real phenomena' that leadership research may address, the idiosyncrasies of all the researchers (in particular if they are not all Euro-Americans), and the ambiguities of language, ways of think- ing and doing research. One and the same formal definition is likely to be accompanied by a variety of different meanings, since people belonging to different intellectual traditions and cultural contexts read and use the words. The more universal and totaliz- ing the definition proposed, the greater variation in meanings and language use. Further, the more dominant the definition, the more likely that the 'phenomenon' is only understood as it is preferred by some limited and dominant group (see Calás and Smircich, 1991; Martin, 1990a).

We may illustrate the shortcomings of definitions by discussing the one used by Yukl, an authority in the field. Here, 'leadership is defined broadly in this article to include influencing task objectives and strategies, influencing commitment and compliance in task behavior to achieve these objectives, influencing group mainte- nance and identification, and influencing the culture of an organi- zation' (1989: 253). This definition is thoughtful and certainly not inferior to other efforts to define the subject matter. Knights and Willmott (1992), for example, cite it and adapt it in their article, even though they come from a completely different research tradi- tion than Yukl. But one could very well let the words 'leadership' and 'culture' change place and then have a definition of culture. Or swap leadership and strategy and the definition still makes a lot of sense. One could also replace leadership with organizational struc- ture, job design, social identity, management or something else. (Weick, 1985, has used this trick to show how some definitions of strategy and culture are roughly the same.) Actually, the definition could be used almost irrespective of which sub-area of manage- ment is being studied. Still, the word 'leadership' triggers associa- tions different than those triggered by 'culture' or 'strategy'.

Claiming 'leadership' as a general, distinct phenomenon, concep- tualized in a uniform manner and having clear relationships to other particular, distinct phenomena is difficult. The two problems pointed out in this section are interrelated: the social worlds of inter- est for leadership researchers do not easily lend themselves to neat categorization and ordering, and language use has its limitations in relation to the goal of fixing meaning through definitions. This relates to the distinction used in Chapter 2, on elite/a priori versus local/emerging approaches. The former approach tries to fix research themes in advance, imposing definitions on ambiguous social reality, thereby aiming to control it and subordinate it to a generalized theoretical and methodological apparatus. The impossibility of mobilizing language so that it works according to this logic – even at the level of formally defining the subject matter – provides a strong case for a move to a more local/emergent approach.

Other key concepts in management and other social research face the same problem when authors try to fix and standardize meaning. For example, culture, strategy, communication, social institution, structure, management, and manager cannot be defined once and for all. No simple one-to-one relationship between the word and a distinct part of social reality can be established across a wide variety of social and organizational contexts.

As we have argued, instead of language being capable of mirroring or fixing part of social reality, it works through providing a way of engaging phenomena or illuminating phenomena in a particular way. Language operates through how the author and reader construct meaning based on the local context, on how discursive logics form associations, how one writes and reads between the lines, and through appealing to a prestructured understanding associated with culture and tradition. When we talk about leadership – or anything else – we sometimes achieve a fair amount of common understanding through the insights, experiences, blind spots and biases associated with cultural belongingness and general language use. The reader (as well as the researcher) 'knows' in advance what 'leadership' is and can, therefore, separate it from 'culture' or 'strategy' due to commonsensical cultural conventions. The latter form a vital, mainly non-explicit and extra-academic resource for intellectual work, but they also mean prejudices, taken-for-granted assumptions and tend to lock researchers and others into closed, conservative and uncreative modes of thinking. Breaking up established ways of using language is, therefore, a vital task for critical research.

Problems with questionnaires

Quantitative research may be defined as research aiming at reducing ambiguity through transforming perceptions into prestructured, quantifiable categories. Typical methods include using existing statistics, observation scales, tests, questionnaires and experiments. A wide array of variations and possible combinations of methods are possible. Still there are common themes. Much research is governed by an ambition of objectivity. To accomplish this, empirical material often becomes quite artificial or artefactual. Sometimes experiments are seen as the most rigorous method, because the researcher is supposedly in a position to control the variables involved and isolate pure effects. In the human studies, however, such research has considerable problems. Often they may be simply the study of the behaviour of students in simplified and artificial settings. It is thus a question of what, exactly, can be learned from laboratory studies. What seems to hold true in the laboratory does not necessarily correspond with what might be going on in the outside world. Extended critiques of neo-positivist research are readily available so we will not provide another here; however, we would like to look at a specific case of leadership research to illustrate the more general issues.

Seltzer and Bass (1990) have studied what they and others refer to as 'transformational leadership'. Their work, published in a relatively prestigious journal, appears to be a relatively good study and representative of many studies. 'Transformational leadership' has received considerable attention during recent years and is often seen as one of the most promising areas within leadership research.

Seltzer and Bass delivered a questionnaire to 84 managers participating in an MBA education asking them to instruct three subordinates each to respond to it. Measures included issues such as 'charisma' (for example, 'My manager makes me proud to be associated with him/her') and 'leader's effectiveness' (for example, 'overall effectiveness of your unit'). The respondents were quite positive in their responses. On average they score the next highest response alternative on the four or five point scales used on most issues; on average their unit is 'very effective' (3.9 on the 5 point scale), the manager makes the respondent proud to be associated with him/her 'fairly often' (2.9 on a 4 point scale), etc. One may draw the conclusion that these results show that the 84 managers participating in the education are, on average, an exceptionally competent bunch of people leading high-performance units. After all, not everybody can be 'very effective', as the word has a relative connotation; for someone to be effective, someone else has to be less effective. An interpretation equally plausible would be that the sample, on average, has poor judgement, strongly overestimating themselves (their units) and their managers. Or perhaps the procedure, where subordinates are instructed by their managers to fill in the questionnaires, makes the former produce positive responses. Many plausible interpretations exist.

Further, the choice of statements in the study indicate some of the difficulties associated with letting the researcher decide what respondents should reply to. The statement, 'My manager makes me proud to be associated with him/her' may well be in a rather awkward relationship to the words and statements that most employees may feel relevant to describe their experiences and relations. By singling out 'proud' as a key dimension of the relationship, other ways of describing the relationship are silenced. This may be seen as a direct expression of the arbitrary choices of the researcher or a culturally specific manner of experience. The subordinates' 'X' in square 'fairly often' may be interpreted in various ways. It may be understood as an expression of a wish to oil the relationship with the boss (who is said to get an aggregated summary of the responses of the three subordinates by the researcher. The respondents may also suspect that the manager may look at individuals' answers). The subordinates may feel that putting the 'X' in that square may be appropriate, given norms in Western society about the subject matter. If it should say anything whatsoever about the experiences and feelings of the respondent, it may equally well be seen as an expression of their immaturity or lack of autonomy with regard to the charisma of the manager. In general, for someone to appear as 'charismatic' a crucial prerequisite is probably the right kind of subordinates/followers (Alvesson, 1995). Well-educated people, developing a self-image as being 'autonomous' are probably not particularly easily affected by the rhetoric of those business heroes often described as charismatic in popular and scientific literature. Information which would help sort out these different interpretations is absent from the questionnaire.

Unpacking leadership
The entire structuring of the research object as 'leadership' is another matter of dispute. Leadership is implicitly defined as something which characterizes the formal superior in relation to subordinates. This is, of course, far from unquestionable. In the Seltzer and Bass (1990) sample, 11 'managers' indicated that they had no subordinates which meant that they were eliminated from the study. In many other cases, it was probably ambiguous as to the extent to which clear-cut superior–subordinate relationships were present.

Borgert (1994), working as a consultant, led a 'leadership' course for people who according to their superior (who believed that they needed the course 'in order to strengthen them in their leadership role') were 'managers'. The course members on the whole did not seem to experience themselves in that way, even protesting against this attribution through exhibiting resistance to the course, for example expressing doubts as to its relevance for them. Many in the group were perhaps best described as seniors in small work groups. And further, most of the participants were female. Leadership may be quite different for women and they may be less prone to emphasize and associate their identity with formal superiority than many men (Billing and Alvesson, 1994). Watson (1994) also shows that managers above the more junior levels experience their situation as contradictory, and that elements of superiority and being in control are often not salient.

In the Seltzer and Bass study, as in many other questionnaire studies, there is limited space for discovering the ambiguities of work tasks and social relations. If people do not directly report that they have no subordinates, then they are defined as managers and engaged in 'leadership'. This construction of social reality is, of course, far from being unproblematic. The research methodology simply produces a particular version of social relations, against which multifaceted, contra-intuitive empirical indications have problems in materializing. Given the strong initial assumption that the course participants are 'managers' and that they are supposed to 'have' subordinates, most of those asked to give questionnaires to the latter probably were inclined to find some people who could be seen to be subordinates. It is likely that this approach led to constructions which were quite different to what would have been the case given a more open approach, sensitive to the meanings of the people involved instead of the rigid structuring of the social relations concerned in terms of fixed asymmetrical relations associated with the notions of leader and subordinate.

One could also, as a thought experiment, consider the possibility of dropping the 'manager/leader' construction and replacing it with 'the most senior colleague' or something to that effect. Perhaps that person makes the respondent 'fairly often' feel proud to be associated with him or her, 'provides advice to those who need it', etc. Here one could, of course, talk about informal leadership but the value of that interpretation/labelling is not self-evident. In many workplaces probably there are people who are not managers, not inclined to exercise systematic influence from the position of 'informal leader', but who still have a good reputation – capable of and willing to give advice on certain issues, etc. This is often salient in professional organizations where formal managers may score lower than some other participants on the measures employed by Seltzer and Bass of 'transformational leadership' without being perceived as exercising (informal) leadership. It is not an unknown phenomenon in other contexts either.

A final point with regard to how this research design impresses a certain commonsensical, but questionable, normative structure on the research subjects. When exposed to the statement 'My manager makes me proud to be associated with him/her', the respondent may read it as a message from social science that it is normal or good for subordinates to feel in a particular way about their managers, 'once in a while', 'sometimes' or 'fairly often'. The two alternatives 'frequently, if not always' and 'not at all' tend to be seen as extreme. The impression may be created that one should be proud of and admire the boss, at least occasionally, if one is not abnormal or the manager a complete failure. A particular view of managers is thus created and communicated to (a) research respondents and (b) uncritical readers of the study. Managers becoming familiar with the results may feel that they should behave in a way that makes subordinates 'proud' of working with or for them. This standard may have disciplinary effects, that is creating a norm to which the subject orientates and monitors her- or himself (see Foucault, 1980a, 1982).

Much more can be said about the Seltzer and Bass study – or about other examples of normative research – but that would go well beyond the purpose of this text. One could perhaps argue that it is in some ways weaker than the best examples of positivist research on leadership, but many of the problems are probably common. It is important to realize that leaders, subordinates, and measurements of various qualities, feelings and outcomes are social constructions – they are not simple reflections of objective reality. The activities of the researcher constructs in various ways the 'reality' that takes the superficial appearance of being stable and real. Many of the problems mentioned also characterize qualitative work, but such research includes better possibilities of being open and reflective about these moves/constructions. These possibilities are far from always utilized, as a lot of qualitative studies also reproduce commonsensical notions of social reality. We will come back to this.

We feel that it is important to move from abstract, general categories and efforts to standardize meaning towards an increased focus on local patterns, where the cultural and institutional context and meaning creation patterns are driven by participants – or jointly by participants and researchers – rather than being one-sidedly, indeed authoritarianly, decided by the researcher. A more open kind of study, in which complex social relations and processes are treated as such and not transformed beyond recognition through the application of standardized measures and abstract categories, is much more rewarding.

This would mean that aspirations to develop a grand theory, in which a limited number of variables and causal relations are seen as being relevant for the formulation of laws or law-like patterns about a subject matter (for example, leadership), are forgotten or at least downplayed and that the researcher takes seriously the ambiguity of that which may be interpreted as 'leadership', to continue using this example. This term covers a wide diversity of actions, feelings, thoughts, relations and social processes; and the merits of applying this concept – interpretive device – are seldom self-evident. To understand what it is about requires care to be taken with respect to the vocabulary applied and respect for the contextual character of language and meaning. This calls for intimacy in relation to the phenomenon under study and depth of understanding at the expense of abstraction, generalizability, and the artificial separation of theory and data.

Qualitative methods offer far better possibilities in this enterprise (for example, Smircich and Morgan, 1982). Many versions of this methodology are, however, unaware of some basic difficulties with data construction – for example, in interviews. We spend the remainder of this chapter looking at the ways qualitative work has been contrasted with quantitative. Some of the contrasts and self-conceptions make if difficult for qualitative researchers to do work that is significantly different from normative work. Much of the contribution is lost. We will look at these differences and discuss limitations. In the next chapters we formulate constructive principles and ideas for the redirection of research taking seriously the interpretive and linguistic turns in contemporary social science.

Problems with the qualitative/quantitative division

Generally, one can say that qualitative research is increasingly popular in the various fields of social science, including management studies. Arguments for this shift include claims that qualitative research makes possible broader and richer descriptions, sensitivity to the ideas and meanings of the individuals concerned, increased likelihood of developing empirically supported new ideas and theories, together with increased relevance and interest for practitioners (Denzin and Lincoln, 1994; Martin and Turner, 1986). Practitioners in many fields often view questionnaire studies as superficial and the abstractions of quantified material and statistical correlations as very remote from everyday practice and, therefore, of little use – at least when dealing with human aspects of organizational life. Apart from the relative merits and claims, the last three decades have been filled with debates between quantitative and qualitative researchers and many attempts to form a happy marriage between them.

As was implicit in the discussion in Chapter 2, we do not find the quantitative/qualitative distinction terribly insightful or useful. The crucial issue for researchers is not the choice between quantitative or qualitative methods, but involves much more fundamental ontological, epistemological, and axiological concerns (Alvesson and Sköldberg, 2000; Deetz, 1996; Guba and Lincoln, 1994). Drawing the great battle line between quantitative and qualitative may be quite misleading as it draws attention to less crucial aspects of research. As Morrow (1994: 207) writes, 'the predominant distinction between quantitative and qualitative methods in sociology serves primarily to conceal and confuse theoretical positions. This distinction focuses our attention on the techniques through which social life is represented in the course of research, as opposed to the process of representing social reality.'

Many, indeed most, as shown in our dissensus–consensus contrast, variations of qualitative methodology share with normative (neo-positivist) researchers a number of assumptions and commitments which are problematic and narrow research agendas. Research, as we have argued, may aid human development by highlighting the precarious and debatable nature of knowledge rather than unidimensional and accumulative 'truths'. Many versions of qualitative method do not deviate radically from nineteenth-century positivist assumptions:

- an objective external reality awaits the discovery and dissection by science;
- scientific methods give privileged access to this reality;
- language is a transparent medium for categorization, measurement and representation;
- the observer-scientist stands outside and above the social reality;
- he or she authoritatively develops or validates robust theories about social reality.

Strauss and Corbin, for example, argue that grounded theory – one of the more prominent versions of qualitative method – 'is a scientific method' that 'meets the criteria for doing "good science": significance, theory-observation compatibility, generalizability, reproducibility, precision, rigor, and verification' (1990: 27). Grounded theory's claims to power here implicitly deny the value of research methods that do not aim for this 'ideal'. As Strauss and Corbin point out, qualitative research (as they propose it) varies from other forms of 'science' (which they seem to use as a synonym to normative research) in terms of how these virtues are realized – the precise version of the general virtues is contingent upon the specific methodological approach used – although they do not question, challenge or radically reformulate conventional ideas about science. Like many qualitative researchers, they do not suggest alternative criteria. While grounded theory focuses on qualified descriptions and empirically generated theory development rather than deductive hypothesis testing, verification is central to their criteria for good research.

Neo-empiricist qualitative methods, like grounded theory, share with neo-positivist hypothesis-testing an appreciation of the difficulty of achieving objectivity, accumulative knowledge and science as a completely rational project.[1] Problems with the neo–empiricism project, arising from insight into the constructed, interpretive nature of empirical material and the impossibility in keeping data and theory/research language apart, are occasionally mentioned (for example, Huberman and Miles, 1994; Strauss and Corbin, 1994). But they tend to be minimized and are claimed to have a limited impact on practical research in empirical as well as theoretical work. Clearly to them these are technical problems to be overcome, or at least to be coped with in a satisfactory way, rather than central concerns which call into question the entire neo-positivist project.

In practice, awareness of the critique of positivism and empiricism leads to lip service responses and is almost neglected in terms of implications for research practice. Most conventional researchers probably neither know nor understand the more fundamental critiques directed against positivism and its modern variants by an increasing number of philosophers, language students, and social and behavioural scientists (for reviews, see Alvesson and Sköldberg, 1999; Denzin and Lincoln, 1994; Steier, 1991). Often they dismiss such concerns as non-constructive rather than rethinking the new and potentially positive role of their work if understood within the larger context of knowledge and society.

Here we intend to go beyond neo-empiricist qualitative methods by reviewing and incorporating some of the major onto-logical and epistemological critiques of mainstream understanding. We wish to take seriously a qualitative approach that takes in the social, political and constructed nature of social phenomena, that is all kinds of empirical material of interest in the social and behavioural sciences.

Forgetting rather than rejecting 'objectivity'

Problematizing language and the hope for neutral representation is a cornerstone in critical research and, according to an increasing number of researchers, any form of reflective research (Alvesson and Sköldberg, 2000; Deetz, 1992). The conventional views on language and the attached ideal of research as an activity developing objective knowledge of an objective social reality through methods maximizing objectivity/minimizing subjectivity are misleading at best.

Objectivity as the principal virtue of research is hard to sustain under examination and creates a number of problems. We are not denying in anyway the existence of – or the importance of taking seriously – an external reality, or the ability of normative researchers to produce reproducible results if they sufficiently constrain either the external world or their attention to aspects of it. As we argued in regard to theory and showed simply in the 'cat, dog, tree, squirrel' problem in Chapter 2, perception requires both an interest or way of relating to the world and a world that can be related to in that way. The world, in itself, is fundamentally indeterminant; it is made determinant in specific ways by human interests in and ways of relating to it. Facts and data are produced and make sense only in the context of a particular framework that allows and guides us to see certain things and neglect others. A genuinely disinterested researcher would have no world, or at least not one world that would be of interest to anyone. The researcher is part of a socially constructed world. What passes as a neutral, remotely distanced position is a particular shared social position. The questions of interest are: 'Whose position is it?', 'What does it allow us to see?' and 'What does it overlook?' This does not mean that all research is subjective in any simple way. The important point is that subjective–objective distinctions generally, as they are often used in discussing differences between quantitative and qualitative research, are not particularly useful when thinking about differences between research programmes.

The old subjective/objective fight could be had. Something called subjectivity could be demonstrated in all research programmes. For example, studies of management are partly a result of cultural tradition and of 'subjective' interests, values and pre-structured understandings. One's own life history, belongingness to a specific research community, and everyday experience inform how one thinks and acts in relationship to the subject matter. These have an impact on the questions asked, the language used and, by implication, the results produced. The area in which an individual works also affects them in terms of values and preferences. A number of studies of (US) economists have, for example, showed that they seem to be affected by the (utilitarian) assumptions of their knowledge area – they behave in a more self-interested way than other academic groups (Frank et al., 1993). Researchers of leadership and other management topics often take a managerial point of view and are more inclined to favour asymmetrical social relations and managerial 'rights', even when recommending 'teams' and employee involvement/participation. Any tendency in this direction would definitely have an impact on the management knowledge produced – and possibly account for some of the peculiarities of the field. For example, much management research assumes somewhat rigid principles of dividing human beings into leaders and followers (managers/subordinates) and thus produces knowledge salient for strategic management and leaders' advancement.

Normative researchers have well-rehearsed answers to these claims. Much of the understanding of science itself is composed of its stands against these potential subjective elements. The idiosyncrasies of researchers should be balanced against the judgements of others; a wide spectrum of viewpoints should be considered before a specific one is celebrated; and empirical claims, arguments and theoretical ideas should be subject to independent replication and/or refutation. We have total sympathy with idiosyncracy-reducing moves and safeguards against bias and contrived results, but nevertheless find the ideal of objectivity to be deeply problematic. Too much is not accounted for to warrant the sacred position given to objectivity by many conventional researchers. Rules for science that claim to show the ultimate or superior way to objectivity and rationality have so far not proven to be uncontested or reliable in the long run (Bernstein, 1983). And the larger systematic biases coming from dominant theoretical frameworks, pre-structured personal and cultural understandings, vocabularies and dominant group interests are rarely counterbalanced (Harding, 1991; Alvesson and Sköldberg, 2000).

Actually, the very idea of framing intellectual positions in terms of objective versus subjective is deeply problematic. People and positions tend to be ascribed in a misleading way. There are several good reasons for avoiding either aspiring for an 'objective' approach or negating it, labelling an alternative position as 'subjective', as for example Burrell and Morgan (1979) have done in their seminal work on paradigms in organization theory.

First, the meaning of the objective–subjective labels is already socially contrived. Not only is the subject–object split a cultural conception rather than a natural fact, the 'objective' practices are those that Husserl (1962) and others (see Apel, 1979; Bernstein 1984) have shown to be the most 'subjective'. Many versions of 'objective' research are actually more vulnerable to critique for being more 'subjective' than a lot of qualitative research. While widely misunderstood, from the start the primary critics of positivism found the natural science model to be too subjective, not too objective. In so-called 'objective' research, concepts and methods are held a priori; they are unknown projections of researchers' own ways of encountering the world, they constitute the world as observed without ownership or critical reflection and are not subject to the 'objection' of the 'outside' towards possible alternatively constituted worlds, including the understandings of others (see Deetz, 1973 for further development).

In methods and research practices in which the researcher tries to achieve 'objectivity' through isolating the work from the outside world and its contaminations, the latter unavoidably creeps in. Efforts to accomplish 'purified' social (as well as many other forms of) research builds on non-recognized cultural assumptions and social conventions – assumptions and conventions held by the researcher, the people being studied and the readers/consumers of the study. A denial of the social nature of research means that the idiosyncrasies of the researcher – the particular mix and dynamics of social influences affecting his or her subjectivity – and the research community are hidden behind a false image of objectivity. Relying on an established tradition is no bastion as 'we thereby *bundle into our work the values, biases, and assumptions of the paradigms laid down by (unknown) others* (philosophers, methodologists, and system experts) who have done the groundwork from which we borrow' (McGrath et al., 1993: 29; italics in original).

What warrants exploration is the subjectivity and implicit desire to dominate others and nature, through making sense fit into a framework of a particular set of variables and predefined meanings, rather than the objectivity, of the 'objective' research programmes. Probabilistic and law-like claims are artefacts of a particular peer group's shared language game or set of constitutive activities. That a specific community of researchers agree about methods, definitions and viewpoints does not mean that they have privileged access to objective reality. The idea of defining leadership in terms of two sets of activities – initiating structure and personnel orientation – is an outcome of social conventions, it does not mean a 'natural' or superior way of mirroring the social world.

Questions of determining which problems to study, the relevancy of findings, and the translation back to the subject's world have always posed constitutive and value-laden issues at the very heart of any 'objective' research that intends to have a social effect (Gergen, 1978). The control orientation of much 'objective' research (see Hamnett et al., 1984) can be seen as the domination of a particular group's desires over and against existing communities and the natural environment (Harding, 1991). In both respects, in practice so-called 'interpretivists' and others often labelled as 'subjective', often have the better claim to 'objectivity' through the way they allow alternative language games and the possibility of alternative meanings and understandings arising from existing communities, denying both research community conceptions and preferred methods as privileged and universal. (More about this later in the chapter.) Thus, we treat the claim of objectivity or subjectivity as a rhetorical move in a research programme's system of justification rather than as a useful descriptive label. Our point is thus that subjectivity and objectivity are simply not interesting ways of thinking about research programme differences (see Bernstein, 1984; Natter et al., 1995).

Secondly, the subjective–objective conception, rather than describing a meaningful difference, reproduces a neo-positivist philosophy of science and obscures the nature of other research programmes. While few claim to be a positivist any more (given more than fifty years of critique), the retention of the discourse of the subject–object split (even given a hundred years of critique) leaves most researchers still practising a kind of neo-positivism celebrating neutrality, accumulation of knowledge and an emphasis on rules, protocol and procedure for the optimization of scientific rationality, in which extra-scientific distortions are minimized. This is not only the case with hard-core abstracted empiricists; in certain respects many subjective humanists also adopt such a stance. Actually, the majority of all qualitative researchers still tend to do that, even though this has started to change (Lincoln and Denzin, 1994).

The subjective–objective distinction persists partly because of the identity protection and privileges given to powerful groups, both in the academy and other organizations. Mainstream functionalists find a bastion in the notion of objectivity and their interpretive opponents have an easy target in this outdated and unreflective effort to ground science. In many ways, interpretivists gain as much identity and group stature in their oppositional identity as do the functionalists.

Thirdly, the retention of the conception of subject–object separation has led to the continuation of rather misleading conflicts and equally misleading presumed relations between qualitative and quantitative research. The association of qualitative research with the subjective label collapses the distinction between purely impressionistic musing and rigorous interpretive work and differences between studying practices, which are materialized in behaviour, and meanings, which call for the study of the ideas, understandings and the sense-making processes of people. Further, neo-positivist researchers accepting dualism (whether called interpretivists or functionalists) often reduce the difference in qualitative and quantitative research to different ways to collect data and, thereby, retain the dream of triangulation as if different research programmes simply provided additive insights into the same phenomenon.[2] This hides the real conflict. More important than data collection techniques are the questions asked and the intent of analysis, how social reality is understood and the cognitive interest pursued. At root, what the research is trying to do is different. The modes of analysis do not work from different points of view on the same thing; they are producing and elaborating in the act of research different phenomena for different reasons.

Clearly both qualitative and quantitative research can share a neo-positivist set of assumptions. Both can accept objects as constituted as if they were given in nature (as in any 'realist' description) rather than explore their constitution. A more basic qualitative–quantitative difference is not insignificant and should be retained. Both types of work are important for different purposes. Normative work can provide important insights into constrained problems and in situations where there is considerable openly-arrived-at linguistic consensus. Verification is also important. It is, however, vital that normative researchers recognize that their 'natural' objects of a presumed external world are 'produced' objects for temporary methodological convenience. The value of normative research is reclaimed as part of a much larger research agenda and discussion without the closure, resulting from the pretence of objectivity. Interpretive researchers, even when following neo-positivist lines, can contribute significantly as long as they see that their 'natural' objects of another's social world are emergent and interactionally formed.

Both benefit from greater clarity as to the social origins of their language and procedures. Social factors simply enter at different places and in different ways. It is impossible to prevent this entrance, not only because research work takes place in a social context and is carried out by people, but also because this personal/subjective element provides the researcher with the understanding and skills necessary to do research: to decide what questions to raise, what literature to connect to, how to write research texts, and so forth. Both kinds of objects are socially shared, historically produced, and general to a social group. In this sense all research is basically intersubjective. Quantitative research itself could be greatly improved if freed from pretences of positivist ontology. Many human questions admit of numerical answers and these answers should be good ones. There is certainly no reason for denying the value of counting in certain cases (Silverman, 1989); some things can and should be counted. But when codification, counting, and statistical reduction are separated from the full process of constituting objects, determining problems and influencing communities, when only one slice of the research process is claimed as science, research loses relevance and critical parts of the process are not investigated. The subjective–objective conception contributes to this problem.

Moves to secure 'objectivity' are often more successful in hiding the significance of human judgement and its contingencies on cultural and intellectual tradition, including a specific research language. Inter-rater reliability is one preferred mode to try to chase the demon of 'subjectivity' away from the research process. It is sometimes assumed that if more than one evaluator agrees, then subjectivity is avoided and objectivity is assured. If a number of individuals – differing in age, gender, cultural background, theoretical preferences, etc. – agree on a particular set of categories and classification, the case for accepting what they agree upon as a matter of objectivity in the sense of a high degree of intersubjectivity is, arguably, strong. Such strong cases are rare, at least in social science. We are much less impressed if two US students, having undergone the same training and socialization with a particular professor, agree in their judgements. Two or more persons may easily share the same biases or, to put it differently, employ the same vocabulary, ignorant of alternative languages and ways of making sense of what they see or hear. A high degree of intersubjectivity across cultural and theoretical variations, is less likely to occur with complex and interesting issues than trivial and uninteresting ones.

The norm of normative research is to arrive at a robust truth, backed by a research community whose results, hopefully, are gradually synchronized and show consistency. In order to make this case economically, to avoid variation, particular procedures aimed at standardizing responses are used. This 'ideal' permeates objectivity-seeking research on all levels. Standardization reduces the significance of researcher judgement and facilitates comparisons, but it does so by reducing possible competing subjectivities to a single one which is now hidden by the claim of objectivity. But the problem is deeper still. High reliability hides the social interaction of the research process, and the social context of research questions and goals.

Subjects in experiments and respondents to questionnaires are forced to subordinate themselves to expressions of the researcher's 'subjectivity' (Deetz, 1992, 1996), for example his or her opinion of what is relevant, the way that he or she has chosen to structure the position and provide response alternatives for the subjects. Even if a study utilizes another person's questionnaire or other technique, that other person's 'subjectivity' – more or less arbitrary choices aided by a mix of judgement and preference – still puts an imprint on the study. The hiding of researcher subjectivity and false pretence to superior rationality, liberated from the tastes, arbitrariness, emotionality and unreliability of social life in general, through forcing the research objects to respond to pre-structured, standardized, easily processed response alternatives is a major problem with the ideal of objectivity in social science.

Another major fault is the neglect of ambiguity. In order to achieve something that appears to be objective, variation must be reduced and standardization and simplification sought for. The rich variety and diversity of the social world is suppressed in order to make it fit procedures that give the impression of objectivity. Quantification has this quality, that is the rhetorical appeal of numbers obscures the processes of construction and interpretation they are built upon. The standardization of social phenomena risks involving a basic distortion of social reality, not in the sense of portraying 'reality' falsely in opposition to accurately, but in terms of imputing certainty and order at the expense of openness, ambiguity and indeterminacy. Another problem with the ideal of removing the researcher as an acting-constructing subject and letting scientific methodology and technique dominate the scene concerns the constraints for ideas, imagination, theoretical novelty, indeed progress, associated with the far too heavy emphasis on procedure, techniques and, at worst, data-dredging.

Arguing against objectivity as a possibility as well as an ideal that one should take any measure to approximate does not, of course, mean that anything goes. Sloppiness, the expression of opinion not grounded in argumentation, arbitrary use of empirical material, reluctance to engage in dialogue with the literature, and careful consideration of alternative interpretations before deciding which one to favour, are all certainly not to be tolerated. Formalization, procedure and technique may, however, be replaced by interpretive and theoretical awareness and sensitivity as means of achieving 'qualitative rigour', and thus avoids problems of relativism and arbitrariness. As we have argued, the alternative is not to celebrate 'subjectivity'; the entire objectivity–subjectivity dualism, at least as it is normally framed, is a dead end. We will come back to the issue of how to assert quality assurance in research.

Critique of mainstream ideas on qualitative method

Qualitative research has become increasingly popular. Much of this has come about due to the weakness of quantitative work in terms of the thinness of data, the control orientation often displayed, and issues surrounding the relevance of findings. Qualitative methods are often defined through what they are not, that is they do not quantify. A more productive view is provided by Van Maanen who defines qualitative methods as 'an array of interpretive techniques which seek to describe, decode, translate and otherwise come to terms with the meaning, not the frequency, of certain more or less naturally occurring phenomena in the social world' (1988: 9). In this section we will briefly discuss three basic difficulties associated with interviews and long-term participant observation in naturally occurring situations, that is ethnographies.

Quite often this means trying to see the world from the 'native's point of view'. Bryman et al. (1988: 61), for example, say that 'the most fundamental characteristic of qualitative research is its expressed commitment to viewing events, actions, norms, values, etc. from the perspectives of the people being studied'. There is, however, an expanding body of literature emphasizing observation of social process as the most fundamental element of qualitative research and here the interest is in what goes on (practices) rather than what things may mean to the people involved (for example, Silverman, 1993, 1997; Dingwall, 1997). From the point of view of critical research, there is a clear interest in the level of meaning but balanced by awareness that discourse and ideological as well as structural forces may operate 'behind the back' of the subjects being studied, thus calling for broader considerations than just focusing on the ideas and meanings of these subjects. There are, therefore, problems in trying to give a firm definition of what qualitative research is. We have no interest in emphasizing the distinct character of qualitative research but are more concerned with evaluating research practices that may be labelled qualitative, that is loosely structured, with a relatively open interaction between researcher and research subjects.

A qualitative approach is often exclusively, or mainly, made up of interviews. Interviews may, of course, mean very different things and be used in different types of research, for example case studies, or in order to cover a broader empirical terrain. Highly structured interviews may be used in a quantitative study, but almost all material may, in principle, be quantified. Of interest here are interviews which aim to get richer accounts. They are, typically, relatively time-consuming and lead to varied responses from interviewees. Qualitative interviews – as opposed to 'talking questionnaires' (Potter and Wetherell, 1987) – are relatively loosely structured and open to what the interviewee feels is relevant and important to talk about, within the bounds of what appears to be relevant given the interest of the research project. This approach is beneficial in as much as a richer account of the interviewee's experiences, knowledge, ideas and impressions may be considered and documented. Interviewees are less constrained by the researcher's pre-understanding and preferred language. The researcher may get perspectives, information and ideas that he or she has not thought of before (or is not documented in the earlier research literature). There is space for negotiation of meanings so that some level of mutual understanding may be accomplished, making data richer and more meaningful for research purposes. Much more complex and varied descriptions are possible (Bryman et al., 1988; Fontana and Frey, 1994; Martin and Turner, 1986).

We have not produced an overview of types of qualitative interviews, nor do we discuss technical and practical aspects on all the issues of importance for gaining good access, establishing contact, developing trust, structuring the situation to an appropriate degree, getting clarification, coping with the expectations of the interviewee, and so forth (see, for example, Easterby-Smith et al., 1991; Fontana and Frey, 1994; Kvale, 1996). Most of the literature on interviewing deals at length with how this practice may be utilized as effectively as possible. While realizing the complexities involved, the literature generally assumes that skills may be developed and an approach taken in which errors are minimized, enabling qualified empirical material to be produced.

Nevertheless, there are some serious problems with interviews that cannot, realistically, be avoided by making interview work as rational as possible.[3] There are always sources of influence in an interview context that cannot be minimized or controlled. There are problems and/or complexities going far beyond what may be seen as pure 'errors'. As Silverman (1989, 1994) has stressed, the value of interview statements is in many cases limited, in terms of their capacity to reflect both reality 'out there' and the subjective world of the interviewee (beliefs, attitudes, psychological traits, etc.). This is partly the case because the statements are liable to be determined by the situation, that is they are related to the interview context rather than to any other specific 'experiential reality', and partly because they are affected by the available cultural scripts about how one should normally express oneself on particular topics (see also Potter and Wetherell, 1987; Shotter and Gergen, 1989, 1994). An interview is a social situation – a kind of conversation – and that which is said is far too context-dependent to be seen as a mirror of what goes on outside this specific situation, either in the mind of the interviewee or in the organization 'out there'. Interviewees speak in accordance with the norms of talk and interaction in a social situation. The research interview is, therefore, better viewed as the scene for a conversation rather than a simple tool for collection of 'data'.

Critics object to the naïve and rather romantic view of research which believes that genuine experiences can be captured with the help of unstructured interviews. Silverman, for example, claims that 'only by following misleading correspondence theories of truth could it have ever occurred to researchers to treat interview statements as accurate or distorted reports of reality' (1985: 176). Like people in general, individuals put in an interview context are not just 'truth tellers' or 'informants', but 'use their language to do things, to order and request, persuade and accuse' (Potter and Wetherell, 1987: 32). In the research interview the intended effect of the interview is often to give a good impression – or just to make the situation work. (A good conversation calls for efforts to be made.) There is often a positive bias in interviews. Some studies do, however, seem to have avoided this tremendous problem. Two excellent examples are Jackall's (1988) work on the formation of moral consciousness in corporations and Watson's (1994) study of the work situation of managers.

These same problems are, of course, also present in questionnaires. As illustrated above in the Seltzer and Bass (1990) study, the inclination to give positive answers is strong, at least in some cultures. Even if the respondents may feel more free when they fill in the forms than when being interviewed (and often more so in other questionnaire studies than in the one carried out by Seltzer and Bass) they are still behaving according to social norms and responsive to the temporary subjectivities produced by the language used and what it triggers in people.

Most proponents of qualitative methods probably agree about the significance of expectations of what the researcher wants to hear and social norms for how one expresses oneself. Many would, however, believe that establishing close personal contact with respondents – who then are seen as 'participants' rather than respondents – may minimize this problem. Fontana and Frey (1994), for example, suggest that the researcher may reject 'outdated' techniques of avoiding getting involved or providing personal opinion and to engage in a 'real' conversation with 'give and take' and 'emphatic understanding'. 'This makes the interview more honest, morally sound, and reliable, because it treats the respondent as an equal, allows him or her to express personal feelings, and therefore presents a more "realistic" picture that can be uncovered using traditional interview methods.' (1994: 371)

We have considerable sympathy for this kind of interviewing, but it does not guarantee 'truthful' interview statements that give a 'realistic' picture. All experiences and social phenomena may be represented in a variety of ways and there is always the element of arbitrariness, chance and availability of a particular mix of discourses guiding a specific interview statement. While an interview technique trying to maximize neutrality and minimize interviewer influence may lead to shallow, convention-guided and not very honest answers, closeness-maximizing approaches may lead to answers in which the orientations of the researcher more strongly guide responses. A feminist woman emphatically interviewing a woman may bring the latter to express a more pro-feminist opinion or feminism-supporting accounts of experiences than would otherwise be the case. Feeling sympathy for an interviewer may simply increase the likelihood of the respondent wanting to agree with and please him or her.

Even if somebody should manage to maximize honesty and minimize the desire to adapt to the assumptions of the researcher's anticipations and values or to comply to social norms for expressing oneself, honesty and independence do not restrict how one can represent the experiential or external world – there is always a plethora of aspects, words and empirical illustrations to choose between when accounting for non-trivial issues. Words used – by the interviewer or the respondent – may trigger certain associations and lines of accounts. There is an element of coincidence determining how an interview runs, what is included and what is not aired. After the interview, the respondent may recall other aspects or examples in addition to those that have been picked up on the tape recorder and which will later serve as data. In addition one can never know for certain what expectations research subjects have, how honest they are, etc. To appear 'honest' – and not socially incompetent or odd – calls for impression management.

A basic aspect here is the identities that are called upon in interview work. These frame the situation and guide responses. If one interviews somebody as a 'woman', a 'leader', a 'middle level manager', different identities are invoked and different answers are produced. Quite often these identities are not clearly signalled, and the researcher may be totally unaware of how language use and other signals may operate on the person being interviewed in terms of identity.

Many researchers show some awareness of some of the problems mentioned above, and have suggested repeat interviews in order to establish better contact, check for consistency over time/ between situations and/or giving interviewees as well as inter-viewers an opportunity to reflect upon what has been said before (for example, Acker et al., 1991; Collinson, 1992). We sympathize with this, but it contributes only moderately to the overall ration-ality of the project and reiterates the more basic problem concern-ing the goal of presumed correspondence, a mirror of a presumed stable world.

Most likely, accounts show a complex mix of similar, more or less different and ambiguous statements. Seldom is there a clear con-vergence or divergence, for the reasons mentioned above. (Potter and Wetherell, 1987, show that actually there are often inconsistencies within a particular account.) Even when consis-tency seems to dominate, it may be an outcome of the same norm or vocabulary (discourses) being in operation at both or several occasions. When inconsistency appears it may be an outcome of the interviewee wanting to avoid repetition, adding nuances or complexities. In a company there may be a wide array of decisions, practices, values, intentions and processes that may point in differ-ent directions, thus leading to inconsistent and confusing but still 'correct' interview accounts. But inconsistencies may also reflect random processes: variations in mood and associations of the interviewer or what he or she has read in a newspaper just before the interview, for instance.

Although Silverman, Potter and Wetherell and other discourse and conversation analysts probably underrate the potential of the interview method and the capacities of the interview subjects to provide valuable information, the drawbacks and risks of the method must be taken seriously. Naïve romanticism – the view that true subjective experiences or other truths come through with the skilfully carried out interview – must be rejected. A possible response to the complexity of the effects of researcher–interviewee interaction and compliance with social norms for expression on interview statements and other accounts is careful interpretation of how such accounts may be used for research purposes (Alvesson and Kärreman, 2000). They provide uncertain but often interesting clues for the understanding of social reality and ideas, beliefs, values and other aspects of 'subjectivities'. They may also inform the researcher about language use – an interesting topic in itself. As Mills (1940) noted, we cannot really investigate motives but we can study vocabularies of motives. In the same way, organizationally dominating talk about motives, leadership, etc. and – related to it – work and leadership ideologies in various contexts may be an interesting subject matter. Such talk is important and has effects in terms of expressing/reinforcing norms for working and for leadership. However, investigating talk remains difficult as talk varies, due to setting and the variety of discourses available and because of different interviewees' verbal skills and creativity in producing accounts.

These considerations lead to a more modest, more reflective approach to interviews. The latter cannot be reduced to simple instruments – this metaphor for interviews is simply misleading – but must be carefully considered as social phenomena of their own; social norms for talk, scripts for discourses available, the relative autonomy of discourses in relationship to other phenomena (beliefs, social reality out there), anticipations of the intentions and uses of the interview material, and mutual identity constructions and interactive dynamics in the researcher–interviewee interaction are crucial to consider.

Ethnography

An ambitious alternative to solely or mainly relying on a set of interviews is to carry out an ethnography. An ethnography is a method – for some it is even a paradigm – on a more general level than interviews, as interviews in one form of another are, typically, an important part of an ethnography. An ethnography usually includes several methods (techniques), of which the most important are (participant) observations over a long time period and non-structured interviews (Atkinson and Hammersley, 1994; Fetterman, 1989; Prasad, 1997; Rosen, 1991; Schwartzman, 1993; Van Maanen, 1995). It is common that the ethnographer establishes close contact with one or a few key informants who then guide the researcher and help him or her with crucial information.

There are, of course, different opinions about what is included in the concept of ethnography. Some people define it broadly as a study of an exploratory nature, working with unstructured data, and being case oriented and interested in meanings (Atkinson and Hammersley, 1994) or any study involving observation of naturally occurring events (Silverman, 1985). We think that the term serves us best if reserved for studies involving a longer period of fieldwork in which the researcher tries to get close to the community (organization, group) being studied, relies on their accounts as well as on observation of a rich variety of naturally occurring events (plus other material, for example documents or material artefacts) and has an interest in cultural issues (meanings, symbols, ideas, assumptions). Unlike Atkinson, Hammersley and Silverman, some authors view an interest in cultural analysis as a crucial criterion for an ethnography (for example, Prasad, 1997; Wolcott, 1995).

An ethnography is typically broader and gives richer, more qualitative material than, for example, behaviourally oriented research on managerial work accomplished through (participant) observation. The focus is typically on a specific site, for example an organization or a part of it. A close and deep contact with it is aspired for. Elements of distance, theoretical abstraction and overview are necessary ingredients, but the kind of strong emphasis on objectivity preventing all identification and real contact with the research subjects being studied is considered to obstruct genuine understanding. An ethnography often includes the study as well as reports of a set of events or situations which have been observed by the researcher. Thick description, that is careful accounts of social phenomena in which layers of meaning are expressed, is one element (Geertz, 1973). Sometimes people emphasize two major elements of an ethnography: the process of fieldwork and the writing of a text (Van Maanen, 1995). The term ethnography actually has two meanings: the empirical work and the completed study (text).

A study design focusing on the observation of a naturally occurring event avoids – or, more usually, reduces – the researcher's dependence on the perceptions, understandings and accounts of respondents. The researcher may discover aspects which interviewees may be unaware of or which, for other reasons, they find difficult to articulate. Interviews or less formal, more spontaneous talks between researcher and informants are almost always an important complement to this method. Without the accounts of the people being studied, it is very difficult to say something about the meanings of and ideas guiding particular behaviours and practices. Interviews may provide richer results as the researcher, over time, gets an improved pre-structured understanding, can ask better questions and may get better contact with the 'natives'.

Ethnographies are difficult because they are very time-consuming, and often personally tiresome and stressful to carry out. They are too ineffective for most research purposes (Wolcott, 1995). More significantly, in terms of research results, there is a risk that the researcher 'goes native', that is becomes caught in details and local understanding without being able to say something systematic of wider theoretical interest. The opposite problem concerns the difficulty encountered by a representative of one culture in fully – or even very successfully – understanding another culture. In the case of management studies, the latter problem is often less significant as the study of companies within one's own country represents fewer barriers in terms of different languages and overall cultural orientation than, say, anthropologists – studying foreign communities – face. In the case of international business, cross-cultural barriers may, however, be similar to those faced by anthropologists studying 'exotic' societies. On the whole, students of corporate culture suffer from a lack of imagination, making it possible to accomplish studies not caught up in the taken-for-granted assumptions and ideas that are broadly shared between management researchers and management practitioners (Alvesson, 1993a). Too much of corporate life is often too familiar and researchers do not always succeed in making the familiar strange.

A more fundamental problem, which also characterizes other qualitative research, concerns the difficulties in handling all the empirical material and in producing a text that does justice to it. Even if the ethnographer claims that his or her first-hand experiences of the object of study are a strong basis of authority, the text produced is not just a document mirroring something 'out there'. The problems of 'writing the study up' have received enormous attention in anthropology and other ethnographically oriented research areas (Clifford and Marcus, 1986; Geertz, 1988; Marcus and Fischer, 1986; Van Maanen, 1988, 1995; Watson, forthcoming). Ethnography has gone from a relatively unreflective, closed and general description of 'a whole way of life' – not too difficult to picture in a text – to a more tentative, open and partial interpretation, drawing attention to matters of uncertainty and style in writing (Geertz, 1973, 1988). Recent critique has drawn attention to the fictional nature of ethnographies – and, for that matter, all social research. The text is seen as central. It tells a story, it adapts a particular style, the author makes all kinds of moves in order to create certain effects, for example trustworthiness, brilliance and so on. All these go far beyond simply reporting data and describing objective reality; they may inspire the author but put highly uncertain imprints on the text. We have every reason to be wary of the realistic or naturalistic mode of writing 'in which the production of understanding and construction of the text are hidden by a form of account that purports to present what is described simply "as it appeared"; this being treated, with more or less conviction, as "how it is"' (Hammersley, 1990: 606).

This aspect may be concretized through emphasizing the selectivity of the empirical material reproduced in the published text. The output of a set of (open) interviews and long-term observer participation aspiring to describe a complex reality is always difficult to transcribe in research texts. Along with a whole host of other problems, some of which are indicated above – for instance, that interview answers are often partially determined by the interviewer, and that the interviewees are inclined to follow scripts allowing themselves to appear moral and rational – the presentation of the material inevitably becomes a question of selection and discretion or arbitrariness. This is a particular problem of non-formal, broader studies utilizing first-hand experiences, extensive interview and observation material, much of this collected in a non-structured and non-systematic way. Only a very small portion of all that has been said by the interviewees and observed, usually during several weeks or months, can be reproduced in a publication or even fully considered in analysis (see Clifford, 1986). If one conducts, tapes and carefully transcribes, say, 25 interviews each lasting for one to two hours, one easily gets 500 pages of transcript. If one has 'been there' for 200 days and written 10 pages of field notes per day, one has 2000 additional pages of empirical text. Of that material, perhaps 2 per cent at most may be presented directly, after editing and framing it, in a research book and less than 0.2 per cent in a journal article. It becomes necessary to be highly selective in what is emphasized in analysis and documented in text. In order to present a coherent description and analysis, the rich varieties typically found in interview accounts must be treated with a certain bias so that a lot of the inconsistencies and ambiguities presented for the reader are avoided (Potter and Wetherell, 1987). Writing conventions typically prevent a text from appearing too contradictory and confusing for the reader. (The presentation of material pointing in different directions is acceptable, but only to a certain degree, and the author is supposed to get it all together at one level or another at some point.) To achieve a completed text that gives a good account, in the sense of 'mirroring' a reality represented in all this empirical material, may be very difficult – even if one disregards the problem of treating language as standing in a one-to-one relationship to other phenomena.

For these and other reasons, ethnography, has lost some of its innocence and self-confidence in terms of authority. As Van Maanen says, 'ethnography is no longer pictured as a relatively simple look, listen and learn procedure but, rather, as something akin to an intense epistemological trial by fire' (1995: 2). Of course, these problems are not only valid for ethnography, although possibly more pronounced and apparent there, but are relevant for all research – especially qualitative research.

This chapter has pointed out basic limitations and shortcomings found in the most common methods employed for management and social research. Our sympathy is with qualitative methods, but the conventional understanding of these is far more problematical than most advocates of these methods seem to acknowledge. Recently there has been more awareness, however, regarding these matters. Also qualitative work – even when carried out by people trying to maximize the rationality of the process – has difficulties in claiming good access either to social reality 'out there' or to the level of meanings, ideas, values, cognitions or subjectivities of people being studied. Rather than searching for a superior method-ology solving problems with the interactive, language- and norm-governed nature of interviews, the theory- and language-impregnated nature of observations, and the selectivity and the fic-tional character of the use of empirical work in all research when 'writing it up', the challenge is to develop a way of thinking which is not overburdening a method with naïve expectations and unre-alistic purposes and which tries to interpret all empirical material in terms of multiple meanings and fruitful ways of utilizing it.

Summary

This chapter has provided a critical review of mainstream method-ologies. Instead of repeating the well-known critique of positivism on a programmatic level, we have concentrated on illuminating some of the basic problems in relationship to a specific research field: leadership studies. One such problem is the tendency to sup-press variety and impose an essence on a multitude of diverse phe-nomena; a standardized, abstract concept of leadership imposes unity and 'freezes' parts of what goes on in organization under its label. Another problem is the inherent difficulties with the favoured method: questionnaires. These typically overburden lan-guage with demands of clarity of meaning and assume that the ticks or crosses that are put in the choice alternative boxes say something definitive about how people think, feel, relate and act. Arguably, in order to understand 'leadership' one should study the processes in which it may occur rather than questionnaire responses (or interview statements). The same goes for (almost all) other management phenomena.

Despite our preferences for loosely structured interviews and observations of 'naturally occurring' (rather than laboratory) events, we are not happy about some of the ways the differences between qualitative and quantitative research typically are repre-sented. The idea of framing social research in terms of objective and subjective is deeply problematic. Good research acknowledges that there is a researcher making an immense number of choices affecting the research results. Good research also struggles with the problems of personal (and group) bias or idiosyncrasies. The problem becomes elevated when the problematic distinction is equated with the quantitative–qualitative distinction. Much quantitative research is one-sidedly driven by the personal preferences of the researcher concerning the questions that are of interest and what language the research objects should subordinate themselves to. Many (perhaps most) qualitative researchers are struggling to persuade their readers (and perhaps themselves) that their reliance on procedures, techniques, rules and the reliability of their numbers in the data make their research 'objective'.

Notes

1 Neo-empiricism means a treatment of theory and interpretation as separate from data and a strong reliance on empirical evidence as capable of telling us the objective truth. This is also a key feature of neo-positivism, but this label is normally used in a somewhat more narrow way that also includes other characteristics not necessarily involved in other versions of empiricism, that is, approaches which do not embrace the ideal of discovering laws through hypothetico-deductive methods, for example neo-empiricist qualitative methods.

2 Triangulation means the use of a combination of different methods in order to reduce reliance on a single method. The idea is that through the combination of different data, one 'homes in' on the topic of study. Critics say that it does not work like this. Different methods produce different kinds of result, rather leading to a 'homing out' (Potter and Wetherell, 1987).

3 Problems here are seen in the context of the typical purpose of interviews, that is getting empirical material saying something accurate about either (a) social reality out there-strategies, decisions, goals, organizational structures, interorganizational relations, etc. or (b) subjective meanings – values, intentions, ideas about competitors, technology or the market. As we shall come back to, interviews may be used for other purposes. Interviews in themselves are, of course, not problematic. Problems emerge in the context of various uses of interview material for making different kinds of empirical claim.

4

The critical tradition: critical theory and postmodernism

In Chapter 1 we focused on the social and historical context giving rise to critical management research approaches and why the themes they address are becoming increasingly important to management studies. In Chapters 2 and 3 we have focused on the differences between conventional and critical research approaches. Here we build, more positively, a picture depicting the nature of critical research. We consider different ways of doing critical work as exhibited in critical theory and postmodernist writings. In addition to reviewing and discussing existing work, we sketch some fruitful lines of development between and within these two approaches. Despite their importance, neither in the treatment of critical theory nor in that of postmodernism do we discuss gender issues in any specific or detailed way, despite the ways feminist work has influenced and been influenced by these traditional critical approaches. Given the complexity of the task at hand, feminist contributions will be blended into rather than held apart from the body of works considered.

Theoretical sources of inspiration and distinction

Both critical theory and postmodern writers position their work with regard to four specific developments in Western thought. The ways they respond to and partly use mixes of these developments account for many of the differences between and within postmodernism and critical theory. These are:

- the power–knowledge relation arising from Nietzsche's perspectivalism;
- a non-dualistic constructionist account of experience and language arising from phenomenological hermeneutics and structural linguistics;
- a historically based social conflict theory arising from Marx;
- a complex human subject arising from Freud.

The first posed a challenge to any possible foundations for knowledge; all knowledge claims primarily reference social communities filled with specific power relations rather than an essential world or knowing subjects. The second situated all perspectives within specific social/historical/linguistic contexts; the intersubjectivity preceding any subjectivity or objectivity is structured in specifiable ways. The third removed the innocence of social/historical/linguistic perspectives by positioning them within materially produced social divisions and denied any smooth unitary historical development. The fourth provided for a complex, conflict-ridden and often mistaken *subject* in place of a knowing, unitary, autonomous *person*, thereby challenging any claim to simple rationality and a clear and fixed identity. Together people, realities, and social relations become non-essential constructions, constructed under specific conditions of power and contestation, and filled with opacities, contradictions and conflict suppression. These different concepts provide the historically specific tools for encountering the dominant discourses of the time.

These shared intellectual heritages should not prevent us from emphasizing the differences between how critical theory and postmodernism draw upon them. Postmodernists typically, for example, use Freud much more unconventionally than critical theorists, and merge psychoanalytic ideas with language philosophy in efforts to deconstruct and show the fragmentation of the subject. Important sources of inspiration that are clearly different for critical theory and postmodernism include structuralist language theory (Saussure), which postmodernism draws heavily upon, and Weberian notions of the rationalization process of modern society, which is central for critical theory. In addition, critical theory is inspired by German moral philosophy and its faith in autonomy and reason (Hegel, Kant). Embedded in these choices are long-term oppositions between French and German cultural contexts. If it were not for this historical context some of the differences would not be as clear. For example, Adorno and Horkheimer's (1979) cultural criticism of administratively induced control contingent upon the conception of progress in the Enlightenment can be read as sounding as close to Foucault as to Habermas's recent writings. But few would think of them in that way. It is interesting to note that Foucault, when towards the end of his life he became acquainted with the Frankfurt School, expressed himself very positively, almost over generously, about it: 'if I had been familiar with the Frankfurt School ... I would not have said a number of stupid things that I did say and I would have avoided many of the detours which I made while trying to pursue my own humble path – when,

meanwhile, avenues had been opened up by the Frankfurt School'
(Foucault, 1983: 200).

Critical theory and organizational research

As outlined in Chapter 2, critical researchers see organizations as
social historical creations accomplished in conditions of struggle
and domination. General social theories and especially theories of
decision making in the public sphere are seen as especially useful
since organizations are largely described as political sites. Various
forms of power and domination have led to skewed decision making, and fostered social harms and significant waste and inefficiency. Critical theorists try to show how commercial organizations
could be positive social institutions providing forums for the articulation and resolution of important group conflicts. Two principle
types of critical studies can be identified in organization studies:
ideology critique and communicative action.

Ideology critique
The earliest ideological critiques of the workplace were offered by
Marx. In his analysis of work processes he focused primarily on
practices of economic exploitation through direct coercion and
structural differences in work relations between the owners of
capital and the owners of their own labour. However, Marx also
describes the manner in which the exploitative relation is disguised and made to appear legitimate. This is the origin of ideology critique. Economic conditions and class structure still were
central to the analysis whether, this misrecognition of interests was
a result of the domination of ruling class's ideas (Marx, 1964 [1844]),
or the dull compulsions of economic relations (Marx, 1967 [1867]).

The themes of domination and exploitation by owners and later
by managers has been central to ideology critique of the workplace
in this century by Marxist–inspired organization theorists (for
example, Braverman, 1974; Clegg and Dunkerley, 1980; Edwards,
1979; Salaman, 1981). Attention by analysts from the left focused
on ideology since workers often seemed to fail to recognize this
exploitation and their class-based revolutionary potential in the
industrial countries. Gradually these later analyses became less
concerned with coercion and class and economic explanations
as their focus changed to why coercion was so rarely necessary
and they became involved with systemic processes which
produced active consent. Issues of 'workers' self-understanding of
experience' become more central (for example, Gramsci, 1971;
Burawoy, 1979; Willmott, 1990).

To an increasing degree, ideology critiques do not address only or even strongly class issues but broaden the picture and study how cultural-ideological control operates in relationship to all employees, including levels of management (Hodge et al., 1979; Czarniawska-Joerges, 1988; Deetz and Mumby, 1990; Kunda, 1992). Ideology produced in the workplace would stand alongside that present in the media and the growth of the consumer culture and welfare state as accounting for workers' failure to act on their own interests. Ideology would also account for professionals' and managers' failure to achieve autonomy in relationship to needs and wants and the conformist pressure to standardize paths for satisfying these (conspicuous consumption, careerism, and self-commodification, see Heckscher, 1995). This would fill out the tradition of ideology critique.

A considerable amount of critical work has addressed management and organization theory as expressions, as well as producers, of ideologies which legitimize and strengthen specific societal and organizational social relations and objectives (Burrell and Morgan, 1979; Alvesson, 1987; Alvesson and Willmott, 1996; Steffy and Grimes, 1992). Academics, particularly those in management studies, are often viewed as ideologists. They serve dominant groups through socialization in business schools, support managers with ideas and vocabularies for cultural-ideological control at the workplace level, and provide the aura of science to support the introduction and use of managerial domination techniques.

Four themes recur in the numerous and varied writings about organizations working from the perspective of ideology critique:

- the naturalization of social order, or the way a socially/historically constructed world would be treated as necessary, natural, rational and self-evident;
- the universalization of managerial interests and suppression of conflicting interests;
- the domination by instrumental, and eclipse of competitive, reasoning processes;
- hegemony, the way consent becomes orchestrated.

Naturalization   In naturalization a social formation is abstracted from the historical conflictual site of its origin and treated as a concrete, relatively fixed entity. As such the reification becomes the reality rather than life processes. Through obscuring the construction process, institutional arrangements are no longer seen as choices but as natural and self-evident. The illusion that organizations and their processes are 'natural' objects and functional responses to 'needs', protects them from examination as produced under specific historical conditions (which are potentially passing) and out of specific power relations. In organization studies, organismic and mechanistic metaphors dominate, thereby leading research away from considering the legitimacy of control and political relations in organizations (Morgan, 1986). Examining the naturalization of the present and the reifications of social processes helps display the structural interrelation of institutional forces: the processes by which they are sustained and changed, and the processes by which their arbitrary nature is concealed and hence closed to discussion. Ideology critique reclaims organizations as social-historical constructions and investigates how they are formed, sustained, and transformed by processes both internal and external to them (see Lukács, 1971; Benson, 1977; Giddens, 1979; Frost, 1980, 1987; Thompson, 1984; Deetz, 1985, 1994d). The self-evident nature of an organizational society, basic distinctions and division of labour between management and workers, men and women, and so forth are called into question by ideology critique – critical studies which demonstrate the arbitrary nature of these phenomena and the power relations that result from and sustain these forms for the sake of discovering the remaining places of possible choice.

Universalization of managerial interests   Lukács (1971) among many others (see Giddens, 1979) has shown that particular sectional interests are often universalized and treated as if they were everyone's interests. In contemporary corporate practices, managerial groups are privileged in decision making and research. Management is ascribed a superior position in terms of defining the interests and interest realizations of the corporation – and thereby of wide segments of the population. The interests of the corporation are frequently equated with specific managerial self-interests. For example, worker, supplier, or host community interests can be interpreted in terms of their effect on corporate – that is, universalized managerial – interests. As such they are exercised only occasionally and usually reactively, often being represented simply as economic commodities or 'costs' – for example, the price the 'corporation' must pay for labour, supplies, or an environmental clean-up (Deetz, 1995b). Central to the universalization of managerial interest is the reduction of the multiple claims of ownership to financial ownership. The investments made by other stakeholders are minimized while capital investment is made central. Management by virtue of its fiduciary responsibility (limited to monetary investors) speaks for (and is often conceptually equated with) the corporation (Storey, 1983). In such a move, since the *general* well-being of each group is conceptually and materially tied to the *financial* well-being of the corporation as understood by management, self-interest by non-managerial stakeholders is often ironically reinterpreted as being accomplished by minimizing the accomplishment of their own self-interests. In ideological critique, managerial advantages can be seen as being produced historically and actively reproduced through ideological practices in society and in corporations themselves (see Tompkins and Cheney, 1985; Knights and Willmott, 1985; Lazega, 1992; Deetz, 1992). Critical studies explore how interest articulation is distorted through the dominating role of money as a simple and powerful medium (Offe and Wiesenthal, 1980), and confront productivity and consumption with suppressed values such as autonomy, creativity and pleasure as objectives for the organization of work (Burrell and Morgan, 1979; Willmott and Knights, 1982; Alvesson, 1987).

The primacy of instrumental reasoning   Habermas (1971, 1975, 1984, 1987) has traced the social-historical emergence of technical rationality over competing forms of reason. Habermas described *technical reasoning* as instrumental, tending to be governed by the theoretical and hypothetical, and focusing on control through the development of means–ends chains. The natural opposite to this is conceptualized by Habermas as *practical interest*. Practical reasoning focuses on the process of understanding and mutual determination of the ends to be sought rather than control and development of means of goal accomplishment (Apel, 1979). As Habermas described practical interest: 'a constitutive interest in the preservation and expansion of the intersubjectivity of possible action-oriented mutual understandings. The understanding of meaning is directed in its very structure toward the attainment of possible consensus among actors in the framework of a self-understanding derived from tradition' (Habermas, 1971: 310).

In a balanced system these two forms of reasoning become natural complements. But, in the contemporary social situation, the form and content of modern social science and the social constitution of expertise align with organizational structures to produce the domination of technical reasoning (see Stablein and Nord, 1985; Alvesson, 1987; Alvesson and Willmott, 1992, 1996; Mumby, 1988; Fischer, 1990). To the extent that technical reasoning dominates, it lays claim to the entire concept of rationality and alternative forms of reason appear irrational. To a large extent studies of the 'human' side of organizations (climate, job enrichment, quality of work life, worker participation programmes, and culture) have each been transformed from alternative ends into new means to be brought under technical control for extending the dominant group interests of the corporation (Alvesson, 1987). Sievers, for example, suggests:

> motivation only became an issue – for management and organization theorists as well as for the organization of work itself – when meaning either disappeared or was lost from work; that the loss of meaning is immediately connected with the way work has been, and still is organized in the majority of our Western enterprises. (1986: 338)

The productive tension between technical control and humanistic aspects becomes submerged below efforts towards the efficient accomplishment of often unknown but surely 'rational' and 'legitimate' corporate goals.

Hegemony   Although Gramsci's (1971) analysis and development of the concept of hegemony aimed at a general theory of society and social change with the workplace as simply one component, his conceptions have been widely used as a foundation for an examination of the workplace itself (for example, Burawoy, 1979; Clegg, 1989). Gramsci conceives of hegemony as a complex web of conceptual and material arrangements producing the very fabric of everyday life. Hegemony in the workplace is supported by economic arrangements enforced by contracts and reward systems, cultural arrangements enforced by advocacy of specific values and visions, and command arrangements enforced by rules and policies. These are situated within the larger society with its supporting economic arrangements, civil society (including education/intellectuals/media), and governmental laws.

   The conception of hegemony suggests the presence of multiple dominant groups with different interests, and the presence of power and activity even in dominated groups. The integration of these arrangements, however, favours dominant groups and the activity of both dominant and dominated groups is best characterized as a type of produced 'consent'. The hegemonic system works through pervading common sense and becoming part of the ordinary way of seeing the world, understanding one's self, and experiencing needs (see Angus, 1992). Such a situation always makes possible a gap between that inscribed by the dominant order and that which a dominated group would have preferred. As Lukes argued, 'Man's wants themselves may be a product of a system which works against their interests, and in such cases, relates the latter to what they would want and prefer, were they able to make the choice' (1974: 34). A number of studies have investigated a variety of 'consent' processes (for example, Vallas, 1993; Burawoy,

1979; Kunda, 1992). Several studies have shown how employees 'strategize their own subordination', achieving marginal gains for themselves through subordination but also perpetuating dominant systems which preclude their autonomy and ability to act on their own wider interests (see Burawoy, 1985; Deetz, 1995a; Willmott, 1993).

Organization studies in the 1980s and 1990s have exhibited a rather wide body of critical theory addressing corporate culture or proceeding from cultural perspectives on organizations, where culture and cultural engineering are defined as pointing towards hegemony (for example, Alvesson, 1993a; Deetz, 1985; Jermier, 1985; Knights and Willmott, 1987; Mumby, 1988; Rosen, 1985). Willmott, for example, has explored how 'corporate culture programmes are designed to deny or frustrate the development of conditions in which critical reflection is fostered. They commend the homogenization of norms and values within organizations ... Cultural diversity is dissolved in the acid bath of the core corporate values' (1993: 534). In practice, as Willmott and other critical theorists point out, management control strategies are seldom totally successful. Resistance and some level of cultural diversity normally prevail. The role of critical theory, but even more so postmodernism, can be seen as trying to preserve and reinforce this diversity.

A critique of ideology critique   Each of the above four concerns raised in various ideological critiques has value. However, limitations of ideology critique have been demonstrated by many. Three criticisms appear to be the most common. First, ideology critique often appears to be ad hoc and reactive. Most studies explain after the fact why something did not happen rather than making predictive and testable statements about the future. Second, it appears to be elitist. Concepts such as false needs and false consciousness, which were central to early studies, presume a basic weakness in insight and reasoning processes in the very same people it hopes to empower. The irony of an advocate of greater equality pronouncing what others should want or how they should perceive the world 'better' is not lost on either dominant or dominated groups. And, third, the accounts from early studies of ideology critique appear to be far too simplistic. According to the critique by Abercrombie et al. (1980) of the 'dominant ideology thesis', the conception of the dominant group remains singular and intentional, as if an identifiable group had worked out a system whereby domination through control of ideas could occur and its interests could be secured.

A more sophisticated critique, coming from postmodernism, indicates that the idea of the centred agent–subject is as central to ideology critique as it is to dominant groups and the systems that advantage them. The hope for a rational and reflective agent who is capable of acting autonomously and coherently may in itself be a worthy target of ideology critique. The modern corporation's legitimacy is based on (a) the assumption of the existence of such an individual and (b) a belief in its ability to foster that individual's development. Ideology critique does not, on the whole, question this basic notion of the individual, even though authors are quick to point to the discrepancy between actual production of people and a potential development.

Clearly the power of ideology critique can be maintained without falling to these criticisms and many critical theorists have accomplished this as they have pulled the concept of ideology away from traditional Marxism. They have responded to the critics by:

- advocating research that empirically investigates expressions of dominating systems of thought in particular communicative situations rather than explains outcomes (for example, Alvesson, 1996; Knights and Willmott, 1987; Rosen, 1985);
- refraining from directive statements regarding what people should do (revolt, liberate) but emphasizing the problematization of dominating beliefs and values (Deetz, 1992);
- recognizing pluralistic qualities, but still insisting that there are strong asymmetries between various interests and perspectives;
- treating ideologies as dominating without seeing them as a simple instrument or in the interest of an elite group, thus showing that elites may have internalized and may suffer from the effects of dominating sets of ideas (such as pollution or through work processes, Heckscher, 1995).

Another response to the problems of ideology critique is the development of a communicative perspective within critical theory. It represents a development from a focus on socially repressive ideas and institutions to the explorations of the communicative processes through which ideas are produced, reproduced and critically examined, especially in decision-making contexts.

Communicative action
Unlike earlier advocates of critical theory, Habermas's work since the late 1970s has reduced the significance of traditional ideology critique and has concentrated instead on building a systematic philosophy in which theory and communicative action are of

pivotal importance (Habermas, 1984, 1987). This project retains many of the features of ideology critique, including the ideal of sorting out constraining social ideas from those grounded in reason, but it envisages procedural ideas rather than substantive critique and thus becomes quite different from traditional ideology critique. It also introduces an affirmative agenda, not based on a Utopia, but still a hope of how we might reform institutions along the lines of morally driven discourse in situations approximating an ideal speech situation.

Habermas separates two historical learning processes and forms of rationality: (a) the technological-scientific-strategic, associated with the system world, and (b) the communicative-political-ethical, associated with the lifeworld. He tries to contribute to the second. Habermas argues for the systematic improvement of the lifeworld through an expanded conception of rationality focusing on the creation and re-creation of patterns of meaning. The lifeworld can be regarded as fully rational (rather than instrumentalized or strategized) to the extent that it permits interactions that are guided by communicatively achieved understanding rather than by imperatives from the system world – such as those contingent upon the money code or formal power – or by the unreflective reproduction of traditional cultural values (Habermas, 1984).

Communicatively achieved understanding is dependent on undistorted communication, the presence of free discussion based on goodwill, argumentation and dialogue. On the basis of undistorted, rational discussion he assumes that consensus can be reached regarding both present and desirable states. He maintains that in language itself and the way it is used there are certain conditions for achieving this ideal: the expectation and the wish to be understood and believed, and the hope that others will accept our arguments and other statements (see Thompson, 1984; Deetz, 1992: chs 6 and 7). Without such expectations and ambitions there is little point in either statements or discussions. Undistorted communication provides the basis for the 'highest' (or perhaps the widest, most reflective) form of rationality, namely communicative rationality. Here it is not power, status, prestige, ideology, manipulation, the rule of experts, fear, insecurity, misunderstanding or any other form of mischief that furnishes a base for the evolving ideas. Decision making becomes based on the strength of the good, well-grounded argument provided in an open forum rather than authority, tradition, ideology, or exclusion of participants.

> This concept of communicative rationality carries with it connotations based ultimately on the central experience of the unconstrained, unifying, consensus-bringing force of argumentative speech, in which

different participants overcome their merely subjective views and, owing to the mutuality of rationality motivated conviction, assure themselves of both the unity of the objective world and the intersubjectivity of their lifeworld. (Habermas, 1984: 10)

Communicative rationality thus denotes a way of responding to (questioning, testing and, possibly, accepting) the validity of different claims. Communicative action thus allows for the exploration of every statement on a basis of the following (universal) validity criteria: comprehensibility, sincerity, truthfulness and legitimacy. Communicative action is, therefore, an important aspect of social interaction in society, in social institutions and in daily life. The ideal speech situation, which enables communicative rationality and is in turn pervaded by it, exists under the following conditions: 'the structure of communication itself produces no constraints if and only if, for all possible participants, there is a symmetrical distribution of chances to choose and to apply speech-acts' (Habermas, cited by Thompson and Held, 1982: 123). Of course, the ideal speech situation is not a quality of ordinary communication, but a counterfactual anticipation we make when we seek mutual understanding, trying to accomplish the form of argumentation we presuppose we are able to step into when we seek to step aside from the flow of everyday action and check a problematic claim. As we suggest when looking at critical theory's contribution, such an ideal when used as an analytical frame in organization studies can provide much guidance to restructuring discussions and decision making in organizations (for example, Lyytinen and Hirschheim, 1988; Power and Laughlin, 1992).

We will not repeat the critique of Habermas's theory here (see Thompson and Held, 1982; Fraser, 1987; Burrell, 1994), but simply mention that it overemphasizes the possibility of rationality as well as the value of consensus (Deetz, 1992) and puts too much weight on the clarity and rationality potential of language and human interaction. To some extent, it relies on a model of the individual as potentially autonomous and clarified, but this assumption plays a less central role in comparison to that in earlier critical theory, as the focus is not on consciousness but on the structure of communicative interaction as the carrier of rationality. But still Habermas can be criticized for his 'benign and benevolent view of human kind' (Vattimo, 1992) which counts on knowledge and argumentation to change thought and action, a position about which postmodernists are highly sceptical.

The contribution of critical management studies
Critical studies in organization theory and management have utilized the ideas sketched above, developed these and illustrated

their relevance for the understanding of modern organizations, in particular corporations. Alvesson and Willmott (1996) have pointed to some metaphors for organizations and management from critical theory: management as technocracy, mystification, cultural doping and colonizing power. These draw attention to the role of management expertise leading to passivity on the part of other organizational participants, how ambiguity and contradictions are masked, how the engineering of values and definitions of reality tend to weaken low-level and other marginal groups in the negotiation of workplace reality and, respectively, how the codes of money and formal power exercise a close to hegemonic position over workplace experiences and articulated values and priorities. As indicated above, two basic foci can here be indicated: one content-oriented, emphasizing sources of constraints; one process-oriented, emphasizing variation in communicative action in organizations.

Critical theory draws attention, for example, to the narrow thinking associated with the domination of instrumental reason and the money code. Potentially, when wisely applied, instrumental reason is a productive form of thinking and acting. However, in the absence of practical reason (aiming at political-ethically informed judgment), its highly specialized, means-fixated and unreflective character makes it strongly inclined to also contribute to the objectification of people and nature and thus to various forms of destruction. Most salient are:

1 Constrained work conditions where intrinsic work qualities (creativity, variation, development, meaningfulness) are ignored or subordinated to instrumental values (Alvesson, 1987; Sievers, 1986).
2 The development and reinforcement of asymmetrical social relations between experts (including management elites) and non-experts (Alvesson and Willmott, 1996; Fischer, 1990; Hollway, 1984).
3 Gender bias in terms of styles of reasoning, asymmetrical social relations and political priorities (Alvesson and Billing, 1997; Calás and Smircich, 1992a, 1992b; Mumby and Putnam, 1992; Ferguson, 1984; Hearn and Parkin, 1987).
4 Extensive control of an employee's mindset and a freezing of their social reality (Deetz and Kersten, 1983; Frost, 1987; Mumby, 1987).
5 Far reaching control of employees, consumers and the general political–ethical agenda in society, through mass media and lobbying advocating consumerism and the priority of the money

code as yardstick for values and individual and collective political decision making (Alvesson and Willmott, 1996; Deetz 1992).

6 Destruction of the natural environment through waste and pollution (Shrivastava, 1993; Stead and Stead, 1992).

In the guise of technocracy, instrumental rationality has pretences to neutrality and freedom from the value-laden realms of self-interest and politics. It celebrates and 'hides behind' techniques and the false appearance of objectivity and impartiality of institutionalized sets of knowledge, bureaucracy and formal mandates. Not surprisingly, technocracy is promoted by each of the management 'specialisms' as they claim a monopoly of expertise in their respective domains. Human resource specialists, for example, advance and defend their position by elaborating a battery of 'objective' techniques for managing the selection and promotion of employees (Hollway, 1984; Steffy and Grimes, 1992). Strategic management institutionalizes a particular way of exercising domination through legitimizing and privileging the 'management' of the organization–environment interface, producing some actors as 'strategists' and reducing others as troops whose role is to subordinate themselves and to implement corporate strategies (Shrivastava, 1986; Alvesson and Willmott, 1996). The concept of technocracy draws attention to some of the darker and more disturbing aspects of so-called 'professional management'. It points to a restricted understanding of human and organizational goals – those that are identified and validated by experts. By associating management with technocracy and its instrumentalization of reason, the domination of a narrow conception of reason is at once exposed and questioned.

The domination of groups, ideas and institutions producing and drawing upon the idea of technocracy leads to a technocratic consciousness (Habermas, 1970; Alvesson, 1987). Here basic conflicts between different ideals and principles are seen as dissolving as a consequence of the development of more and more rational methods. In work organizations, conflicts between practical reason (emphasizing the removal of repression) and instrumental reason (focused on the maximization of output) are portrayed as avoidable through the use of optimal management methods such as job enrichment quality of working life (QWL), total quality management (TQM), corporate culture and so forth – which simultaneously produce human well-being and development, and high quality and productivity. Basic political issues are then transformed into technical problem-solving.

Habermas's ideas may also be used in a pragmatic way, more suitable for social science and organization studies than the original philosophical-theoretical version. With the communicative turn in Habermas's work, there follows possibilities for a more applied and empirical development in the use of critical theory. This means, as Forester argued, 'putting *ideal* speech aside' and expanding the exploration of 'the *actual* social and political conditions of "checking", of political voice, and thus too of possible autonomy' (1993: 3; italics added). Forester (1985, 1989, 1992, 1993) has developed a 'critical pragmatism' based on an independent and creative reading of Habermas. Forester's work is particularly interesting as it combines theoretical sophistication with an empirical and applied orientation and can serve as an example here of what critical theory can look like in organizational practice. To Forester, an empirically–oriented critical theory should be: '1) empirically sound and descriptively meaningful; 2) interpretively plausible and phenomenologically meaningful; and yet 3) critically pitched, ethically insightful, as well' (1993: 2).

In following this through, Forester (1989) distinguishes between unavoidable and socially unnecessary disturbances, between socially ad hoc problems and more socially systematic, structure-related sources of distortions. Organizations may be understood as structures of systematically (that is, non-accidently and possibly avoidable) distorted communication or as social/communicative infrastructures mediating between structural relations and social actions in economic and working life contexts. Irrespective of the extent to which distortions can be avoided in practice, knowledge and insight of distorted communication are certainly of value. From a communication perspective, organizations can be assessed and evaluated according to whether they approximate dogma (closed communication) or dialogue (open communication) (see Deetz, 1992: ch. 7). As Forester argued:

> When organizations or polities are structured so that their members have no protected recourse to checking the truth, legitimacy, sincerity, or clarity of claims made on them by established structures of authority and production, we may find conditions of dogmatism rather than of social learning, tyranny rather than authority, manipulation rather than cooperation, and distraction rather than sensitivity. In this way critical theory points to the importance of understanding practically and normatively how access to, and participation in, discourses, both theoretical and practical, is systematically structured. (1983: 239–40)

Forester views the organizing of attention as a crucial feature of administrative and organizational processes of social reproduction.

He draws upon Habermas's (1984) model of reproduction, which includes:

- cultural reproduction of world-views (ideas, knowledge, beliefs);
- social integration, in which norms, obligations and patterns of social membership are reproduced;
- socialization, in which social identities, motives and expressions of the self are altered and developed.

At stake in specific communicative/organizational acts (and struggles) are thus the reproduction/challenging/reformulation of beliefs, consent and identity. Crucial research as well as practical questions include 'what makes possible or impedes a worker's finding out information at the workplace, challenging rules or norms, or expressing needs, feelings, his or her identity, way of being?' (Forester, 1993: 131). The problem here, Forester notes, is to link control structures to daily experience, voice and action. Such an account becomes a structural phenomenology: it is structural because it maps 'the systematic staging and framing of social action; it is phenomenology because it explores the concrete social interactions (promises, threats, agreements, deals, conflicts) that are so staged' (Forester, 1993: 140). Forester (1992) illustrates his approach through a sensitive reading of a mundane, seemingly trivial empirical situation: a city staff planning meeting. He explores his data – 12 lines of transcript from the meeting – and shows how Habermas's pragmatic validity claims are productive in exploring how social and political relations are established, reordered, and reproduced as the staff talk and listen.

Postmodernism and organizational research

Much has been made of the multiple uses of the term postmodern and the different versions of it (Alvesson, 1995; Thompson, 1993). We do not here deny the variation within the stream. Nevertheless, in contexts such as the present one it can be helpful to produce common themes in which variation in key authors' agendas are downplayed and commonalities highlighted. In postmodernism as a philosophically based research perspective, which is our major concern in this chapter, the following, on the whole interrelated sets of ideas are often emphasized:

1 The centrality of discourse – textuality – where the constitutive power of language is emphasized and 'natural' objects are viewed as discursively produced.

2 Fragmented identities – emphasizing subjectivity as a process and the death of the individual, autonomous, meaning-creating subject where the discursive production of the individual replaces the conventional 'essentialistic' understanding of people.
3 The critique of the philosophy of presence and representation where the indecidabilities of language takes precedence over language as a mirror of reality and a means for the transport of meaning.
4 The loss of foundations and the power of grand narratives where an emphasis on multiple voices and local politics is favoured over theoretical frameworks and large-scale political projects.
5 The power/knowledge connection where the impossibilities in separating power from knowledge are assumed and knowledge loses a sense of innocence and neutrality.
6 Hyper-reality – simulacra – replace the 'real world' where simulations take precedence in contemporary social order.
7 Research aimed at resistance and indeterminacy, where irony and play are preferred to rationality, predictability and order.

Let us consider each briefly.

The centrality of discourse
Postmodernism grew out of French structuralism by taking seriously the linguistic turn in philosophy. In this sense postmodernists in the French tradition made a move on structuralist thought similar to the one Habermas made on ideological critique in the German tradition. As systematically distorted communication replaced false consciousness in critical theory, textual/discursive fields replaced the structure of the unconscious in postmodern thought. Both used these to fight a two-front war, the objectivists on the one hand with their science aimed at predicting/controlling nature and people, and humanists on the other privileging the individual's reported experience, unique human rights, and advancing a naïve version of human freedom. Focusing on language allowed a constructionism which denied the objectivist claim of certainty and objective truth, and the humanists' reliance on essential claims positions which led objectivists and humanists to miss the social/linguistic politics of experience. As discussed later, the linguistic turn enabled a postmodern rejection of humanism through a critique of autonomy and unitary identities, and a rejection of objectivism through a critique of the philosophy of presence and representation.

To note the primacy of discourse is to suggest that each person is born into ongoing discourses that have a material and continuing presence. The experience of the world is structured through the ways discourses lead one to attend to the world and provide particular unities and divisions. As a person learns to speak these discourses, they more properly speak him or her in that available discourses position the person in the world in a particular way prior to the individual having any sense of choice. As discourses structure the world, they at the same time structure the person's subjectivity providing him or her with a particular social identity and way of being in the world. The person, contra humanism, is always social first and only mistakenly claims the personal self as the origin of experience.

There are two major versions of this theme. One version emphasizes discourses in a special linguistic sense, where language in use is intrinsically related to meaning and perception. All perception and meaning entails a 'seeing as' and this 'seeing as' is described as a fundamental 'signifying' or 'language' relation. The distinctions historically carried in language enable a reproduction of specific 'seeing as' relations. Different discourses are always possible – although they may be more or less powerful or marginal. As a linguistic phenomenon, discourse is weakly coupled to material practices in this version (Weedon, 1987). Another, Foucauldian version views discourses as systems of thought which are contingent upon as well as inform material practices, which not only linguistically but also practically – through particular power techniques (clearly visible in prisons, psychiatric hospitals, schools, factories, and so forth) – produce particular forms of subjectivity (Foucault, 1977, 1980b). In both versions, human subjectivity can be relatively open or closed. Discursive closure according to the first version is temporary, though often continually reproduced, while Foucault tends to emphasize a more systematic fixation of subjectivity as a result of the network of power relations in operation.

Many organizational researchers have used this insight productively. Most, but not all, have followed Foucault in their development. For example, Knights and Morgan used Foucault's discursive practices to show the construction of person and world in the discourse of corporate strategy. They argue that 'strategic discourses engage individuals in practices through which they discover the very "truth" of what they are – viz. "a strategic actor"' (1991: 260). They point to a number of power effects of corporate strategy discourse, including the sustaining and enhancement of the prerogatives of management, the generation of a sense of personal security for managers, the expression of a gendered masculinity for (male) management, and the facilitation and legitimization of the exercise of power.

Fragmented identities

The position on the 'person' follows directly from the conception of discourse. Postmodernism rejects the notion of the autonomous, self-determining individual with a secure unitary identity as the centre of the social universe. Even though many other traditions have also done so (for example, behaviourists, structuralists), post-modernists have pushed this point strongly and in a sophisticated manner.

There are two versions of this critique of a secure unitary identity. The first suggests that the Western conception of *man* has always been a myth. It represents a rather ethnocentric idea. Freud's work on tensions and conflicts as central for the human psyche is used to show the growing awareness in Western thought of the fundamental inner fragmentation and inconsistency, but postmodernists go further in their deconstruction of the Western self-image. The conception of a unitary self is considered a fiction used to suppress those conflicts and privilege masculinity, ration-ality, vision, and control. To the extent that dominant discourses spoke the person (and produced the person as the origin of thought), the person gained a secure identity but participated in the reproduction of domination, thus marginalizing the other parts of the self and other groups. The sense of autonomy served to cover this subservience and give conflict a negative connotation.

The other version suggests that the view of the individual as coherent, integrated and (potentially) autonomous has become false in the contemporary historical and cultural situation. If iden-tity is a social production, identity will be relatively stable in homogeneous and stable societies with few dominant discourses. In contemporary, heterogeneous, global, teleconnected societies the available discourses expand greatly. They also change rapidly. The individual comes to be spoken by so many discourses that fragmentation is virtually inevitable (Gergen, 1991). As society becomes more fragmented and hyper-real or virtual (discourse is disconnected from any world reference, images reference images) the identity-stabilizing forces are lost.

Such a position suggests the possibility of tremendous freedom and opportunity for marginalized groups and aspects of each person to enter the discourse, but also suggests insecurities which lead to normalization strategies in which people 'voluntarily' cling, or attach themselves, to consumer identities offered by commercial forces or organizational selves through the orchestration of corporate cultures (Deetz, 1995a; Willmott, 1994). This loose self is also very susceptible to manipulation and can be jerked about in the system, leading to ecstasy but domination without any dominant group, as in Baudrillard's (1983, 1988) conception of simulation. These two versions – emphasizing human nature per se or only the contemporary Western variant as discursively produced and fragmentary – are often a matter of emphasis (see Gergen, 1991, 1992).

This view of the human subject, however, creates difficulties in developing political action. Flax (1990) for example, shows the awkward position in which it leaves women. If gender is treated as a social construction and dominant discourses have produced marginality and a sense of women being an 'other' – taking all the negative terms in the linguistic system and discourse – then ridding society of strong gender ascriptions (making gender irrelevant in many situations) is a good idea (Alvesson and Billing, 1997). One should simply stop talking about 'men' and 'women', and stop reproducing this pervasive and powerful distinction (except in specific situations where it makes practical sense, that is in relationship to childbirth and a few diseases). But to accomplish such a move in the contemporary situation requires women to organize and show that gender is an issue across nearly all social situations. And similarly with the issue of experience. If women's experience arises out of an essential difference (bodily and/or socially produced), it cannot be denied as important and needing to be taken into account, but to make the essentialist argument denies social constructionism and can easily be used in a society where men have resources to further stigmatize women. Theoretical tensions are not easily escaped (see Fraser and Nicholson, 1988). Ironically, however, this type of deep tension and inability to develop a single coherent position appears at the same time both to weaken postmodern work and to give it its reason for being. Such tensions have led some researchers to borrow from critical theory conceptions to add a more clear political programme (see Martin, 1990b) and others to focus on more local forms of resistance (see Smircich and Calás, 1987).

Important implications for organizational analyses follow from the destabilization of human actors and their organizing processes. Linstead suggests that 'organization then is continuously emergent, constituted and constituting, produced and consumed by subjects,' and argues for investigations that move 'towards those processes which *shape* subjectivity rather than the process by which individual subjects act upon the world' (1993: 60). Knights and Willmott (1989) have provided such work demonstrating the way being subjected leads to particular forms of subjugation. Pringle (1988) has shown how the identity of a 'secretary' becomes constructed and reproduced. Deetz (1994c, 1997, 1998) has shown how the nature of 'knowledge-intensive' work situates the production of specific work identities. In a similar way, Townley (1993) applied Foucault's analysis to the discourse of human resource management/HRM. In this work, Townley argued that the basic unit of analysis in understanding human resources management was 'the nature of exchange embodied in the employment relation'. Since this relation in itself is indeterminant, the exchange relation is organized through imposing order on the inherently undecidable. The construction of knowledge in human resource management 'operates through rules of classification, ordering, and distribution; definition of activities; fixing of scales; and rules of procedure, which lead to the emergence of a distinct HRM discourse' (Townley, 1993: 541). This body of knowledge operates to objectify (determine) the person thus both constraining and subordinating the person's fuller social and personal character.

The critique of the philosophy of presence
Normative social science as well as most of us in everyday life treat the presence of objects as unproblematical and believe that the primary function of language is to represent them. When asked what something is we try to define it and list its essential attributes. Postmodernists find such a position to be illusionary in the same way as is the conception of identity. The *stuff* of the world only becomes an *object* in specific relation to a being for whom it can be such an object. Linguistic and non-linguistic practices, thus, are central to object production. Such a position has been familiar for some time in works as varied as Mead, Wittgenstein, and Heidegger, but continues to lead to misunderstandings; the most common is the claim of relativism. The position is not, however, relativistic in any loose or subjective way. Those making the charge misunderstand the conception of objects or the strength of the conception of discourse. Most postmodernists are not concerned with the chance of being called relativistic, they are more concerned with the apparent stability of objects and the difficulty of unpacking the full range of activities that produce particular objects and sustain them.

As mentioned in the section on fragmented identities, postmodernists differ in the extent to which they describe discourse in textual versus a more extended form. On the whole, however, they start with Saussure's demonstration that the point of view creates the object. Saussure meant this to attend to the importance of the value-laden nature of the system of distinctions in language, but the linguistic and non-linguistic practices quickly interrelate. Let us use a brief example. A 'worker' is an object (as well as a subject) in the world, but neither God nor nature made a 'worker'. Two things are required for a 'worker' to exist: (a) a language and set of practices which makes possible unities and divisions among people, and (b) something to which such unities and divisions can be applied. The questions – What is a worker really? What is the essence of a worker? What makes one a worker? – are not answerable by looking at the something that can be described as a worker; they are a product of the linguistic and non-linguistic practices that make this something into an object. In this sense, a worker is not an isolated thing. To have a worker already implies a division of labour, the presence of management ('non-workers'). The 'essence' of worker is not the properties the 'object' contains but sets of relational systems including the division of labour. The focus on the object and object properties is the mistake, the attention should be on the relational systems which are not simply *in* the world but are a human understanding *of* the world, they are discursive or textual. The meaning of 'worker' is not evident and present but deferred to the sets of oppositions and junctures, the relations that make it like and unlike other things.

Since any something in the world may be constructed/expressed as many different objects, limited only by human creativity and readers of traces of past understandings, meaning can never be final; it is always incomplete and indeterminant. The appearance of completeness and closure leads us to overlook both the politics in and of construction and the possibilities for understanding that are hidden behind the obvious. Language is thus central to the production of objects in that it provides the social/historical distinctions that provide unity and difference. Language cannot mirror the reality 'out there', nor people's mental states (Shotter and Gergen, 1989, 1994). Language is figural, metaphorical, full of contradictions and inconsistencies (Brown, 1990; Cooper and Burrell, 1988). Meaning is not universal and fixed, but precarious, fragmented and local (Linstead and Grafton-Small, 1992). Management researchers have used these conceptions to deconstruct objects of organizational life, including the bounded concept of an organization itself. Perhaps among the most productive have been those studying accounting practices. The bottom line, profit and loss, expenses, and so forth have no reality without specific practices creating them (Hopwood, 1987; Power and Laughlin, 1992; Montagna, 1986). Others have looked at knowledge and information (Boland, 1987), or at reporting practices (Sless, 1988) and categories of people (Epstein, 1988). Each of these show the conditions necessary for objects to exist in organizational life. Any attempt at representation is thus always partial (one-sided and favouring a side). The making of distinction through language use is a necessary condition of life with others, and yet it is inevitably limiting in that it hides important alternative distinctions (see Bourdieu, 1984, 1991).

The loss of foundations and master narratives

The power of any position has been traditionally gathered from its grounding. This grounding could either be a metaphysical foundation – such as an external world in empiricism, mental structures in rationalism or human nature in humanism – or a narrative, a story of history, such as Marxism's class struggle, social Darwinism's survival of the fittest, or the market economy's invisible hand. With such groundings, positions are made to seem secure and inevitable and not opportunistic or driven by advantage. Certainly much organizational theory has been based on such appeals, as has critical theory in its morally guided communicative action.

Again, like in the case of identity, postmodernists take two different but not incompatible stances: one categorical (valid throughout history and social context) and one interested in recent historical trends (thus overlapping the philosophy/periodization distinctions). Following the first position, foundations and legitimating narratives have always been a hoax. They have been used (usually unknowingly) to support a dominant view of the world and its order. Feminists, for example, have argued that the historical narrative has always been *his*tory. Empiricists' appeal to the nature of the external world covered the force of their own concepts (and those borrowed from elite groups), methods, instruments, activities, and reports in constructing that world.

Following the second position, other postmodernists note the growing social incredulity exhibited about narratives and foundational moves. Lyotard (1984) showed the decline of grand narratives of 'spirit' and 'emancipation'. The proliferation of options and growing political cynicism (or astuteness) of the public leads to a suspicion of legitimating moves. This conception not far from Habermas's idea of legitimation crises in late-capitalist society (Habermas, 1975). In Lyotard's sense, perhaps all that is left is local narratives. Such a position has led to sensitive treatments of how stories in organizations connect to grand narratives and how different ones have a more local, situational character (see Martin, 1990a; Deetz, 1998). Others have used this opening to display the false certainty in the master narratives in management (Jehenson, 1984; Ingersoll and Adams, 1986; Carter and Jackson, 1987; Calás and Smircich, 1991).

Not all postmodernists see this as necessarily positive. Certainly the decline of foundations and grand narratives takes away a primary prop of the dominant group's offer of security and certainty in exchange for subordination. But the replacement is not necessarily freedom and political possibility for the marginalized groups. Lyotard (1984) demonstrated the rise of 'performativity' where measures of means toward social ends become an ends in themselves (see also Power, 1994). Access to computers and information – contingent less upon knowledge integrated in the person ('scholarship') than upon financial resources – has become a significant source of knowledge and power. Along with this comes new forms of control not directed by a vision of society and social good but simply more production and consumption.

Certainly the loss of grand integrative narratives has not been missed by management groups. One could perhaps say that corporate 'visions' and 'cultures' are strategic local narrative constructions to provide the integration and motivation in a pluralistic society formerly provided by wider social narratives. On the other hand, one could say that these forms of management control represent large-scale systematic efforts which resemble grand narratives, though at a corporate level. Perhaps the development of management control can be seen as corporate grand narratives taking over some of the functions of political programmes. The decline of vision, hope and community in politics have paved the way for management ideologies and practices that may fill parts of the vacuum (Deetz, 1992). Postmodernists point to the precarious nature of this kind of project. Corporate cultures, for example, are seen as text and corporate members then become readers who 'bring awareness of other texts, other cultural forms, other evocations and explosions of meaning to their reading of any text, and enter into the text, changing its nature and re-producing it as they consume it' (Linstead and Grafton-Small, 1992: 344).

The difficulty with this in postmodernism, as in the concept of fragmented identities, is how to generate a political stance with regard to these developments. If one rejects an essentialist foundation and believes that more than local resistance is needed, some kind of combination between postmodernism and critical theory may well provide the best remaining option. We will come back to this.

The knowledge/power connection

Within postmodern writings, power is treated far differently than in most writings on organizations. Foucault has been the most explicit (Foucault, 1977, 1980b; see Clegg, 1994). The power that is of interest is not that which one possesses or acquires. Such appearances of power are the outcome of more fundamental power relations. Power resides in the discursive formation itself – the combination of a set of linguistic distinctions, ways of reasoning and material practices that together organize social institutions and produce particular forms of subjects. As mentioned before, language is here less strictly focused than in many other variants of postmodernism. Following the earlier example, the discourse that produces a 'manager' both empowers and disempowers the group of individuals formed as that object. It simultaneously provides a solidarity, interests, material and symbolic resources, self-understandings and sets into play conflict. At the same time others such as professionals and workers receive identities along with the problems and resources that come with them. Power thus resides in the demarcations and the systems of discourse that sustain them, including material arrangements – for example, recruitment and selection procedures, office arrangements, reward and control structures, inclusion or exclusion in significant meetings, and so forth. One of the most useful terms entering into organizational studies from this has been Foucault's (1977) concept of discipline. The demarcations provide forms of normative behaviour supported by claims of knowledge. Training, work routines, self-surveillance, and experts are discipline in that they provide resources for normalization. Normative experts in particular, and the knowledge they create, provide a cover for the arbitrary and advantaging discursive practices and facilitate normalization (Hollway, 1984, 1991). Townley's (1993) work discussed above carefully showed how the development of the human resource expert and human resource knowledge was used as a way to 'determine' and subordinate employees. Such knowledge can also be utilized by employees to engage in self-surveillance and self-correction of attitudes and behaviours toward norms and expectations established by others (Deetz, 1995a: ch. 10, 1997).

Hyper-reality
Postmodern writings vary in terms of how they handle the relation of language to the non-linguistic realm of people and world. A strict linguistic focus and a strict critique of the philosophy of presence leaves little interest in references to a pre-formed and relatively constant extra-textual reality. Most postmodernists treat the external as a kind of excess or 'otherness' which serves as a resource for formations and also prevents language systems from becoming closed and purely imaginary. While the referent has no specific character it always exceeds the objects made of it, and thus reminds one of the limited nature of all systems of representation

and their fundamental indeterminacy (Cooper, 1989). The presence of 'otherness' in the indeterminacy provides a moment to show the domination present in any system, to open it up, and to break the sealed self-referentiality of some textual systems.

Many existing linguistic or representational systems are shown to be self-referential by postmodernists. Such systems are neither anchored in a socially-produced-as-objective world nor do they respect the excess of an outside. They produce the very same world that they appear to accurately represent. For example, contemporary media and information systems have the capacity rapidly to construct images which replace, more than represent, an outside world (Boorstin, 1961). Such systems can dominate the scene with an array of reproduced imaginary worlds. The referent disappears as anything more than another sign, thus signs only reference other signs; images are images of images. Such systems can become purely self-referential or what Baudrillard calls *simulations* (see Deetz, 1994b). In such a world, in Baudrillard's analysis, signs are disconnected from opening a relation to the world and the 'model' response to a 'model' world replaces responsive action in an actual changing world. Signs reach the structural limit of representation by referencing only themselves with little relation to any exterior or interior. Baudrillard expresses this relation as follows:

> The form-sign [present in a monopolistic code] describes an entirely different organization: the signified and the referent are now abolished to the sole profit of the play of signifiers, of a generalized formalization in which the code no longer refers back to any subjective or objective 'reality,' but to its own logic. ... The sign no longer designates anything at all. It approaches its true structural limit which is to refer back only to other signs. All reality then becomes the place of semi-urgical manipulation, of a structural simulation. (1975: 127–8)

The world as understood is not really a fiction in this situation since there is no 'real' outside which it portrays falsely or which can be used to correct it. It is properly imaginary; it has no opposite, no outside. Baudrillard used the example of the difference between feigning and simulating an illness to show the character of this postmodern representation:

> feigning or dissimulation leaves the reality principle intact; the different is always clear, it is only masked; whereas simulation threatens the difference between 'true' and 'false', between 'real' and 'imaginary'. Since the simulator produces 'true' symptoms, is he ill or not? He cannot be treated objectively either as ill, or not ill. (1983: 5)

The only option of the researcher is to 'produce a text that reproduces these multiple versions of the real, showing how each impinges and shapes the phenomenon being studied' (Denzin, 1997: 13). These ideas have inspired some organization studies emphasizing the imaginary character of modern organizations (Berg, 1989; Alvesson, 1990; Deetz, 1994c, 1995a). As is common with postmodern ideas in organization theory, these studies do not follow the source of inspiration to its full (extreme) consequences.

Research as resistance and indeterminacy
As more generally is the case in critically based research, the role of postmodern research is very different from more traditional roles assigned to social science. It primarily serves to attempt to open up the indeterminacy that modern social science, everyday conceptions, routines, and practices have closed off. The result is a kind of anti-positive knowledge (Knights, 1992). The primary methods are deconstruction resistance readings and genealogy. These terms have been used in many different ways and in the limited space here we can do little beyond providing a sketch of them. Deconstruction works primarily to critique the philosophy of presence by recalling the suppressed terms (the deferred terms) which provides the system and thus which allows the positive terms to appear to stand for an existing object. When the suppressed term is given value, both the dependency of the positive term on the negative is shown and a third term is recovered which shows a way of world making that is not dependent on the opposition of the first two (see Cooper, 1989; Martin, 1990b; Calás and Smircich, 1991; Mumby and Putnam, 1992). The resistance reading is less narrowly focused on terms. It both demonstrates the construction activity and provides indeterminacy based in the excess of the outside. The positive and the polar construction are both displayed as acts of domination: subjectivity doing violence to the world and limiting itself in the process. In this move, conflicts that were suppressed by the positive are brought back to redecision and the conflictual field out of which objects are formed is recovered for creative redetermination – constant de-differentiation and re-differentiation. Given the power of closure and the way it enters common sense and routines, especially in simulations, such re-readings require a particular form of rigour and imagination. The re-readings are formed out of a keen sense of irony, a serious playfulness, and are often guided by the pleasure one has in being freed from the dull compulsions of a world made too easy and too violent. A good example of such readings is Calás and Smircich's (1988) account of a mainstream positivist journal article; they start with the question 'why should we believe in this author?' and then point out the rhetorical tricks used in order to persuade the reader. Another interesting example is Sangren's (1992) critical

review of Clifford and Marcus's *Writing Culture* (1986). Sangren, drawing upon Bourdieu (1979), uses their points about the politics of representation – intended to indicate the problems of ethnographies in mirroring cultures and exemplified through important anthropological works – against them, showing how the representations of Clifford, Marcus and co-authors of earlier works can be seen in terms of politics. Particular kinds of representations are used that create the impression that earlier works are flawed and that there is a large and open space for novel contributions (and the career options) of the new heterodoxi (Clifford, Marcus *et alia*) and their more informed view on the politics of representation.

The point of social science is not to get it right but to challenge guiding assumptions, fixed meanings and relations, and to reopen the formative capacity of human beings in relation to others and the world – qualities that Gergen (1978) and Astley (1985) displayed as essential to any important theory. As Sangren (1992) illustrates, the challenges on dogma, fixed ideas and reopenings may easily imply new dogmas, fixations and closures. Postmodernism is in no way immune to such implications (Alvesson and Sköldberg, 2000).

One outcome of the themes reviewed above – in particular the critique of the philosophy of presence and the loss of master narratives, but also hyper-reality and the focus on resistance – is a strong current interest in experimenting with different styles. This is prominent in anthropology (Clifford and Marcus, 1986; Geertz 1988; Marcus and Fisher, 1986; Rose, 1990) and also in organization theory (for example, Calás and Smircich, 1991; Jeffcutt, 1993; Linstead and Grafton-Small, 1990; Watson, forthcoming). Typically, 'realist' ways of writing are superseded or complemented by other styles, for example, ironic, self-ironic or impressionistic ones. In an investigation of texts in organizational culture and symbolism, Jeffcutt shows how it is 'distinguished by heroic quests for closure; being dominated by authors adopting representational styles that privilege epic and romantic narratives over tragic and ironic forms. These representational strategies expose an overriding search for unity and harmony that suppresses division and conflict' (1993: 32). Perhaps the inspiration to develop new ways of writing will turn out to be one of the most powerful and interesting contributions of postmodernism.

Relating critical theory and postmodernism

Critical theory and postmodernism, as has been shown, are both alike and different. Each has much to contribute to organizational studies, and we believe that they have a contribution to make together. Without considering postmodern themes, critical theory easily becomes unreflective with regard to cultural elitism and modern conditions of power; without incorporating some measure of critical theory thought – or something similar that provides direction and social relevance – postmodernism simply becomes esoteric. Both draw attention to the social/historical/political construction of knowledge, people, and social relations, including how each of these appear in contemporary organizations. And they share a view that domination is aided, and that both people and organizations lose much if we overlook these construction activities by treating the existing world as natural, rational and neutral. In critical theory's language, the concern is reification; in postmodernist language it is the philosophy of presence. Based on this naturalization and freezing of contemporary social reality, important conflicts – options for reconsiderations and questioning – are lost, and different groups of people as well as vital values are marginalized and disadvantaged. Both see organizations and the social sciences that support them as relying increasingly on a form of instrumental reasoning which is privileging the means over ends and aiding dominant groups' ability invisibly to accomplish their ends. Habermas describes this in terms of 'instrumental technical reasoning', Lyotard in 'performativity'.

The differences are also important. Critical theory sees the response in terms of an expanded form of morally guided communicative reasoning leading to individual autonomy and better social choices. Through reflections on the ways ideology – taken-for-granted cultural ideas as well as specific messages engineered by powerful agencies – enters into person/world/ knowledge construction and by providing more open forums of expression and a type of discourse aimed at mutual understanding, there is hope for the production of social consensus and social agreements that better fulfil human needs. The grand narrative of the Enlightenment might, according to critical theory, yet be advanced. But postmodernism rejects such reflection and consensus, suspecting the replacement of old illusions with new ones, and the creation of new elites and new forms of marginalizations. Critical theory replies: without reflection, consensus and rationality, there is no politics – no agenda for a constructive alternative. Postmodernism counters: politics are by necessity local and situational – responsiveness is more important than systematic planning. Critical theory responds: local politics is too weak to confront system-wide gender and class dominations as well as global poverty and environmental problems. Postmodernism maintains: organizing against domination both props up and solidifies dominant groups – it creates its own forms of domination. The difference is, in a sense, the same as between a push and a pull theory. Critical theory wants us to act and provides direction and orchestration; postmodernism believes that such a move will be limited by the force of our own subjective domination and encourages us to get out of the way and allow the world to pull us to feelings and thought hitherto unknown; but critical theory does not have enough faith to let go. And so on.

However, there are ways to think them both at once, though not necessarily through some new synthesis. We have a need for both conflict and consensus, for resistance and plans. The issue is not which to choose but the *balance*, choosing the right moments (Deetz, 1992). To say that consensus implies domination does not mean we should not make the best decisions we can together, but that we need to continue to look for domination and be ready to move on. To say that resistance lacks a clear politics does not mean that it is not doing something important and ultimately may be the only way we can see through dominations that we like or that benefit *and* limit us.

One option is thus to work with unresolved tensions within a text where one follows different themes of postmodernism and critical theory without attempting synthesis, working with the tensions and contrastive images. Examples of this include work by Knights and Willmott (1989) and Deetz (1994c). Another option is to allow space for various discrete voices in texts through organizing these around conversations between various theoretical perspectives or interest groups (Alvesson and Willmott, 1996) or to conduct multiple interpretations of the same phenomenon (Alvesson, 1996; Morgan, 1986), such as interpreting a phenomenon from both critical theory and postmodernist (and perhaps other) positions. Another way of combining insights from critical theory and postmodernism is to see both as metatheories, useful as inspiration for reflexivity, rather than as theories directly relevant for guiding and interpreting studies of substantive matters (Alvesson and Sköldberg, 2000). Still another option is to restrict the approach to the careful study of language use and communicative practices in 'real' social settings, which is done by discourse and conversation analysis (I. Parker, 1992; Potter and Wetherell, 1987) and constructivists (Shotter and Gergen, 1994; Steier, 1991). Such studies can be used to sensitize us to the power effects of language and ground Habermasian and postmodernist ideas in portions of organizational reality (Forester, 1992). Such a language focus avoids the philosophy of presence but maintains an empirical context. (For an overview of the possible reactions to the centrality of language, see Alvesson and Kärreman, 2000.)

Perhaps the greatest criticism of critical theory and even more so of postmodernism is the lack of extended empirical studies. Other versions of critical organization and management studies, such as labour process theory, fare much better (for example, Knights and Willmott, 1990). This is clearly a problem this book hopes to help overcome. Part of the criticism arises due to a narrow view of the notion of 'empirical' but many researchers can still be faulted for writing conceptual essays without extended field experience and reports. Critical theory and postmodernism's strong critique of empiric*ism* and their emphasis on data as constructions open to a multitude of interpretations does not mean that reflective empirical work is not worth doing. Many texts have limited feelings for organizational contexts and the lives of real people. Much can be gained by allowing organizational participants to 'say something' that is not immediately domesticated by theories locating the material in an all-too-predictable 'bureaucracy', 'patriarchy', 'capitalism', 'managerialism' pejorative discourse, an all-embracing Foucauldian power concept, or a pacification and fragmentation of subjects as mere appendices of discourses. An empirical turn may also reduce the tendency of negativity in much of critical theory and some postmodernism. Having said this, we must acknowledge that recently more empirical work is being done, particularly with a critical theory orientation (for example, Rosen, 1985, 1988; Knights and Willmott, 1987, 1992; Alvesson, 1996) but also using postmodern themes (Martin, 1990b, 1995; Deetz, 1997, 1998). What is lacking, in particular, are serious efforts to ground ideas of local resistance in specific empirical contexts. There is a lot of talk about resistance in the postmodernist industry, but it is highly theoretical, often underdeveloped and generalized, and it remains quite esoteric. We need to go further than repeating programmatical slogans and use and refine the idea in close contact with the lives of subjects in organizational settings.

For space reasons, we shall not indulge in further discussion of these responses to various critiques of traditional ways of doing research brought forward both by postmodern authors (in particular) and authors not waving the postmodern flag. Suffice it to say, there are various paths that address the middle ground between more traditional realist and hermeneutic epistemologies – where there is a space for empirical studies of organizational phenomena – on the one hand, and a postmodern philosophy threatening to turn all social science into esoteric literary criticism on the other hand.

Summary

In this chapter we have provided an overview of the versions of critical tradition(s) that we find most productive, given contemporary society and the developments of business and working life: Frankfurt School critical theory and a critical, politically committed version of postmodernism (sometimes labelled postmodernism of resistance). We identify two major versions of critical theory: ideology critique and communicative action. Of the various major themes within postmodernism, Foucault's work on knowledge/power and the discursive production of subjects are perhaps most relevant for critical management research. The two streams (where, in particular, postmodernism is very heterogeneous) stand in a tension-laden but productive relationship to each other. We anticipate that the critical theory–postmodernism debates will offer inspiring challenges for critical studies in management in the future.

5
New rules for research

All that has been said in Chapter 3 and in parts of Chapter 4 warns against a naïve empiricism, that is a belief that data can be separated from theory and interpretation, that data and empirically validated claims should be privileged in knowledge development, and that data are capable of revealing the objective truth. Any idea of easy access to or unproblematical accounts providing empirical material reflecting reality must be rejected. 'Data' in the context of social science – except on trivial issues – are never so robust, objective or mirroring as they may appear. Data are constructions made by the researcher, to a higher (interviews) or lower (observation) degree in interaction with research subjects (Alvesson and Sköldberg, 2000; Denzin and Lincoln, 1994; Steier, 1991). Language does not stand in a one-to-one relationship to (partially) non-linguistic phenomena such as behaviours, thoughts and feelings (Gergen and Gergen, 1991). The research texts produced, even if anchored in ambitious empirical studies, are literary products. Social reality never determines exactly how words should be composed in a journal article. Texts follow conventions for writing and persuading (Calás and Smircich, 1988; Clifford, 1986; Jeffcutt, 1993; Van Maanen, 1988). Rhetoric is an unavoidable element in research publications (Astley, 1985; Brown, 1990; Watson, 1995). Writers' conformity with dominant norms within the science community should not be confused with objectivity. Texts thus cannot simply mirror objective reality.

This should in no way discourage empirical studies. What has been said does not mean that one should not listen carefully to what people may say nor try to find out what is going in everyday corporate life. However, it motivates deep changes towards a more reflexive understanding of the entire project characterized by awareness of interpretative acts and consideration of alternative ways of describing and interpreting the candidates for empirical material (observations, interview statements, questionnaire responses, etc.). Reflexivity involves the self-critical consideration of one's own assumptions and consistent consideration of alternative interpretative lines and the use of different research vocabularies (Alvesson and Sköldberg, 1999). The mode of study suggested, grounded in the critique offered in Chapter 3, aims at an interpretive, open, language-sensitive, identity-conscious, historical, political, local, non-authoritative and textually aware understanding of the subject matter.

This chapter will offer and discusses some general methodological guidelines for qualitative research of a post-empiricist nature. These guidelines are rather unspecific – the views put forward in Chapter 4 go strongly against a 'cookbook' and bureaucratic approach to social research circling around procedures and detailed rules – and are compatible with, but not very tightly connected to, critical research. This chapter, therefore, presents some general guidelines of relevance for all qualitative research (and a lot of quantitative research also, for that matter), outlines some principles further framing the kind of critical research we are advocating and thus forms a basis on which later chapters can build, dealing more specifically with critical research.

Intensifying interpretation

Recognizing the interpretive nature of research means that no data, except possibly those on trivial matters, are viewed as unaffected by the construction of the researcher. For this reason we prefer the expression 'empirical material' and think that the metaphor 'data collection' is directly misleading. It sounds as if social studies resemble the picking of mushrooms. But 'in the social sciences there is only interpretation. Nothing speaks for itself' (Denzin, 1994: 500). The researcher does something active in order to produce empirical material. Observations, even when leading to detailed descriptions, call for immediate interpretations and the forming of gestalts of what is going on. That somebody instructs, jokes, plans, or asks for information are interpretations – not plain facts. Interviews, at least of a qualitative nature – in contrast to what Potter and Wetherell (1987) call 'talking questionnaires' – call for consistent interpretations before and during the interaction with the respondent. Without interpretations of the respondent's person and his or her previous accounts, the social interaction will not work; the researcher will appear as rigid and strange – an impression that will colour (and restrict) further responses. An interview is thus an event characterized by highly intensive interpretation, much of it unreflective and nonconscious, not only on the part of the interviewer-researcher, but also on that of the interviewee – who actively tries to make sense of who the interviewer is, what he or she is characterized by in terms of framework and pre-structured understanding, what the research project is about, what may come out of it of relevance for the interviewee, etc.

Taking the interpretive nature of research seriously means that one avoids prematurely applying conventional ideas and words such as leader and leadership (and manager and management, man and woman, strategy, culture, etc. for that matter). These interpretations – it is seldom self-evident that a person, a behaviour or a relationship are best conceptualized in these terms – must be applied with care. To continue with the example of leadership, the degree of asymmetry of a specific relation – normally seen as a major criterion for talk about leadership – may be ambiguous, inconsistent, contradictory and even transcend formal relations (as when a former subordinate has a larger impact on a superior than the other way around). The subtleties of the relationship, as well as the variations, must be noted in qualified research. Of course, the leader is hardly exercising leadership over subordinates all the time. 'Leaders' interact with customers, suppliers, colleagues, superiors, etc. Also, when interacting with subordinates they do not 'lead' all the time (unless they are obsessed with being a 'leader'). They also work. (Managers are workers.) Especially in qualified work settings, simple ordering or manager-led control of meaning are not necessarily salient or crucial. Managers do not just work top-down, but are also passive and receptive. One manager describes his work in terms of 'listening to people'. Social processes involving planning, giving advice and support, encouragement, providing of information, persuasion, solving problems, discussing ideas, etc. may seldom be easily or best fitted into a leadership–follower pattern, unless the researcher has this interpretive formula rigidly anchored in his or her head and vocabulary, allowing it command over the social reality that he or she will make sense of without seriously considering other interpretations (theoretical vocabularies).

Instead, what is vital is an *open attitude*, perhaps best being described as what we in Chapter 2 labeled a local/emergent research orientation. This ideal may be reframed as the postponement of closure in the research process as well as the written text. It is likely that careful interpretive work will show that the 'leader' holds a position that is far from always being salient in everyday work, and that leadership as a quality of behaviour/social relations is often ambiguous and precarious and that it is only relatively rarely present. It is possible, for example, that competence asymmetries on particular issues mean that a (group of) former subordinates take a leading role, have a more powerful impact on group discussions, the framing of the problem situation and the highlighting of route for further action. This is in line with recent ideas saying that 'leadership' is a shared social process, involving a group of people rather than a single individual standing out as being superior to the rest (Yukl, 1989). The point of labeling this 'leadership' may be disputed. If leadership is not prematurely tied to a formal position or defined as a fixed quality but seen more openly in relationship to that which goes on in the work organization context and the relations being formed and reformed in processes of sense making, attribution and negotiation, then it is likely that much more variation becomes salient than is the case in interview accounts in which 'leaders' are interviewed as 'leaders' about leadership. The risk of a heavy bias is especially great in questionnaires where subjects are pressed into the fixed leader–follower structure from the very beginning, with few possibilities of social reality kicking back (encouraging the researcher to re-think his or her basic ideas and categories). But also in qualitative research similar biases, locking the research project into imposing certain interpretive inclinations, may be strong. It is in a sense unavoidable as natural language builds upon arbitrary distinctions and certain ways of constructing the world – the self-evident appropriateness of dividing up the corporate world into managers and workers, centralized and decentralized organizations, planned and emergent strategies, etc. makes many accounts of natives or interviewees deeply problematical. In the context of being interviewed by a representative of management science, a person producing 'data' to a research project may be inclined to try to adjust their accounts so that they fit into what is assumed to make sense for the management researcher, which may well be the vocabulary and models that the interviewee has learned in business school. Even though the interviewee may well express viewpoints that deviate from the textbook view of the management world, the basic framework and the vocabulary used may be strongly affected by this conventional management knowledge. Such shared knowledge facilitates smooth management researcher–practitioner interaction – in, for example, research interviews – but it also effectively obstructs the questioning of these frameworks and vocabularies, preventing new interpretive possibilities from emerging.

Care in employing or accepting conventional words such as leadership, strategy, motives and services, will help keep the interpretation process open. It is, however, likely that what is conventionally and commonsensically labeled in these terms may sometimes be more productively interpreted in other terms. Naturally enough, one may always question the value of general concepts such as leadership, culture, motives, and strategy – and the problems of references to commonsensical ideas and prejudices associated with the signifier should not be underestimated – but it is also important to recognize that the linguistic ambiguities of broad concepts provide unifying symbolic functions for researchers: 'they are robust mechanisms for generating scientific communion' (Astley, 1985: 501).

The researcher may recognize and confirm this function without fixing his or her identity as a leadership (service management, feminist) researcher. An open attitude to the subject matter – including considerations of alternative research vocabularies or lines of interpretation before, during or after the research process (Alvesson and Sköldberg, 2000; Rorty, 1989) – may benefit the intellectual inquiry. Here, of course, it is important not to adopt the naïve idea of being 'non-theoretical' or blank as a means of being open. This simply means that cultural taken-for-granted assumptions and other implicit theories take precedence. Illiteracy does not lead to an open mind. Openness, the consideration of alternative routes of interpretation and analysis, is better accomplished through familiarity with a span of theories and vocabularies. Openness is thus a matter not of avoiding theory, but challenging it, broadening the repertoire of vocabularies and theories that can be mobilized in order to consider more and less self-evident aspects and also by challenging those that come to mind, a particular interpretive bias following from a closed theoretical/ cultural/private orientation may be counteracted.

An important methodological rule is thus to develop access to and use several vocabularies and theoretical perspectives which, in a systematic way, may facilitate insights leading to the view that there are no (or very few and often trivial) 'facts', but only interpretations. Further, insights may be given that all observations and interview outcomes are constructions and results of more or less superficial and conventional interpretations – or perhaps novel and open interpretations. Rather than pretend that one postpones interpretation until the 'data' have been 'collected', it is fair to say that the empirical material is, throughout the fieldwork, the object of intensive and explicit interpretation in which the empirical material is opened up through theoretical awareness rather than fixed through conventional language use and reproduction of social established beliefs and categorizations. 'Descriptive' interpretations are thus made in such a way that they do not easily fall into conventional categorizations and distinctions. Such opening up goes hand in hand with the use of multiple interpretations.

Not all of these have to be reported in research texts, but can be used by the researcher in decisions on how to produce qualified constructions of 'data'.

Let us take a brief example. We are interviewing a person. It may be tempting to establish as objective facts that this is a 50-year-old male manager. But chronological age, sex and formal position may be rather misleading – the person may appear to be much younger, the biological sex may lead the associations in the wrong direction if the person scores highly on female values in terms of work values and family life, and the person's work activities do not mainly seem to be about 'managing' other people. Stating that the person is a 50-year-old male manager is hardly wrong, but it may be a poor, unproductive even misleading claim about what is relevant. Other interpretative possibilities – emphasizing other qualities – may offer an initial understanding which is less destructive for the associations and further interpretations of the researcher, as well as for the reader of research texts.[1]

As said, this point of recognizing the interpretive character of empirical work is basic and, to varying degrees, overlaps the points discussed below. However, they all add other vital aspects and foci.

Evaluating language use in an action context

Another vital aspect of reflexive research, carrying what we have discussed above further, is that it should be *language sensitive.* This is not, as in conventional research, a matter of precise definitions and operationalizations. Some basic characteristics of language and, in particular, language use complicate how accounts of interviewees as well as actors observed (a great deal of what is observed is linguistic behaviour) can be used in research. These involve the metaphorical and contextual nature of language, that language use typically is functional (oriented to effects) rather than truth-oriented, and that social norms and conventions guide and constrain language use. We will discuss all these three aspects in this section.

The ambiguities, and contextual and constructive character of language have been stressed above. Language cannot easily transport meaning across the local settings in which statements are made. To some extent this is inherent in the awareness of the interpretive character of inquiry, but this point goes beyond that. As Deetz (1996: 2) puts it, 'conceptions are always contests for meaning. Language does not name objects in the world; it is core to the process of constituting objects. The appearance of labeling or categorizing existing objects is derived from this more fundamental act of object constitution through language.' Also, the outcomes of qualified interpretations can only with care and pain be compared or aggregated according to a logic of knowledge accumulation. That people in two organizations describe ongoing changes in terms of 'decentralization' does not mean that material changes or changes in social relations are well illuminated through this vocabulary or that what goes on in the two organizations have anything in common – except that the signifier decentralization is currently used with a certain frequency. Empirical material is normally primarily linguistic phenomena and the relationship between these and something else, 'outside' language, is obscure. Language use does not mirror any such reality, at least not in any simple, straightforward way.

As stated above, language is used in order to accomplish something, to produce effects. Language use is always an action and it needs to be understood in its context, rather than a carrier of abstract truths to be evaluated against objective reality. Accounts by, for example, interviewees may therefore more appropriately be understood in terms of a desire to create certain impressions – of rationality, brightness, smartness, morality – or to get the conversation going without too much confusion or disruption. When interviewees appear reliable – which they often do – such appearance may be understood in terms of the desire to appear trustworthy rather than as a certain sign of them essentially being so. Without the mutual feeling of this quality being there – for example, the researcher feels that the interviewee is not trustworthy or the interviewee feels that his or her accounts do not create such an impression – the social situation does not work; the persons involved are likely to see the interview as a failure.

This is not to imply that interviewees are necessarily dishonest, manipulative or eager to do anything to communicate a favourable impression or self-image. Many studies report a large number of interview accounts in which interviewees openly discuss negative behaviours (for example, Jackall, 1988; Watson, 1994). But it is also important here for interviewees to give an impression of being trustworthy when they talk about manipulations, cheating and other immoral behaviours (typically conducted by others, not the interviewees themselves). In an organizational context, it is not inconceivable that people being interviewed are politically conscious and may use the research project for their own purposes, for example slant their descriptions of organizational reality so that their own units or functions may benefit. However, specific language is used for more than simply pushing one's own political interests. People interacting with strangers – and researchers, despite being around for some time and doing follow–up interviews, are still basically unknown persons – in uncertain, ambiguous situations normally want to make a good impression and cope with the interview situation so that it does not become embarrassing or awkward. This calls for a careful balancing of one's words. A person who does not censor any feelings or observations about him- or herself or the workplace may appear odd, socially incompetent or immoral rather than trustworthy and honest. Someone airing many critical views about the organization may easily be seen as disloyal or a complainer.

Contextuality and language use as accomplishment are not, however, the only problems. Social norms for expression guide the use of language, further constraining how language can be used as a simple tool for the researcher. Take, for example, the following summary of research on traits related to leadership effectiveness:

> Traits that relate most consistently to managerial effectiveness or advancement include high self-confidence, energy, initiative, emotional maturity, stress tolerance, and belief in internal locus of control. With respect to interests and values, successful managers tend to be pragmatic and results oriented, and they enjoy persuasive activities requiring initiative and challenge. (Yukl, 1989: 260)

'Traits' here may be seen as purely linguistic phenomena. It is hard for any researcher to state that a person has high self-confidence, energy, initiative, belief in internal locus of control and enjoy persuasive activities if the person has not stated – in an interview or in a questionnaire – that he or she is 'so and so' and believes or likes 'this' and 'that'. (Also, in tests, the respondent often sees what the items refer to in terms of variables and results.) The individual statements are, as far as we understand the research methodology, expressed on one occasion in an 'artificial' (researcher-initiated) setting (interview or questionnaire). Whether similar statements are expressed in other, everyday settings remains an open question. Whether different respondents mean the same thing or not when they state their beliefs and joys is similarly open to question. It is most likely there are great variations in the original statements in the studies where interviews have been used; how many managers explicitly state, 'I have a strong belief in the internal locus of control'? Also it is probable that most successful managers sometimes talk about recession, Japanese competition and other external factors as well as internal factors associated with company history and the errors made by others. They may talk less about these factors than their less fortunate colleagues. It is likely that people in successful companies are inclined to describe the results as outcomes of their own actions and capacities, while people in less successful organizations point at external factors in order to account for the results. Variations and contingencies of accounts would indicate that the uniform results are an outcome of codification processes where a great deal of variation is cut out. This is what conventional methodology is about (Potter and Wetherell, 1987), and complex relations have been disregarded. Of course, this does not necessarily discredit the results, but it indicates the problems inherent in the aggregation of quite diverse accounts to produce general conclusions.

Being agnostic about any relationship between 'real' phenomena corresponding to the words in the citation, we think that social norms and language conventions may account for the findings of Yukl (1989) discussed above. Inherent in the idea of 'managerial effectiveness' are high self-confidence, energy, initiative, belief in internal locus of control, being pragmatic and results oriented, etc.; so, almost by definition, this is the case. Language rules prevent us from saying something else. A manager can hardly say, unless joking or claiming exceptional originality, that he or she has low self-confidence, is lazy, lacks initiative and hates persuasive activities and is an excellent manager. (Nor can a person promoting a person to a managerial post say something of this sort.) Actually, the prospect of being seen, or viewing oneself, as an 'effective manager' is closely linked to whether one manages to convince oneself and other people about high self-confidence, energy, initiative, results orientation, etc. (Of course, the 'substantive' indications of these somewhat vague qualities, as well as their impact on performance, are often highly uncertain. Mastery of symbolism and impression management is crucial. Performance is often hard to measure and the manager's impact on these is a matter of debate. Promotion is to a certain extent based on impression management and skilful political behaviour (Jackall, 1988; Pfeffer, 1981a, 1981b). More generally, people are probably inclined to emphasize qualities consistent with common social understandings of, and norms for, describing the prerequisites of the job. In a study of advertising agencies one of us found that the people described themselves in accordance with established notions of advertising work. It is, of course, possible that the correspondence between people's psychology and ideas of the work is perfect, but the interpretation that they follow social norms for language use appears to be more credible (Alvesson, 1994). For example, advertising workers often describe themselves as 'emotional'. Researchers normally do not. It is hardly likely that the groups differ that much in personality terms. After all, being emotional is a basic human characteristic and it seems clear that researchers have a strong emotional involvement in their work (Jackson, 1995; Jaggar, 1989). The conventions of research and report writing may prescribe a cool detached attitude. The researcher studying a subject may also be inclined not to deviate from the language conventions of the field – partly because he or she cannot liberate him- or herself from it, partly for political reasons. For example, the leadership research community – and those agencies funding it or being recipients of its knowledge products – would not reward people for saying that the positive value of managerial effectiveness is predicted by 'negative' values such as neuroticism, belief in external locus of control, low work morale, conformism, etc. We can also understand the findings of Seltzer and Bass (1990) in a similar way. If a person agrees with statements such as 'my manager makes me proud to be associated with him/her' and 'provides advice to those who need it', he or she is probably inclined to put an X beside a high score on 'overall work effectiveness of your unit' and the supervisor's a effectiveness; this is simple prediction because language rules point to a strong correspondence between these statements. To this picture belong problems in assessing the effectiveness of a unit. It appears odd to report that one feels proud of an ineffective manager. In a sense, it appears to be unnecessary to do the empirical research; language analysis would do a large part of the job (Gergen and Gergen, 1991). In general, tautologies seem to be rather common in studies focusing on performance and/or effectiveness. (For some illustrations in organizational culture studies, see Alvesson, 1993a.)

The overall picture of language becomes more complicated if we include recent arguments – often launched under the banner of post-structuralism (postmodernism) – that, as described in Chapter 4, oppose the idea of the individual as autonomous and consistent, as a bearer of meaning and intentionality. Instead the subject is perceived as constituted by discourses – more or less systematic forms of knowledge, ways of reasoning and definitions of reality entrenched in linguistic practices – and as fragmented in relation to the multiplicity of its constituent mechanisms and processes (for example, Deetz, 1992; Geertz, 1983; Linstead and Grafton-Small, 1992; Shotter and Gergen, 1989; Weedon, 1987; Willmott, 1994).

Language is the central focus of all postmodern work.

In the broadest terms, language defines the possibilities of meaningful existence at the same time as it limits them. Through language, our sense of ourselves as distinct subjectivities is constituted. Subjectivity is constituted through a myriad of what post-structuralists term 'discursive practices': practices of talk, text, writing, cognition, argumentation, and representation generally. … Identity is never regarded as being given by nature; individuality is never seen as being fixed in its expression. (Clegg, 1989: 151)

It may not perhaps be necessary to dislodge the individual quite so emphatically from the centre – that is locating the origin of action and the creation of meaning firmly outside the individual (in language and discourse) – as has become popular in post-structuralist circles, but it does seem reasonable to show at least a little scepticism regarding the consistency and non-ambiguity of the subject in relation to meanings, values, ideals, discourse processes, etc. Particularly in the context of method, where the language used has a strong impact on the responses produced, the language-sensitive nature of human subjectivity must be taken seriously. If we once again take Seltzer and Bass's (1990) example of proudness in relationship to being associated with the manager, we may doubt whether 'proud' is a real feeling existing prior to the language triggering certain reactions. A person is not made 'proud' by the manager 'fairly often', 'sometimes', etc. in the same way as he or she may eat potatoes at certain intervals. Being asked to monitor oneself and categorize perhaps vague, ambiguous, non-explicit orientations in relationship to a particular signifier for a feeling – indicated to be 'normal' – a particular response is constructed that is contingent upon the discourse invoked in the situation, rather than anything just being there, spontaneous, self-evident and extralinguistic. Where the respondent puts his or her X on the form may thus be seen as a temporary response to a word rather than an indication of a clear-cut feeling being there before the word provided a particular form to relate to. At least this possibility of discursive constitution of subjectivity must be taken seriously in reflexive research.

All this calls for a strong interest in language and language use per se. There is a strong case for focusing solely on language use – apart, perhaps, from observations of simple behaviour – as the only target of inquiry of which we can develop fairly robust empirical knowledge (Potter and Wetherell, 1987; Silverman, 1985, 1989). Seeing accounts as reflecting 'objective reality' or people's values, intentions or beliefs may be viewed as naïve. Despite the strong arguments for focusing exclusively on language and language use, we see this as too strict and narrow a position (Alvesson and Kärreman, 2000; Alvesson and Sköldberg, 2000: Chs 6 and 7). Paying attention to language use as an important area of study is, however, motivated. The issues discussed here may be responded to by taking a larger interest in talk about leadership, motives, strategic changes, gender relations, etc. Such talk is central in organizations. What do 'leaders' do? As many studies have shown, they talk in meetings – are involved in spontaneous interactions (Mintzberg, 1975; Watson, 1994). Investigating talk in a variety of settings – from research interviews to public speeches and informal interactions between peers – and mapping regularities as well as variations, with a strong sensitivity to the contextuality of all language use, should be a part of the researcher's agenda. Sometimes moving beyond a language focus may be called for. Here, careful consideration of when and how accounts may permit the researcher to say something about actions, structures, ideologies, beliefs, and so on is central. (Statements about non-ambiguous issues such as number of employees, turnover and simple behaviours may be accepted at face value.) Treating a statement as a proof (strong indication) of something non-trivial thus calls for careful consideration and argumentation in the research text.

The implication is that the researcher must be aware of how important and precarious, as well as powerful, language is. It must be made an important area of reflection as well as being an object of study before producing interpretations and conclusions that aim to go 'beyond' language. The researcher must systematically consider all empirical material before deciding what it can be used for. The researcher must critically evaluate the empirical material in terms of situated meaning versus meaning that is stable enough to make transportation beyond the local context (for example an interview conversation), and thus comparison, possible. Three interpretations are possible:

1 Statements say something about social reality (for example leadership behaviour, events).
2 Statements say something about individual or socially shared 'subjective reality' (experience, beliefs, stereotypes, cognitions, values, feelings or ideas).
3 Statements say something about norms for expression, ways of producing effects (for example impressions, identity work, legitimacy) or something else where accounts must be interpreted in terms of what they accomplish rather than what they mirror – as action rather than in terms of true/false (Alvesson and Sköldberg, 2000).

The researcher must rely on his or her clinical judgement and capacity for reflection and, of course, compare different empirical materials. Material from observation is important here, not to give the truth in comparison to subjective beliefs (observation material is also limited and ambiguous), but in order to provide richer material for reflection and puzzle solving.

Relating interview and other accounts to identity constructions

What we have said so far means that great care must be taken in interpretation of the local meanings produced and that caution and reflection should guide any generalizations to other contexts than the temporary one of the interview or questionnaire. It is of particular importance here to appreciate how actors' accounts may be seen as expressions of their identities. Identities frame and structure how we provide accounts of complex phenomena, they affect what we focus on, what we neglect and how we describe what we focus upon. It makes sense to assume that how a person describes their company, work, relations, etc. reflects their identity, for example ideas about who they are, what they are characterized by and how they differ from other people. But this does not mean that accounts reflect one stable, well-integrated identity, existing prior to the production of a specific identity in intension. As discussed in Chapter 2, identity is better understood as unstable, multiple and responsive to the discourses interpellating the subject.

The interviewer must be aware of how responses are coloured by the identities triggered by the language used in, for example, a research interview (or a 'naturally' occurring situation for that matter). If a person is asked to describe his or her work, and the interviewer explicitly or implicitly interpolates that person as a manager, employee, woman, 40-year-old person, accountant, black, mother, religious, or whatever, different accounts are likely to be produced. Of course, technical details, income, etc. remain the same (though even income can be quite complex) but it is likely that the story of work experiences of a manager with an accounting background may differ from that produced by a black woman, even if these identities are harboured in the same person. This is the case even if the area of inquiry is held constant; even if the topic is, say, decision-making processes, the accounts of it may vary depending on which of the characteristics listed above are invoked.

The extent to which people express such a multiplicity in their accounts of themselves and their situation is of interest. Laurent (1978) notes, for example, that managers often describe themselves as superiors but do not mention that they are also (and may be described as) subordinates, that is they have 'higher' managers as superiors. This hardly reflects their work situation, nor their firm beliefs about it, but the kind of subjectivity – feelings, values, self-perception and cognitions – associated with the managerial/superior identity triggered in the research situation. Sometimes researchers explore more ambiguous and multiple identities. In the depth study by Watson (1994) a more nuanced picture of the contradictory situation of many managers' work position is portrayed. Here being a manager – in an existential-experiential ('real') rather than a formal sense – is, for most people, not seen as mainly occupying a position of superiority but also as including experiences of equality, subordination and ambiguity. The multiplicity of identity in complex organizations comes through rather clearly in this empirical material.

Given that all statements – in research interviews as well as other situations – emerge from a position implying a perspective, and that positions are associated with identity and unstable, all empirical work must consider the identities – positions constituted in the interaction and interpellations in the specific situation. In a research interview, the kinds of positioning must be carefully interpreted, before, during and after the interview. The interviewer must be aware how he or she contributes to invoking a particular identity through the questions raised and the responses made (for example signals of what the researcher finds interesting and uninteresting). The leadership researcher may be inclined to address the interviewee as a leader while the feminist addresses the female leader as a woman (and, perhaps, more specifically as a victim or a brave fighter against patriarchy). The researched subject (interviewee) may be more or less inclined to adopt a certain position irrespective of the researcher's signals, even though we assume that human responsiveness may make this 'autonomous' approach relatively rare. Normally, the research subject will constitute him- or herself in a way that is responsive to the specific situation. Identity constitutions in the researcher–subject interaction are seldom unilateral, reflecting not only the researcher's and the subject's initiatives and moves, but also the subtle interaction involved. (Sometimes this interaction is not so subtle, as when the two parties differ in interests – as in terms of what the interview should be all about.) Not only explicit references to positions/identities but also more subtle clues, such as the areas addressed and the language used, are significant here. The sex, age, academic background and style of the researcher may also matter.

The skilled researcher may be good at intellectually grasping the identity dynamics during interviews, thus avoiding errors such as prematurely fixing a certain position (encouragements such as 'please describe your leadership style' may illustrate this kind of error), and encouraging more multifaceted accounts before gradually – and after careful reflection – attaining a focus and exploring themes of particular interest. However, there are limits to the extent to which interviews can be rationalized. The most significant element concerns how one deals with the accounts that have been produced when they are available for careful interpretation, that is when they have been transcribed. The researcher must carefully interpret all empirical material in terms of how it emerges from, and is impregnated by, certain identity positions. This is better to evaluate the accounts in terms of context and what they accomplish. One possible accomplishment is to constitute and sustain a particular identity. Interviews may be seen as identity work (Alvesson, 1994). It is through assessments of the presence of identities that one may better clarify in what sense (from which position and in which context) accounts may tell us something about a particular chunk of social reality or a person's ideas and beliefs. But one may also want to see identity issues as important objects of study; most areas of qualitative-critical research in the traditions of critical theory and poststructuralism would suggest that some attention is paid to identity issues. Rather than, or in addition to, explicitly addressing identity and subjectivity concerns in interview questions, one may see how these emerge in the responses. In other words, identity can be tracked through how identities are expressed and positions taken *in* the interview, rather than the interview being *about* these themes.

Incorporating historical context

Related to the language problems associated with contextual meanings is another crucial aspect stressing the significance of the local, compared to the universal. Not only the ambiguities and changing circumstances of language but also those of economic, social and cultural conditions motivate a trend from grand theory to local theory. The historical character of social phenomena motivates agnosticism to the grand theory project of developing a single theory of leadership, corporate strategy, service management or whatever. Even though universal concepts such as leader, management, service, decentralization, woman, etc. may appear to make completely different phenomena comparable, they are more likely to suppress diversity and, thus, counteract local understanding. (On these issues, see Alvesson and Billing, 1997; Fraser and Nicholson, 1988; Lyotard, 1984). If they are to be used – and there are social and symbolic rather than empirical reasons for this, as Astley (1985) points out – local grounding is necessary. To some extent this is accomplished through the general principles outlined in the previous sections. But the historical, social and cultural character of the phenomena concerned must also be emphasized. Language use – apart from it being context-dependent at the micro-level – varies over time and place. In addition the economic and material context, the socialization patterns and produced self-identities, the ideologies and generalized meaning patterns differ greatly from one historical period to another and also between different organizational sites in the same period. That organizational forms change throughout history is self-evident. The significance of information technology, automation of work, internalization of trade, multinational companies, the expansion of the service and knowledge-intensive sectors is commonly recognized.

Allow us briefly to illustrate how empirical results and theorizing may be contextualized in a historically conscious way. One of us has conducted an in-depth case study of a middle-sized (500 employees) Swedish computer consultancy company and, inspired by the empirical material, developed the idea of social integrative leadership (Alvesson, 1995). The concept refers to efforts by managers to accomplish a social identity associated with employment, loyalty to the employer, a sense of community within the groups of employees – which also includes managers – and some general ideas of ways of working that are typical for the company. One purpose of this kind of leadership is to counteract fragmentation effects contingent upon loosely coupled work tasks and to reduce staff turnover. In this kind of company, particularly at the time of the study – with a scarcity of computer experts and a growing market – this concept appeared especially to illuminate behaviours and practices observed as well as interview statements from managers and other employees. The concept apparently has some relevance for understanding leadership behaviour in other contexts as well – presumably more so in knowledge-intensive and/or professional work than work which is more easily controlled from above through bureaucratic means. However, in many other historical and present work contexts, this concept is probably less salient or useful for understanding organizational practices and relations. To emphasize the historical and cultural-institutional context of this concept of leadership – to establish the domain in which it works – is more important than trying to test it as a generalizable theory of leadership.

Historical changes, however, go further than the level of the relatively easily observable. Human nature does not remain constant. The meaning of periods viewed as crucial for the constitution of humans, such as childhood and adolescence, have changed over history; adolescence, for example, is actually a new construct. The expression 'teenager' as a common term emerged as late as during the 1950s. In the context of management and organization studies, issues such as motives, leadership, women-in-management, etc. need to be conceptualized as historical and changing – as moving targets. Maslow's ideas about human needs may have made sense in the US in the 1940s and 1950s, but their relevance a few decades later in other cultures is uncertain. The lack of historical conscious-ness among large parts of the social and behavioural sciences means that these ideas are regurgitated in textbooks all over the world with little or no feeling for their historical origin and context. Sensitivity regarding the institutional and cultural context of, for example, motivation or leadership does not obstruct generalizable theories, but leads one to be cautious about premature efforts to produce such theories. It is very possible that the historical roots of, for example, US leadership theories (according to Lipman-Blumen [1992] inspired by myths about the frontier leaders) or strategy ideas (originating from the field of the military [Knights and Morgan, 1991]), mean that a lot of less fortunate meanings and associations follow the use of these theories and concepts. In the worst cases, they may carry historical baggage which prevents a fine-tuned treatment of current empirical material and the development of new ideas and aspects.

Awareness about the historical nature of social phenomena has implications for how a variety of issues are conceptualized. On a general level, established theories and earlier empirical research results must be evaluated in terms of their relevance to the under-standing of contemporary phenomena. Their relevance may lie in that they offer an interesting point of reference and comparison rather than as bricks in a wall of knowledge which may be built up higher. If a new study produces different results to a previous one it may be seen as calling for further studies in order to find out about empirical matters – to solve the inconsistencies – or it may be taken as an indication of changes that have occurred. Of course, different results may also be ascribed to local variations rather than to broader historical changes. If, for example, a Canadian study of the cognitive styles of female supervisors in restaurants in the 1970s showed different results to a German study of a similar pop-ulation in the 1990s, this may be seen as (a) an inconsistency to be solved through further research, (b) being due to national differ-ences, (c) resulting from historical changes, (d) expressions of local circumstances (for instance, studies in the same country at the same period of the same or similar populations also often show different results). The point is, one can never take it for granted that the empirical phenomena one wants to investigate will remain constant enough for empirical results to be valid over time. Surprisingly sometimes, they do. A study of advertising agencies in London at the beginning of the 1960s indicated many similar findings as a study of Swedish agencies carried out 30 years later (Tunstall, 1964; Alvesson and Köping, 1993). At a deeper level, there may still, however, be substantial differences. Sometimes more salient changes take place. Research on women and leadership indicated few if any differences between men and women in the 1970s and early 1980s while more recent publications sometimes indicate some differences (Alvesson and Billing, 1997, Ch. 6). The changes may reflect new constructions of gender, or they may reflect new norms for how women in relationship to leadership are talked about. Earlier writers on the topic were engaged in trying to prove that women are as good as – and similar to – men in managerial jobs; in the late 1990s, in contrast, there is an interest in promoting the specificity ascribed to women. Irrespective of how we understand the changing trend, this example illustrates how important it is to consider the historical context of research and research results.

Not only research results, but also the ideas and meanings – indeed the very construction of the research subjects – must be evaluated in terms of historical situatedness. The vocabulary and norms for expression may reflect a conservative tendency. Quite often apparent and superficial changes are focused by the entire 'change-industry', that is those having an interest in promoting belief in a radical changes process. Mass media, consultants, popular writers, political reformers and some researchers in the news business see to it that some radical changes are brought to people's attention. The researcher is wise to be sceptical and perhaps even adopt a conservative position in relation to some of this talk. But more profound than the changes accompanied by – and reinforced or even accomplished by – the megaphonic voices of the change-industry, are subtle and deep changes affecting human subjects and their relationships. This is held to be the case by the poststructuralists and somewhat more moderate researchers also support this view (for example, Giddens, 1991).

In the case of gender, for example, it is likely that deep changes have taken place. A theoretically sophisticated response is not a matter of studying only the behaviour/values/attitudes of women and men in terms of changes, but to involve consideration of the very concepts of women and men as the two genders which we divide humanity into. Gergen (1991) proposes that the idea that there are two genders should be dropped within the social sciences. (See also Fraser and Nicholson, 1988, and Scott, 1991, for expression of similar ideas.) A fruitful response to the changes that have occurred may thus be to refuse to use the terms 'women' and 'men' and, thereby, to refute the biological or biologically-anchored essentialism they imply. Some time ago, when women were women, nurturers and caretakers, mothers, nurses and secretaries, it made sense to talk about women. Today, when 'women' are presidents, police officers and engineers as well as mothers, secretaries and nurses, the label 'women' does not tell us much about social aspects of human beings. The lable is also potentially misleading as it indicates homogeneity among the half of the population with particular biological equipment. This may encourage easily reproduced stereotypical ideas (Alvesson and Billing, 1997). Historical awareness would thus call for care in applying concepts that may have made sense in a historical perspective but does not necessarily facilitate productive interpretations any longer.

Let us illustrate this point with an example from leadership studies. As briefly mentioned above, Lipman-Blumen criticizes dominant American conceptions of leadership for being 'based upon a masculine ego-ideal glorifying the competitive, combative, controlling, creative, aggressive, self-reliant individualist' (1992: 185). She instead proposes a more feminine ideal of leadership, labelled connective leadership. Without denying the value of this contribution and realizing that one cannot achieve everything at the same time, one could question the appropriateness of continuing to talk about leadership. Even a revision of the leadership ideal still carries with it most of the basic features associated with leadership, for example the pronounced or implicit distinction leader–follower and the assumption that there is a systematic, unitary force attached to one person who, being superior to others, exercises this force. This idea is softened but not transcended by Lipman-Blumen. Perhaps a full recognition of the historical roots of leadership talk, and the associations and allusions triggered by this history, would indicate a replacement of the leadership concept with something more sensitive to the present – and future – context It is clearly beyond the scope of this book to offer something radically new in this regard. Instead of connective leadership one could talk about connective organizing processes. The person(s) highly active in such connective actions could be labeled primary organizers or connection initiators instead of leaders.

Emphasizing the political nature of empirical material

Realizing the historical and social nature of social science is not too far from acknowledging its *political nature* (Alvesson and Willmott, 1996; Deetz, 1992). In this context 'political' does not refer primarily to parliamentary politics – or even to explicit workplace politics or other obvious struggles for power associated with espoused interests and materialized conflict (although these are also significant) – but to wider institutional and ideological issues which shape society and social relations. Politics refer to the dominance of certain values and interests, irrespective of whether these are accompanied by consensus or conflict. While conventional understandings of power and politics take an interest in easily observable conflicts of interests and struggles of power, a recognition of the basic political nature of all social science means that politics is not only an object 'out there', but also something that the research project is impregnated with and cannot stand outside of. Values, and thus various ideals and criteria for how social life should be formed (this is what politics is all about), must guide research. What is worth researching? Who do we listen to? Whose viewpoints and meanings get much space in research texts? What vocabulary is used in research texts? Are social institutions and dominating ideas viewed as legitimate and unproblematic or are they met with scepticism and a critical eye? As a general rule social science tends either to confirm and reproduce or to problematize and challenge social institutions, ideologies and interests (Alvesson and Sköldberg, 2000: Ch. 4). Social science is either based in assumptions of, and thus providing impetus to, regulation or radical change (Burrell and Morgan, 1979). Most social research – particularly within management studies – tends to confirm and reproduce dominating institutions and interests, although on minor issues there may be some stimulation to change.

Social science involves studying value-laden phenomena of which the researcher is a part. It is not the leadership of baboons or the organization of the society of ants that we are interested in, but human relations and socially created institutions. Knowledge about the latter – including research results – interferes with the shaping of these relations and institutions, while ants and baboons live their lives quite independent of our developed knowledge about them – to the extent that this knowledge is not followed by human actions. The idea of studying 'effective management' is, for example, hardly neutral – even though some people would argue that truly 'effective management' is in the interests of all. But given different value criteria and varying interests, what is defined as 'effective' may vary dramatically and there is no universal definition of effectiveness capable of meeting all possible value criteria. How value criteria are chosen and balanced against each other is, again, a matter of politics. Therefore, the political nature of management studies must be taken seriously. The ways we conceptualize and write about issues such as management do not simply mirror external reality existing independent of our conceptions and writings about it. Management research creates ways of seeing and valuing, and supporting certain interests (normally those of 'managers' rather than other people); and it has some impact on how management is exercised – through publications and education. Much management thinking has a masculine undertone and is far from gender neutral, for example in the fields of leadership (Calás and Smircich, 1991; Hearn and Parkin, 1987; Lipman-Blumen, 1992) and strategy (Knights and Morgan, 1991). Political awareness – realizing that the research texts tend to support or challenge social institutions, ideologies and sectional interests – thus becomes an important criterion and skill for evaluating social studies. Uncritically to reproduce conventional ideas of, for example, leadership in research exercises a conservative influence. It contributes to the freezing of social reality rather than encouraging an open consideration of it (Knights and Willmott, 1992). It may, for example, encourage the construction of people as 'leader-dependent' rather than autonomous and 'leader-independent'.

In terms of implications for method, the political dimension calls for awareness on a number of points. Of course, paying attention to diverse interests in organizations is basic. Without denying that there are issues and areas within which organizational stakeholders have shared interests, the multiplicity of actors, wills, interests and logics permeating complex organizations calls for consideration of this multiplicity in political terms. A plurality of viewpoints associated with the standard set of variation generating groups – associated with sex, age, class, occupation, position, etc. – but also with more emerging group formations, potentially discovered in the research process, for example networks of people, ideological orientations, and so on (Van Maanen and Barley, 1985). Through the incorporation of a broad spectrum of viewpoints, manifest political conflicts will not go unnoticed. Sometimes these may be difficult to get hold of, as people may feel that they do not want to disclose them. Awareness about such tendencies may also differ among organizational actors.

All interview accounts – and other empirical material as well, for that matter – must be evaluated in terms of the political interests and considerations of the interviewee. Actors in organizations are also political actors. They live in a world of scarce resources and competition for promotion, status and a large budget. In addition, and associated with these struggles, there is competition about alternative world-views and ideas about what is good and important. Such awareness may differ between actors; the more senior ones probably have a better or a more cynical understanding of it (Jackall, 1988).

We are not saying that politically conscious organizational actors are necessarily manipulative or untrustworthy. However, even if they were to tell the 'truth' as they know it, there are different 'truths' to be told and few people are inclined to tell stories that may hurt their own interests. We noted earlier that interview accounts normally give an impression of the interviewee as rational and moral. Most people probably feel some inclination to be – or at least appear to be – loyal to their company or their occupation. They may suspect that what they say could reflect back on themselves or the company. Sometimes employees suspect that the researcher will offer something to top management in return for access; they may even believe that the researcher is a spy for top management (Easterby-Smith et al., 1991). Reassurances that interviews will be treated confidentially and that all quotations will be anonymous may be only partly effective. A lot of interview talk may, therefore, be devoid of much critical material. On the other hand, some interviewees may feel frustrated at the workplace or, for one reason or another, may want to use the researcher as a tool for seeking revenge by telling negatively biased stories.

In a study of promotion patterns in a ministry (within the civil service), interviews with people – both men and women – revealed little information that was able to illuminate what the researchers were interested in: the absence of women in senior positions. Therefore, a number of women who had left the ministry were contacted. They revealed what they saw as a number of discriminatory practices, for example expectations from top management about women eventually giving priority to family over career, and female professionals being given less qualified and meriting tasks. The researchers were left with two rather diverse sets of accounts and it was not easy to evaluate which set was the most trustworthy (Billing and Alvesson, 1994). What is easier to see is how different positions and different interests are responsible for putting some imprints on the accounts.

Addressing manifest workplace politics and the political subtext of all accounts by corporate actors – in interviews and in documents – is much easier than coping with the workings of ground power (that is, ideological, symbolic power). Ground power is the mechanism leading to phenomena being seen as normal, unavoidable and natural – no alternatives can be imagined (Castoriadis, 1992; Lukes, 1978). It also means that it is impossible to locate and isolate the origin or distinct operations of power creating great problems for empirical research. Generally, research deals only with explicit or surface power, which is unsatisfactory. At this point we reach a crossroads and are faced with a challenge for reflexive social science, especially for critical studies. We discuss this at length in Chapters 6 and 7, here saying only a few words. Unless the researcher favours a conservative stance and is content with reproducing the status quo in terms of socially established consensus, some problematization of the effects of ground power and the inertia contingent upon the impact of cultural traditions are called for.

A particular aspect here concerns attaining and keeping some degree of social imagination, making it possible to combine what *is* with what may *become.* Social phenomena are constructions and they may either be reconstructed or undone. Rather than view what exists as something natural that one should subordinate one-self to, the existing phenomena may be seen as strange and research may thus encourage the rethinking and the undoing of what has been done up to now in terms of the social construction of social institutions and relations. If, for example, female managers behave like male managers we may be content with this result – implying that we should expect such behaviour from female managers and even that they would be wise to adopt to this presumable universal standard – or we may ask why they do not behave differently. Or if people say that they become satisfied because of a high level of consumption, this may be interpreted as consumption leading to feelings of happiness; alternatively it may be believed that people have been produced as consumers, oriented to a flow of goods and services which bring about a more or less temporary experience of happiness.

The proposal (as discussed above) to get a broad spectrum of viewpoints on the particular phenomena being studied may, in addition to monitoring diverse recognized interests and more or less espoused conflicts, also give some empirical grounding and encouragement in addressing ground power and repressed conflicts. Through bringing forward 'silent voices' and reinforcing them with critical considerations, the status quo may be critically presented. The problem in addressing ground power is that empirical material is only, at best, moderately supportive of inter-pretations of such efforts. The researcher must make depth read-ings of the accounts of natives and the surface behaviours being observed. More about this and other methods in critical research will follow in Chapter 6.

Activating the reader

A final point concerns the problem of authority in social and management research. Traditionally the researcher has claimed authority: I have done this study according to the rules of science, therefore I can offer you valid knowledge. (See Calás and Smircich, 1988, for an exploration of authority-creating moves in a research text.) Considering all the problems with a linear and empiricist approach to social research (and other research also, for that matter), such an attitude appears increasingly problematical. As mentioned above, following rigorous methodological rules does not prevent different researchers from arriving at different results.

The acknowledgement of ideals such as openness for various representations and interpretations, sensitivity to the complexity of language use, and political awareness, motivate a non-authoritative form of research and writing. Rather than the researcher providing authoritative research results, the entire research approach should be clear about the complex and uncertain nature of the project, how 'results' are dependent on the researcher's more or less conscious preferences and situatedness within a particular political, paradigmatic and linguistic orientation. From this follows a downplaying of researcher authority and a reduction of the asymmetry between researcher and reader. Instead of passively consuming research results, the reader should be encouraged actively to consider various interpretations and ideas. A conversational understanding and style could be sought. Central to this is 'the dialogical character of rationality', and 'the situated, embodied, practical-moral knowledges it involves' (Shotter and Gergen, 1994: 27) These knowledges 'are accountable to an audience' rather than 'provable within a formal system'. We are prone to give this conversation a more critical orientation (Alvesson and Sköldberg, 2000; Deetz, 1992). A conversation indicates something polite, civilized, constrained, and guided by good faith, convention and undisturbing statements. A conversation should not prevent evaluation, critique and challenge, but be, generally speaking, open to the possibility that everything is less stable and clear-cut than it seems and is, therefore, open for discussion and reconsideration. Such reconsiderations are a major element in the development of ideas and the process in which good or better ideas are sorted out from ideas which are less interesting, aesthetically less appealing, pragmatically irrelevant, empirically unsupported, and so on. A reasonable level of rigour is maintained while both conformist authoritarianism and relativism are avoided through debates about criteria and critical evaluation of the appropriateness of various criteria as well as how specific efforts to live up to these succeed.

There are different kinds of styles of writing and ways of using the research text to accomplish this ideal. Instead of the common realistic or objectivist style, a more personal style may be used

(Van Maanen, 1988). Through making it clear that it is not an objective picture of social reality but a set of impressions and interpretations produced by a situated person, and characterized by feelings, imagination, commitments and a particular pre-structured understanding associated with education, intellectual heroes, etc., the reader is reminded that what is offered is one story – at best empirically sensitive and well-grounded, and full of insights and theoretical contributions but still open to other readings, and informed by other perspectives, interests or creative powers. A problem with almost all empirical accounts is that they are, by necessity, structured in a certain way. Interview statements and observations are selectively presented to the reader, who is carefully guided by the researcher through the story. Presenting limited events or interviews in their entirety may be one technique through which the reader may make his or her own interpretations and evaluate what the researcher-author interprets from it. We discuss this at some length in the following chapter.

Conclusion

In this chapter we have, based on the critique of conventional quantitative and qualitative methodologies and insights on the nature of social science, suggested some general ideas and guidelines for an interpretive, open, language-sensitive, identity-conscious, historical, political, local, non-authoritative and textually aware understanding of social research. We refer to such an approach as a reflexive methodology (Alvesson and Sköldberg, 2000).

At a superficial level, some of these general rules may appear to resemble those methodological principles governing many case studies in strategic management and organizational analysis. For example, Pettigrew (1985) advocates an interest in history, context, language and politics and is also well aware of the existence of multiple perspectives. But even if the same or similar key words are used, this says rather little about their specific meaning. Pettigrew mainly sees the dimensions as features of the research object, that is something to be empirically studied, not as an aspect of strong significance for understanding the entire research project and thus as elements of the reflexive research project – that is, the self-understanding of the research project and text. Not only strategic change per se, but also how one writes about it, is a political project which needs to be understood in terms of history and context. Not only the context of the focused research object, but also the social context of the researcher and his or her project call for careful consideration. Like most other qualitative scholars,

Pettigrew has strong faith in empirical evidence; the approach sketched above, however, stresses the constructed and contestable nature of empirical material and calls for another balance between emphasis on the empirical material and meta-interpretations of the research work (Alvesson and Sköldberg, 2000). As argued above, the approach suggested here clearly goes beyond established ideas of qualitative method.

Reflexive methodology does not advocate the following of specific procedures or techniques, but views such a focus as dangerous as it draws attention away from many of the most crucial aspects of research (discussed above) and tends to give priority to accurately processed 'data' as the cornerstone of research work. The most general rule is to develop a certain level of sophistication in how to relate to empirical material. Such sophistication reduces the risk of clumsy, commonsensical and naïve ways of treating the material – for example viewing it as a series of mirrors on reality – and increases the chance of using it for more creative purposes in terms of producing theoretically interesting results. We realize, however, the need for suggestions for putting this sophistication into action and, in the next chapters, produce some ideas in this direction.

Much of what has been said above tends to downplay the role of empirical material as the judge of 'objective reality'. As stated, there is a strong trend away from dataism/empiricism and a realization that data is fused with theory and interpretation in contemporary social science and philosophy of science. There are also strong signs saying that empirical verification has a rather limited relevance for the assessment of the value of a theoretical contribution: 'Theories gain favor because of their conceptual appeal, their logical structure, or their psychological plausibility. Internal coherence, parsimony, formal elegance, and so on prevail over empirical accuracy in determining a theory's impact' (Astley, 1985: 503).

Even though empirical documentation may serve as 'rhetorical support in persuading others to adapt to a particular world view' (Astley, 1985: 510), this is not to say that empirical material is simply a projection of theory or interpretation, or can be used only for illustrative purposes. The depth and plausibility of empirical material should, in our opinion, definitely be one important criterion for evaluating research. Empirical material can occasionally verify or falsify a hypothesis (support or throw doubt on an idea), but this is more likely to work for simple rather than interesting or complex issues. The arguments presented here indicate that empirical research should not be guided by this purpose. Data never stands independent of language and theory. The robustness of the hypothesis-testing project is often illusionary and, anyway, the results are normally contradictory. To provide qualified descriptions illuminating core phenomena rather than abstract indicators of what goes on is one essential purpose of empirical research. Based on such descriptions more advanced interpretations can be made, and ideas and theories developed.

Besides making the general approach outlined somewhat more specific, Chapter 6 deals with how reflexive research with a critical orientation can be conducted in the context of management studies.

Note

1 It may be argued that this example is about choice of dimensions for description rather than interpretation. There is, however, no strict distinction as all interpretation is partly a matter of what is paid attention to and what is given weight in understanding.

6

A framework for critical research

This chapter details the process of critical management research and discusses methodological guidelines for conducting studies. We hope to balance the open-minded, emergent ideal embraced by interpretive and poststructural perspectives with the more critical, theory-driven approach of Frankfurt School critical theory and other approaches informed by an ambitious theoretical framework (see Chapter 2).

Elements in critical research

The intellectual role today, especially for the critical researcher, is more appropriately one of enabling an open discourse among the various social stakeholders than one of either establishing a superior insight or the authoritative establishment of a truth (see Deetz, 1995a). This research ideal should not characterize only the results and their practical impact, but also – and partly in order to facilitate the ideal – guide the research process itself. The research and facilitation activities should themselves be openly participative. A dialogic process will then be a part of the research work, imprinting the research product and, although this is outside the researcher's control, be inspirational for ways of working in companies and other organizations. We shall return to the precise meaning of dialogic processes of knowing later and discuss the elements of participatory critical research here. The intellectual role has three moments. We will call them insight (hermeneutic understanding in the critical tradition, archaeology to Foucault), critique (genealogy to Foucault, deconstruction to the poststructuralists), and transformative re-definition (education in Dewey's sense, *conscientização* in the critical tradition). The last element is absent or, in some versions, diminutive in poststructuralism. We shall account for these three elements and later discuss some methods for working with these in empirical contexts, before saying something more about dialogic processes.

*Insight: hermeneutic understanding and the archaeology
of knowledge*

Most modern social science organizes itself around the production
of cumulative knowledge. This knowledge about the world is held
outside of, instead of being in contact and changing with the world
itself. The results of correctly carried out research are viewed as
robust and valid pieces to be used in the total project of developing
more and more sophisticated systems of knowledge through
which human actors may get reliable guidance for knowing and
mastering human problems. A participatory view of theory leads
instead to the progressive development of distinctions (how we
linguistically and mentally structure the world) and alternative
conceptions – an opening of human dialogue in contact with, or
even integral to and productive of, the variety of the world. It is not
the objectivity of objectified knowledge that creates limitations to
such engagement but, as discussed before, it is subjectivity masked
as objectivity – the hidden privileging of the researcher's and the
research community's way of dividing up and constructing the
world. Related are the constraints exercised by the power which
supports one type of engaging with the world and object production over other equally plausible ones.

Everyday knowledge and scientific research are produced out
of established meanings which are in some degree taken for
granted – to the extent that they are culturally dominant. In everyday life, as in social research, people use culturally dominant
meanings as a paradigmatic point of departure as well as the
resources for thinking, getting data and writing. Most of the time
members of a community, as well as traditional researchers, take
for granted this knowledge and the formed nature of objects and
events. 'Insight' denotes the process of seeing into the various
ways in which this knowledge and the seemingly objective character of objects and events are formed and sustained. The term
recalls the hermeneutic understanding of language as disclosive
and opening a field of consideration rather than the representational view of language which underpins knowledge as truth
claims. Insight can properly be called the leading edge of human
thought. It is structured along the lines of the powerful exemplar
rather than the mass of data. Insight is both the process of producing a meaning of interest in the 'data' – of knowing how to
construct empirical material in an open manner ('gathering data')
and how it fits together – and understanding the conditions for
seeing or pointing to such a meaning. Conditions include tradition
and the socio-economic context which frames how we relate to
and make sense of the world.

Insight is closely related to – integral to and an outcome of – interpretation. An interpretation aims to read something into what is ambiguous – or what can be productively turned into something ambiguous through turning the simple and self-evident into something complex and open. Interpretation draws attention to the open nature of a phenomenon – a text, an act, a statement, physical material. Insight then may be seen as an outcome of a successful interpretation. A successful interpretation, that is insight: (a) addresses something non-obvious, (b) makes sense of something, and (c) is perceived as enriching understanding – it adds something to what the subject understood prior to the insight.

Insight is a type of practical knowing, a seeing of what is important. Insight as suggested in the more general look at language and communication is not into individuals, situations, or their meanings but of the systems of relations which make such meaning possible (Deetz, 1973, 1982). Foucault described his archaeology as:

> an inquiry whose aim is to rediscover on what basis knowledge and theory became possible; within what space of order knowledge was constituted; on the basis of what historical a priori, and in the element of what positivity, ideas could appear, sciences could be established, experience be reflected in philosophies, rationalities be formed, only, perhaps, to dissolve and vanish soon afterwards. (1970: xxi–xxii)

In this sense most ethnographies and cultural studies are, at most, a first step in a much larger analysis. Particular persons and situations are artefacts used to understand the system of meanings through which particular persons and situations are composed and connected to the larger sociocultural context. How are particular kinds of knowledge and members constructed and sustained in discourse?

The 'genuine' experiences and meanings of the subjects of study are neither our only nor our primary interest. Rather the focus is on the social and linguistic processes producing the kind of subjectivity 'behind' or at least being an integral part of these experiences and meanings. This does not mean, we think, that experiences and expressed (espoused) meanings should be disregarded. Doing so easily leads to elitism, in which the subjects are seen as mere appendices to discourses operating through them, triggering experiences, feelings and orientations. The ideal must be to pay attention to experiences and meanings as well as discursive and other processes of an ideological and material nature that may constitute experiences and prescribe meaning. Of course, individual research projects – as well as more practical efforts at understanding – may call for more or less attention to any of these levels, but insight calls for some consideration of both.

Insight in both a hermeneutic and archaeological sense detaches knowledge from the ahistorical 'truth' claim and reopens a consideration of its formation thereby reframing knowledge and giving choices that previously were hidden by the accepted knowledge, standard practices, and existing concepts. The production of insight establishes the possibility of competing discourses through the recovery of conflict and choice. Without such insight members remain, in a sense, victims of meaning structures that were developed in response to past situations and perpetuated in their talk and actions. While as Giddens (1979) argued all cultural members have some degree of 'discursive penetration', that is some insight into the structural properties of knowledge production, they are unlikely to enlarge the penetration on their own due to practical restrictions and various mechanisms of discursive closure. The intellectual is free of some of these constraints, or has at least more time and resources (training, access to books and networks, some institutionalized freedoms) to address critically and reflect upon these mechanisms of closure. And while not privileged, he or she is capable of the distancing required to develop counter-discourses within particular sites of production.

Critique: deconstruction and the genealogy of knowledge

Political, economic, and community forces are inscribed in organizational arrangements, social relations, and in every perception. It is not sufficient to describe these as naturally occurring, they arise historically and arbitrarily advantage certain groups. Participation as a normative foundation for communication draws our attention both to describe and to criticize such systems. The participative ideal does not so much give a norm or criteria for evaluation as provide a set of interests and analytical foci for acting upon them – a way of thinking about these systems. Grossberg described the task as one to 'describe (and intervene in) the way messages are produced by, inserted into, and function within the everyday lives of concrete human beings so as to reproduce and transform structures of power and domination' (1987: 393). Addressing the systematic privileging of certain discourses and meanings associated with forms of power – formal and ideological – is thus a crucial element in critical research.

Foucault, in recognizing the need to go beyond neutral descriptions, presented a 'genealogy' to complement the archaeology. Orders are selected, controlled and distributed within societies along lines of strategy and advantage. Foucault used the term 'apparatus' to denote the heterogeneous forces which direct the presence of certain constitutive conditions. As Foucault described it:

the apparatus is essentially of a strategic nature, which means assuming that it is a matter of a certain manipulation or relation of forces, either developing them in a particular direction, blocking them, stabilizing them, utilizing them, etc. The apparatus is thus always inscribed in the play of power, but it is also always linked to certain coordinates of knowledge which issue from it but, to an equal degree, condition it. (1980b: 196)

Insight into these strategies and understanding them to be deployments of power is itself a strategy toward recovering alternative practices and marginalized alternative meanings. Knowledge is an important part of this relation, for the apparatus both produces knowledge and is extended and sustained by it. Produced knowledge can guide participation or domination; sometimes it can guide both. The difference is often unclear and ideological domination may operate and form the premises of participatory decision making. In such cases only a narrow set of viewpoints and pieces of information are seen as relevant. The point is not to try to disconnect power relations from the production of truth as Gadamer or Habermas would do, but to detach 'the power of truth from the forms of hegemony, social, economic and cultural within which it operates at the present time' (Smart, 1986: 166; see also Knights, 1992). Thus the critique of everyday dominations must always include a critique of the social science, and in the context of organizations, of the management science, which accompanies it.

The Derridian conception of 'deconstruction' is also useful in filling out the concept of critique. The movement of science as production of knowledge, and communication as the transmission of it, share the privileging of the speaker and the known and producing what can be called a centred text – the dominance of a particular unity or point of view over others. The unity appears innocent, as a consensus. Deconstruction shows the manner of historical privilege and recalls the equivocality, the many voices, the alternative texts which become the hidden background for the centred one. As Culler has described:

> deconstruction is not a theory that defines meaning in order to tell you how to find it. As a critical undoing of the hierarchical oppositions on which theories depend, it demonstrates the difficulty of any theory that would define meaning in a univocal way: as what the author intends, what conventions determine, what a reader experiences. (1983: 131)

In the broader terms of this work, deconstruction denies the univocal products of the intellectual, the result of methods and procedures, and common sense of the public; and instead it opens the movements in and between them.

Critique thus is directed at the conventions and structures of social orders and the forms of knowledge and privileged understanding that are complicit with such orders. Critique itself operates as part of a participative communicative act, the act of reopening effective communication to productive conversation.

Critique cannot be separated from insight. In any insight there lies a critical element in the sense that a prior understanding is at least implicitly seen as being insufficient. Critique builds upon insight. The difference is that critique explicitly relates to the conditions of power, constraint, social asymmetries, ideological domination, cultural inertia that give privilege to certain ways of understanding and ordering the world – an understanding which is achieved without full consideration of alternative discourses and guiding principles for social life. Critique thus seeks to undo the more structural and ideological roots of frozen meanings and the frequency with which certain discourses are circulated, others are marginalized and still other ways of describing and prescribing the social world almost never appear.

*Transformative re-definition: concept formation, resistance,
and conscientização*

Transformative re-definition is the natural counterpart to insight and critique. It can easily be claimed that critical writings in both the Enlightenment and post-Enlightenment traditions have placed too much attention on awareness and understanding and not enough on enabling alternative responses. The implicit faith in the view that if people knew what they wanted and the system of constraints limiting them, they would know how to act differently has little basis. Interests and identities do not have the kind of robust, essentialist character that this thesis presupposes. Those who hold out for revolutionary change miss the implications of modern forms of control and democracy. Here the centre, which it is possible to transform through a focused attack, has lost much of the directive powers it perhaps had some decades ago. Meaningful change is in the micro-practices at the innumerable sites of power relations (Foucault, 1980b). Democracy cannot simply be found in some new form of social relations but in an ongoing task of struggle and decision as new forms of control evolve. Higher education, including management, must be involved in the production and distribution of a kind of political competence. Following Simonds, political competence in modern society means, 'not just access to information but access to the entire range of skills required to decode, encode, interpret, reflect upon, appraise, contextualize, integrate, and arrive at decisions respecting that information' (1989: 198). Clearly, as we have seen around the world, increased literacy is more threatening to autocratic rule than an uncensored press. Literacy regarding complex communication systems and technologies is itself a complex phenomenon. The concern is not just that people get wrong or biased information (the propagation of false consciousness) but that they lack the resources to assess what they have. And more importantly, they do not understand the modern means by which control is exerted and participation undermined.

Freire (1970) has provided the most stirring discussion of the role of education to open cultural development. While much of his social theory was caught up in the Marxism of his day and the immediate political realities of Brazil, his conception of *conscientização* locates a meaningful role for intellectuals in the construction of human agents – that is, subjects who chose to make their own history. While many researchers at the end of the twentieth century conceptualize and teach their subjects to be objects – to be known and acted upon – objects can be taught to be subjects who know and act. The point is then not to produce a new theory of domination as knowledge, but to produce ways of seeing and thinking and contexts for action in which groups can express themselves and act.

Thus the movement toward greater participation and democracy is not accomplished by rational arguments and the display of systems of domination alone, but also by helping create responses to the current situation. Members of the everyday community have learned their concepts, practices and skills over a lengthy period of time. Learning competing discourses, embracing conflict, and participating in decision making are skills to be learned. But interaction skills are only part of the matrix. Developing technologies for participation and skills in using technologies and communication media are important parts of the democratizing effort.

Further, the intellectual is not a teacher in any standard sense. We do not know a lot about participation and we certainly do not know the contours of the sites as well as everyday participants. The role Freire ascribed is more appropriate to the need to combine research with education:

> We must never merely discourse on the present situation, must never provide the people with programs which have little or nothing to do with their own preoccupations, doubts, hopes, and fears. ... It is not our role to speak to the people about our own view of the world, nor to attempt to impose that view on them, but rather to dialogue with the people about their view and ours. (1970: 85)

Unfortunately, it is not only the people out there who are not ready to talk with us, it is also the critical researchers who are often not yet ready.

Despite the power in various social formations, there is always resistance to and opportunity for difference and change. Local resistance often fails, owing to trained incapacities, inadequate concepts and unknown structural constraints.

The final goal is the formation of new concepts and practices for social members and researchers in such a way as to enhance understanding of social life. Living and working is a practical activity for members. The choices in the everyday context require a type of practical consciousness or adequate knowledge as suggested by Giddens (1979) or phronesis (practical wisdom) as suggested by Gadamer (1975). Certainly the modern intellectual can aid the production of this. Concepts developed by the academic community need not be privileged to give voice to concerns and understandings which have not been expressed in everyday contexts, and such concepts can be generative thus questioning and reconstituting social experience (see Gergen, 1982; Giddens, 1979). To fulfill this function our concepts must be recovered from operational and textbook definitions and reconnected to ways of seeing and thinking about the world. In the dialectics of the situation and the talk of individuals with different perspectives, the emergence of new ways of talking becomes possible. Such a process both enhances the natural language of social members and leads to the development of new concepts to direct the attention of the research community. It is important for the participative conception of communication which underpins political democracy in the modern context.

Critical methodology: producing insight, critique and transformative re-definition

As suggested in Chapter 1, critical researchers interact with research subjects and use methods (use of documents and statistics, interpretation of material artefacts) much like other researchers. The critical researcher interviews and makes observations, and writes fieldnotes, etc. in ways that are not dissimilar to (other) qualitative researchers. Although the procedure is not very original, in terms of the *content* of empirical material, critical research as a matter of course pays attention to situations, relations, events, institutions, ideas, social practices and processes that may be seen as exercising a surplus repression or discursive closure. Of greatest interest here are not necessarily the most obvious or profound examples of these phenomena, such as greedy capitalists doing things broadly seen as immoral. The more subtle aspects are a better object of critical research – more obvious issues often talk more or less for themselves if they are exposed. What is seen as natural, self-evident, unproblematic and unavoidable – the outcomes of, and preconditions for, discursive domination – is then of interest. The researcher cannot take for granted what is viewed in this way, but this calls for investigation. These qualities need to be established. This calls for careful listening to subjects, in interviews as well as in everyday life talk and action in the organization. Such listening has, in the present context, the following purposes:

1 A general understanding of the focused social reality and dominant modes of order(s) and ordering.
2 Identification of significant themes, the local nature of the phenomena in which the researcher has particular interest (or may develop such an interest).
3 An identification and subsequent exploration of dominant ideas and understandings, vocabularies and discourses.
4 Pointing at variation in ideas, meanings, vocabularies, discourses in relationship to a specific theme, both in terms of voices of the field and in terms of different theoretical ways of making sense of the empirical material.

Instead of one meaning, broadly understood as the self-evident one, variation in aspects that may be adopted opens things up for the consideration of productive alternative understandings. Variation may involve elements of questioning and resistance, they may run against dominant themes. They may, however, run parallel to, be loosely coupled to – or even compartmentalized from – dominant themes.

The exploration of dominant ideas and discourses is a difficult enterprise if one is not content to hold low criteria for determining something as dominant or if one relies on standard, sociological 'fact sheet' kinds of domination (for example, class, gender, race). Elite ideas expressed in public cannot be equated with the dominant, but what is needed are indications on the discourses and meanings that guide everyday life and subjects' understandings. Accounts – in interviews, written documents or observed conversations – normally display considerable variation due to the local context (Potter and Wetherell, 1987). Patterns as well as variety need to be understood. Neither should be privileged. Pattern-seeking often leads to a suppression of variety. This may well be acceptable and necessary in order to understand what appears to be dominant, but it must be done with openness and care for what is hidden (diversity). Emphasizing diversity may mean that attention is drawn to what is not entirely the same and overall tendencies may be neglected. A third interpretative option is to draw attention to ambiguity: confusion and uncertainties that are persistent and thus do not seem to be absolved with more information. Quite often people show neither clear consistency nor apparent diversity in how they express themselves on a specific theme; their accounts may be characterized by a high level of ambiguity. They may, for example, address very specific issues which are difficult to compare with or relate to broader themes. They may express themselves vaguely or incoherently, run along associative lines of argumentation/storytelling which make it difficult to follow them, or they may be uncertain about a particular theme, lack adequate vocabulary and so on.

From a critical perspective, patterns indicating discourses, meanings and social practices that are dominant are of greatest interest to investigate. To some extent, fragmentary and disconnected social phenomena are also worth considering. For example, concern may be directed towards the regulation of consumption through the destabilization of identities: new fashions, new lifestyles, expression of frustration with self-hood (pointing implicitly at imperfections in looks, appearance and social performance) and the tying of self-esteem with commodities (Lasch, 1978). But also here, a 'pattern' of fragmentation and destabilization – the orchestration rather than randomness of these – needs to be highlighted. (Here critical theory and critical postmodernism differ from diversity and fluidity privileging postmodernism as expressed by, for example, Chia, 1995.)

Insight production: the art of interpretation
Interpretation is based on the studying of delimited parts in the context of the whole – or rather a variety of wholes. Interpretation may attend to details or more aggregated kinds of phenomena, based on the combination of specific empirical materials. Normally there is a circling – gradually emerging into a spiral-like movement – around a focus on details and on the whole(s). Interpretation is based on the process of:

- paying attention to something;
- creating a gestalt or image of this something;
- giving a particular 'close-to-surface', but non-obvious meaning to it;
- either exploring this meaning or pointing at an additional, 'depth' meaning of this something, throwing a new, unexpected light on it.

Interpretation may border in a triangle between non-obvious description, the perspectivization/imagination and the insightful revelation of the 'something' – in itself or as a part of a larger theme.

Interpretation calls for careful consideration of all empirical material from a multitude of angles. One of these is the process in which research is produced. All material, at least of an interview nature, may be seen as outcomes of the interaction between the researcher and the interviewee. Empirical material is the result of a complex interplay between research process-induced influence, norms and conventions for expression in particular settings, workplace or market cultures, social conditions (the 'out there'), and the interviewee's experiences, interests (including ideas on how the research may reflect back on the organization and his or her career in indirect ways), intentions, and values.

Of course, even if accounts are seen as outcomes of norms for expression this may still tell us quite a lot about the workplace. If people emphasize long working hours, this may indicate aspects of corporate or professional culture in terms of norms of working, impression management and/or commitment. The exact length of working hours may be less relevant and not necessarily something worth checking: noting that people are inclined to emphasize this, in a particular social context, is of interest in itself.

The multitude of angles also come from theoretical sources. One possibility is to rely on one specific well-integrated framework, based on a theory, but this calls for an appreciation of its drawbacks (blind spots) and an awareness of the risk of projecting the ideas onto empirical material. The interpretative repertoire may also be broader, for example it may be comprised of a rather loose and broad theoretical approach (for example reality is 'socially constructed' and a cultural interest in the level of meaning and symbolism) or a set of distinct theories (for example those reviewed in Chapter 2). It may facilitate doing context-appreciative interpretations. Identity theory may, for example, aid the researcher in viewing interview statements as identity work. We return to the topic of theoretical inspiration later.

The need to consider empirical material from a wide angle of perspectives provides problems due to complexity and difficulties in saying something 'referential' or related to a specific theme. The researcher may become indecisive and too cautious or plague the reader with too much dwelling on what the material may tell us. It also provides possibilities. A rich array of interpretations are possible out of almost all empirical material. This, of course, does not mean that all interpretations should be made in a particular study.

Space, the purpose of the research, problems with attaining a sufficient degree of generalization within the object of study being chosen, etc. – plus problems in grounding or supporting many interesting interpretations – call for self-discipline and the exercise of judgement.

Production of critique
Critique adds political meaning to insight illuminating the elements of constraint and degree of interest carried by particular phenomena. Socially constructed phenomena are thus also politically and morally constructed. Critical studies are inclined to pay attention to and interpret 'raw material' for advanced interpretations in terms of power and domination, broadly defined. Observed events, situations, incidents and social practices, accounts of experiences, social conditions, expressions of ideas, thoughts and beliefs, and indications of economic, structural and technical arrangements are monitored in terms of critical themes such as, for example:

- male domination;
- communicative distortion;
- fixation of subjectivity;
- asymmetrical relations of power;
- conflicts of interests;
- mystifications;
- technocracy and social engineering;
- discursive closure;
- naturalization and/or reification of social reality.

Of course, these issues often overlap. One could also say that some of these vocabularies often work nicely together in specific investigations.

Immediate interpretation may be in these terms. More fruitful are often, however, the first-hand impressions, notes, the reading of transcribed material and so on that are less directly tied to these somewhat abstract critical concepts. We also think it is often wise to postpone these evaluations and fulfillment of interpretations, and, to some extent, separate the element of insight-generated interpretation and formulation of critical interpretation. An open, emergent critical approach avoiding a bias towards elitism means some initial holding back of the critical inclination and the use of critique with care and nuance in a second phase. There are interpretations and insights that should not necessarily be followed up and 'deepened' by distinctively critical interpretations.

Realizing that interpretation and critique cannot be fully separated, critical research means that those interpretations which have a specific bearing on issues of power, domination, constraints, social suffering, lost possibilities for action, etc. are seen as the most important to explore. This does not imply that such issues should be one-sidedly privileged. Also other issues may well be brought forward in final description and analysis. Critical research-relevant issues should appear unobtrusively, that is the researcher must be open to the possibility that the empirical material is not very productive in allowing him or her to say something original, interesting or significant about the case from a specific critical position. This does not mean that conflicts of interest, discursive domination, communicative distortions, masculine power, etc. are absent from most sites of study; in a large majority of cases they are clearly present. But such phenomena may not surface very clearly in the empirical material. In such cases, the researcher may downplay the critical interest and follow a different path. In the great majority of cases, well-thought out and well-executed research work means that there are sufficient candidates in the empirical material available – after a set of interviews or some months of ethnographic work – to say something important about the above mentioned themes.

The researcher then deepens insight-oriented interpretations through more critical theoretically–oriented explorations of these interpretations. These explorations typically attend to detail, but relate these more strongly to institutional macro-oriented themes. A theoretical understanding of economy, ideology, social orders, classes, patriarchy, macro-level discursive domination, and so on form an interpretive frame which is potentially productive in exploring meanings beyond the purely local, micro, action or meaning-near that easily comes to mind (and constrains it) in the interpretation of specific empirical material.

Production of transformative re-definition
The third element in critical research is, in a sense, the most difficult. Having explored issues of domination and constraints, the task is to indicate ways in which subjects may re-think and perhaps also re-feel or re-experience what exists – or the currently dominating constructions of reality. A transformative re-definition means the opening up of a new ways of engaging the social world – ways marked by critical insight and added ethical considerations and inspiration for new forms of practice in which certain biases, blinkers, constraints and frozen orientations are struggled with in a more enlightened and reflective manner, and more social criteria for responsibility are taken into account. Re-definition then aims to support imagination in such a way that a qualitative, different

reality is seriously considered. Re-definition often involves promoting alternative vocabularies. Domination is not 'just' another word for control; it redirects and changes attention. Creative euphemisms may be promoted which reveal conflicts suppressed by historical and management preferred terms.

Inherent in all good interpretations is the casting of new light on the something that earlier has either escaped serious attention or been understood in a conventional and thus partly conservative way. Critique includes stronger seeds to transformative re-definition. Here, to some extent, sources of domination are neutralized or at least weakened. Critique may, however, primarily lead to a rather negative and gloomy view. Action implications may be unclear. Even though critical research refrains from authoritatively telling people what to do, transformative re-definition adds to critique clearer indications of a more positive future or, more cautiously, alternative routes towards engagement with the world. While critique puts some emphasis on the negative by constructing counter-image to a predominant understanding or ordering of social practice, transformative re-definition tends to be more positive, though still emphasizing change.

How do we build on critique in ways which will accomplish transformative re-definition? One possibility is simply to produce a variety of empirically grounded discourses, such as local actors' voices on the subject matter. This may be accomplished by the researcher sensitively registering in the empirical material an intention to select and bring forward, in particular, those that indicate variation. Thus a way for the opening up of a particular chunk of social reality may be constructed and engaged in. This means that weak, hidden, obscured and peripheral voices and discourses are reinforced through the research text. Another possibility is through the use of empirical examples indicating diversity of social forms, social practices and cultural traditions, thus opening up a way for new forms of action. Empirical examples may emerge from other companies or other societies. A third possibility is the theoretical exploration of the issues involved. A specific social construction or dominant discourse may be analysed and theorized. Through pointing out the origin and connections of various economic, social and other forces and mechanisms involved, their – in a sense arbitrary or at least socially accomplished – character is investigated and other arrangements and developments may be imagined.

Transformative re-definition must in some way connect to the ideas, opinions and orientations expressed by the people being studied. Without any openings in terms of discursive pluralism – the existence of some variety in vocabularies, language use and modes of reasoning about constituted reality – the process of stimulating transformative re-definition appears fruitless. Discovering cracks in a seemingly solid, uniform, dominant discursive formation of social reality enables critical research to go beyond critique.

The workplace community must have some value base for the stimulation of new modes of engagement. If not, critique is the last and vital element in the critical research process. Negativity, the production of harsh critique against a frozen, totalizing social order, is what remains but this may be powerful – as the Frankfurt School (Adorno and Horkheimer, 1979 [1947]; Marcuse, 1964) and Foucault (1972) also, for that matter, have shown. The accomplishment of a counter-text is certainly not without implications for transformative re-definitions, but these may not be explicit nor clear. They may, however, be elaborated upon in the community. Without engagement with community values, research may be satisfied with interpretation and insight, and critical studies may well concentrate on critique and abstain from saying much or anything about possible changes. Normally, at least in the context of contemporary corporations, there are signs of values, moral commitments, insights and meanings that are in harmony with a broad critical project, but in specific instances and on certain issues these signs may be weak.

Critical research may have different emphases; interpretive work aiming for insight may be central, complemented by limited elements of critique and transformative re-definitions. Critique may also dominate, but if so the empirical case study is typically used for more limited, illustrative purposes. Transformative re-definition should not dominate empirical research. Texts dominated by this tend to be Utopian and this quality is not salient in studies with research ambitions.

An illustration: a different world with closed doors and quiet corridors

Let us illustrate the points made. We focus here on a limited empirical case study in order to concentrate on the essentials – the elements in critical research. We go through this material in some detail, in order to show specifically how the interpretations and different elements in critical research can be carried out.

The case
This mini case is extracted from a study of a large, Swedish, relatively old industrial company (Alvesson and Björkman, 1992). Here an interviewee, employed as secretary to a divisional manager

heading a production and sales unit of 400 persons, provided the following account. Her initial word 'they' refers to senior managers in corporate and business unit management:

> They are sitting a bit isolated in large rooms with closed doors. You don't go into them without a good reason. It is a bit of a different world. Rather quiet corridors. They don't run down here and talk with people. They meet their immediate superiors, they never go down and sit here. The personnel here has wanted that to happen. Everybody has said: imagine that he could come down here and walk around, and pick up the habit of walk in sometimes and sit down instead of only sending after people. For example, Gustaf (divisional manager) always had to go up. Magnus (his boss, business sector manager) never came down. (Alvesson and Björkmann, 1992: 140)

We should add that a short time before the interview, the company was re-organized. The divisional manager, who was very appreciated by his subordinates, got another job when the unit was merged with two other units into a division. Without going into details, other empirical material in the study tended to support the account, although we have no additional specific material on the details of issues such as the spatial behaviour of senior managers or whether their doors are closed or not.

Producing insight
A number of interpretations may be produced. Some of these may focus on the message produced, that is the dramatic, narrated undertext of the story produced.

The world of power in this company is lifeless, slightly alienated, even a bit scary. It is inhabited by people who somehow have been robbed of parts of their humanity. Senior managers are asocial. They limit social relations. They want to sit alone behind closed doors and not be disturbed. They are socially unresponsive: they refuse social calls. They emphasize social borders and show little interest in their subordinates. But also, within their own social categories, interaction is highly limited. Spontaneity and emotion seem to be absent.

The interview is then treated as a narrative, not as telling us something of organizational reality 'out there', nor about the interviewee's beliefs or feelings. The account is seen as literature, as fiction. We then examine the structure and plot of the interview seen as a dramaturgical text.

Another set of interpretations draws attention to the subject performing the account. One possibility is to see how the interviewee constitutes herself – expresses the claim – as a sharp social observer and as a humanistic critic, exploring the constrained, alienating individualism of male senior managers. The sociability and outgoing nature of the interviewee implicitly came through.

The subject may also be seen as expressing negativity to top management and sympathy for Gustaf, her earlier boss, who was both well known and well liked for his social and communicative style. The interviewee may, therefore, use the interview and the researcher as an occasion to express feelings, although in covert form. The account of senior managers make them appear as a highly negative counter-image of Gustaf. The interview may serve as an occasion for the interviewee to work through emotions. Interviews may well fulfill therapeutic functions. The (good) interviewer is, in many respects, similar to the non-directive therapist: she or he asks few, open questions, is patient, emphatic, client-centred, has time at his or her disposal, and promises anonymity.

Another interpretation, related to the last one, draws attention to the political nature of the account. The interview subject may use the interview for their personal (political) purposes, to exercise influence on the company. It could be argued that the interviewee here is not happy with the state of the work situation and may very well expect the research report to be read and perhaps be acted upon by her management. Convincing the researcher about organizational conditions and shortcomings may be seen as a political move. As an employee with limited authority, the researcher may be a valuable ally or channel for allowing her voice to be heard.

A third line of interpretation takes an interest in the level of meaning of the group of people to which she belongs to. Collective meanings are cultural phenomena. In the present case, we may assume that the account reflects shared meanings; the cultural understandings of the collective the interviewee belongs, interacts with, and thereby constructs a shared social reality. At this point we do not dwell further on the possibility that the account reflects personal, idiosyncratic beliefs, ideas and meanings, but focus instead on what it tells us about workplace culture – that is, shared meanings and understandings.

Workplace culture may be more or less stretched and refer to smaller groups or larger collectives. We may see it as local phenomena, an expression of group-based developments of meaning, or we may talk about macro or grand cultures – for example organization-wide or, in other words, corporate, industrial or even business sector cultures (Alvesson, 1993a). From a more local perspective, the account says something about the images, ideas and fantasies of people located some way down the corporate hierarchy and positioned in a unit. Top management is constructed as distant, asocial, individualistic, atomistic, rational, and emotionally constrained. The corporation is seen as hierarchical. The observation that Gustaf has to walk 'up' to his superior, who never visited the unit, is viewed as a symbol of a clear-cut hierarchical relationship and the emphasis on power. It also indicates that the top management is unreceptive to the wants of the subordinates or, perhaps, even of what is going on in the units of the company. (They certainly monitor results, but this is not the same as taking an interest in the knowledge, ideas and viewpoints of unit personnel.) This interpretation resembles the narrative interpretation, the principle difference is that a narrative does not address the cultural level. The narrative approach looks at the text as a text not as, as in culture theory, a reflection of beliefs, ideas, meanings and symbolism. The cultural interpretation would then emphasize the understandings of (some) low-level organizational members that this company characterized by social distance.

A cultural analysis going beyond the group and addressing wider cultural patterns (corporate culture) does not so much concentrate on and limit interpretation to the beliefs and meanings of the interviewee and people around her, as much as emphasize beliefs and meanings shared broadly in the organization – including senior managers. Ideas about hierarchy, distant or rather shallow social relations between different sections of the company, and the value put on individual, analytical concentrated work – presumably best conducted 'in rooms with closed doors' surrounded by 'quiet corridors' – are then seen as characterizing the company. Here the statement is seen as reflecting corporate culture rather than a specific local, unit staff understanding of the company. The account indicates variation and the existence of subcultures in the company. The values, ideals and understandings expressed by the interviewee are at odds with what she claims characterizes the culture of senior managers, but the latter dominates.

A fourth line of interpretation, in terms of claims, goes further than addressing the statement as text, as an expression of a particular subject and her (political) interest, or as an indication on workplace or corporate culture. The interview account may also be viewed in terms of what it says about behaviour and social practices. It then is viewed as mirroring or rather saying something significant about specific, observable behaviour patterns and structures in the company. The statements then inform us not so much about the interviewee's personal, group or more company-wide beliefs, meanings and ideas, but about what takes place in terms of specific, observable behaviours and regularities in social patterns. We then come closer to refer to 'objective' conditions. If the person has witnessed the context of say 25 face-to-face interactions between Gustaf and Magnus and all of these were preceded by Gustaf leaving his office and informing the secretary that he would go to divisional headquarters, then it makes sense to treat the statement as a factual account (on condition that we trust the interviewee). The behavioural regularities of the senior managers may also be described in ways that come closer to the 'objective' noise level in corridors and the structures of interaction among senior managers and other organizational participants. (Who meets whom? With what frequency? Who initiates the contact?) Interpretive work may thus move away from a cultural level and take seriously specific events, acts and behaviours which take place. Still, it should be emphasized that critical research is not satisfied with mapping body movements or counting frequencies. The objective is to go beyond this level and interpret how these specifics are part of social orders and represent ordering processes, where specific behaviours and events interact with and have consequences for meanings, consciousness and discourses, that in their turn may freeze an ordering of social reality.

We thus have produced a number of interpretations of the interview account. The order of presentation goes from those being more text-near to those in which the account is read as saying something about phenomena of a quite different nature than the account itself. The first interpretation points at the study of the account as an account, later we addressed the account as an expression of beliefs and meanings, and, finally, the account is viewed as reflecting corporate reality ('out there'). Of course, possibly apart from the first interpretation, further interpretations and conclusions claimed to be valid for the organization – or at least a part of it – call for additional empirical material. It would be too space-consuming to go into this here. As mentioned, in the study in which this account was produced, there was a fair amount of additional empirical material pointing in a similar direction as the interpretations conducted above in terms of group and corporate culture as well as structured practices. For example, one interviewee, a blue-collar worker, remarked that 'most people at higher levels have their noses in the air. They hardly want to pass the shop-floor. They prefer to walk outside it' (Alvesson and Björkman, 1992: 141). This suggests that it makes sense to treat the material as of relevance in order to address organizational conditions.

Producing critique
Let us now continue and address the element of critique. We evaluate the interpretive lines above in terms of the relevance for critical research.

The narrative focus appears somewhat limited from this viewpoint. Given the purpose of this research, our greater interest is to go beyond studying the plot of the story and view the account as saying something about the company or groups and relations within it. Viewing the account in terms of the interviewee's desire to work through feelings or as an effort to exercise political influence is of some interest from a critical perspective. It may well remind the researcher about how empirical material is always loaded with expressiveness and interest orientations. Critical research may respond positively to the voices and claims of the underdog, although only after careful consideration. If these voices appear to make sense (underdogs may be ignorant, unrealistic, prejudiced, and so on), given the broader understanding emerging after considering aspects and criteria other than social need-fulfilling, the researcher may give the proposals in the account some impact in framing parts of the entire research project. Feelings and interests evaluated to be legitimate and expressing a voice silenced by dominating corporate practice may well be represented in the researcher's text.

Of greater interest, perhaps, is the exploration of some aspects of the account viewed as an expression of the hierarchical relations in the company. A critical interpretation of the discourse and consciousness expressed by the account may then concentrate on how the interviewee and like-minded people relate to the world, that is a particular kind of cultural orientation in terms of authorities. We then read how the account tells us something about a specific way of constructing the corporate world. Here more or less well-grounded ideas (that is, originating in observations and interactions) about the senior managerial world are developed. There seem to be some elements of fantasy involved here. The image of the mausoleum-like corporate headquarters may be viewed as being beyond the clearly true or false and involving a dramaturgical character. The interviewee constructs senior managers so that they are distant from her reality. They almost belong to another world ('It is a bit of a different world.'). In this world slightly alien people live. Distance and 'foreigner-ship' are thus emphasized. Accompanying this construction of the 'Other', the one different from myself, are mixed feelings or, at least, slightly contradictory orientations. First, the higher status, authority and social significance of senior managers are emphasized. They are busy and you do not disturb them without a very good reason. Secondly, they appear as rather negative characters: unresponsive, socially isolated and dry. Thirdly, they are portrayed as very important to get in contact with or at least receive attention from. In the account, people 'here' really want 'them' to come down and visit. (The image of the UFO enthusiast comes to mind.) The combination of distance, alien character and the desire to have contact may indicate some mystification. The importance of senior managers is elevated. With 'them' being different, contact and initiatives become difficult. But if contact could be established it would be very valuable. Senior managers showing interest in, and wanting to interact with, unit people would be much appreciated by the latter. The social value of the senior managers is thus underscored.

All this leads to a construction of a world in which the preconditions for participation – initiative, dialogue, proposals – are undermined. A dominant discourse in which top management is viewed as isolated, unable to be contacted, socially significant and as a source of social gratification (in addition to all other resources and rewards controlled by top management) means that unit people construct themselves as different, passive, dependent and those that desire the contact of a more valued Other. The account means that initiative is ascribed one-dimensionally to senior managers. Unit people have no real impact on the quality of social relations. These are not seen as being created through a variety of actions from different positions as much as being established top-down.

We can thus emphasize how the account illuminates the construction of a reality in which people freeze the pyramid as a metaphor for social relations and build their organizational reality accordingly. We can here talk about a psychic or cultural prison in which projections, fantasies, the expressions of desires and fears reinforce a certain kind of dependency and passivity. This does not mean that this is solely a matter of fantasies. Material arrangements, cultural traditions (also involving senior managers and people other than those in the interviewee's position) and social actions are probably crucial here, but that does not prevent the constructed nature of the different worlds – the value of visits from senior managers, the passivity of unit people – from being central in itself as well as something guiding observable phenomena.

Critical research could then focus on prison-building constructions without falling victim to psychological or shared fantasies-reductionism. Specific actions, for example closed doors or senior managers regularly asking or ordering subordinates to walk to their offices, may thus be interpreted in terms of the consequences for ideas, beliefs, and meaning constructions among subordinates.

Critical research may also focus on a broader symbolic-cultural level. Here the entire corporation or a particular well-sliced and targeted part of it, for example senior–middle management interaction, could be investigated in terms of critique. The critical focus then proceeds not so much from the account seen as an expression of the beliefs and fantasies of the group culture of the interview, but uses the account as information about management culture and practices. Critique may then develop the interpretations of senior managers as distant, asocial, individualistic, atomistic, rational, and emotionally constrained in style. This may be seen as an expression of the ideological domination of the Western business world in which subjects are disciplined as carriers of an hegemonic instrumental rationality, fitted into the logic of machine bureaucracies which are impoverishing human relations. Here humans are moulded so that feelings and relations are controlled and minimized.

Critique may here also incorporate ideas from feminism and gender studies, pointing out how a dominant form of masculinity has taken shape locally which guides the orientations of managers. Adopting the mentioned values and practices means that managers create or uncritically express an identity of being masculine which, in business life, is a source of meaning, self-esteem, identity and status. As management traditionally has been constructed as masculine, the ability to adapt to this norm may be significant in order to carry out successful managerial work – at least in a traditional organizational setting. In the context of gender studies, the position and expressed values and desires of the interviewee are of significance, as the account may well be seen as an expression of female values and criteria. Thereby, a counter-image to masculine domination is, although somewhat cautiously, expressed. The interviewee is here interestingly located, being marginalized as well as being placed in a situation with good insight into parts of managerial relations and politics.

A final line of critique may deepen the interpretations made above on the behaviours and social practices described in the interview. For example, the observation that Gustaf has to walk 'up' to his superior, who 'never' visited the unit, may be viewed as a symbol of a clear-cut hierarchical relationship and the emphasis on power in senior managerial action. The symbolism of this behaviour clarifies:

- who is in command;
- whose time is most valuable;
- the general asymmetry of the relationship;
- the relative lack of interest in the unit's personnel and its internal operations.

From a Foucauldian perspective on the disciplining of bodies, this particular habit may be seen as one detail in the network of micropower mechanisms creating docile subjects. We may suspect that structured context around interactions may act in a distorting way. Of course, we have not developed here the mechanics involved in the process of this focused behaviour leading to social consequences. While different intentions may be involved, in this account the symbolic meaning of this routinized behaviour is viewed in the ways mentioned and presumably has effects which regulate the asymmetry of the relationship between the senior manager and his subordinate, between the division and the unit.

In the critical interpretations sketched here, each draws attention to some aspects of the organization and people employed in it. The interpretations show how employees have mystifying relations to senior managers in which the manager's significance is elevated at the same time as one's own initiative is downplayed. The employee becomes caught and constrained in certain conceptions of rationality, with atomistic and alienating effects, asymmetrical relations of power, and unnecessarily strict and rigid hierarchies. And further, they become caught in masculine conceptions of rational organizational life.

Transformative re-definition
Critical analysis leading to transformative re-definition means encouragement of the development of competing discourses, embracing constructive conflict, and participating in agenda setting, reality definition and decision making. Critical work thus aims to contribute to intellectual as well as interaction skills. Offering alternative ways of accounting for what exists and sketching alternative realities are thus central.

According to the interviewee, the world of senior management is populated by slightly alien people. Distance and 'foreigner-ship' are emphasized. As mentioned above, accompanying this construction are mixed feelings, or at least slightly contradictory orientations. These issues may be worked through, aided by further empirical material on the different world. Through, for example, accounts of senior managers, their goals and priorities, viewpoints, everyday work life, expectations and beliefs about lower-level organizational employees, a better understanding of this different, alien world may be accomplished. Material from other studies of managerial work may be included. The resulting review and presented original material may indicate a de-distanciation or de-alienation of corporate managers, from the perspective of the interviewee and her peers. From the perspective of senior managers, research in which a variety of perspectives – organizational subcultures – are related to each other may also facilitate a better understanding, including some new insights. This is not to suggest that knowledge indicating the perspectives from the other side will lead to drastic changes. Knowledge inputs may, however, lead to improved understanding and better chances to act in a slightly different and perhaps more productive way.

Analysis of the feelings about, and views of, relations with senior managers may also lead to insights about assumptions bringing about unnecessary passivity. If senior managers seldom or never appear in person within the domains of the unit's offices and factory, this may be seen as partly an outcome of a relationship and not solely as a self-contained, one-sided lack of interest. Perhaps the unit may be partly responsible for the state of affairs, perhaps people here involuntarily and unreflectively reproduce certain unwanted patterns. Perhaps the unit may make senior managers interested. Perhaps they can communicate the desire for superiors to visit, to locate meetings at the unit's offices. Showing how a particular superior–subordinate structure does not simply exist 'out there', beyond any influence from the 'weaker' part, but is actually co-constructed by both parties, may encourage rethinking of the situation and a better appreciation of chances for initiative.

So far, some ideas for transformative re-definitions that proceed from the constructions of unit staff employees' corporate reality indicate how their construction may be re-made. Of course, this does not in itself transform the corporation at the level of action and interaction, but it may, to the extent the interpretations are taken seriously, encourage the re-definition of the action base of this group of people.

Transformative re-definition may then develop the critical interpretations of senior managers' – according to the interview account – distant, asocial, individualistic, atomistic, rational, emotionally constrained style. Of course, the interview material provides only a hint that these qualities dominate parts of the corporation. More indications, including empirical material emerging from the parts of the company primarily characterized by these values and orientations, are needed. Critique may be exercised from a certain distance, but transformative re-definition calls for good grounding among those whose meanings are to be challenged and encouraged for re-consideration. It can never be taken for granted that a set of values and meanings are wrong, inferior and need to be changed without careful consideration and listening to their carriers. A cultural change is difficult to accomplish through appealing solely to those groups within the corporate context that are already sceptical of the cultural manifestations that one wants to problematize and highlight the negative features of. They may be empowered, but critical research does not aim to equip one group with knowledge and/or resources with which to persuade another group. The viewpoints of the sceptics may, however, be brought forward as valuable contrasts to the dominant ones. Alternative values and understandings that effectively contrast taken for granted ones may encourage re-thinking. Alternative discourses of management may also be brought in from other empirical contexts, for example studies of other companies dominated by other cultural orientations or new, more progressive forms of management knowledge. Another possibility is to emphasize the negative features of certain values and orientations. Loyalty, commitment, synergy effects, development of human resources, etc. may, for example, follow from the orientations and practices of management, as they come through in the account. From a critical research position impoverished social relations, and limited capacities for, and tolerance of, the exchange of viewpoints and democracy are more important costs to bring forward. But in a corporate context more instrumental concerns also need to be addressed in the case of transformative re-definition of cultural values and social practices.

Gender discourses offer one type of possibility of challenging dominant discourses. In the present case, the empirical material we have at our disposal indicates that masculine values dominate among the senior managers. If the reader expects that these are men, he or she is correct. (This is the case not only among senior but also middle management in the company; the only exceptions were a few female personnel managers.) Through pointing at the combination of these two features – a group of males work according to almost stereotypically obvious masculine principles – may encourage scrutiny of the self-evident nature of what exists. Feminist counter-pictures may be less effective in much of business life as sources of change than as critique or calls for legal changes. (In the present case most of the employees are men, so the idea of appealing to women's action or radical feminist transformations would be pointless. The issue at stake is hardly to encourage the liberation of women.) While the prospect of suggesting feminist counter-ideals may not be very constructive in the present case, one could imagine the exploration of a de-masculinization of the focused part of the company. De-masculinization means liberation from the construction of identity and social relations in strong masculine terms, acknowledging the sacrifices and constraints involved and the virtues of a freer, less male-norms-guided way of relating to work and life.

Our final issue concerns the form of meeting ritual (the divisional manager always having to go to his superior), where the asymmetrical relationship between division and unit, between superior and subordinate manager is established. Such forms of micro-power work most effectively if they are used quietly. It is then taken for granted, seen as natural, self-evident and never questioned. By drawing attention to this phenomenon and addressing it as micro-power, some of its effect is lost on those who become aware of it (and that are subjected to it). Simply presenting the quote does much of the job; perhaps little more is needed. The interviewee herself in this case does much of the work of drawing attention to interesting empirical material with a critical edge; the impulse to re-define its power effects as well as re-imagine interaction patterns may follow unobtrusively. Nevertheless, more ambitious interpretive work, critique and encouragement to transformative re-definitions may add significantly to this understanding – and in most cases, simply allowing interviewees or descriptions of empirical situations to talk for themselves does only a minor part of the job of critical research.

Even though critical research should offer ideas and insights aimed at transformative re-definition rather than specific advice on what to do, one could add that subordinate actors may disrupt situations through suggestions for a renewal of the meeting ritual. For example, they could say that their personnel complain about senior managers never visiting them and would be happy if they turned up at the site, so perhaps the meeting could be held at the divisional manager's office instead.

Summary

In this chapter we have structured critical research in to three elements or moments: interpretation producing insights, critique exploring domination and repression, and transformative re-definition indicating alternative ways of imagining and relating to what exists. Expressed a bit differently, the first element highlights hidden or the least obvious aspects and meanings of a chunk of social reality, the second shows the problematic nature of these meanings (and the material arrangements and social orders they indicate), and the third undermines their seeming robustness by encouraging alternative ways of constructing this reality. Critical research calls for at least the first two elements. The third may be included in a more or less ambitious version. A lot of critical research halts with the critique.

In research practice, the three (or two) elements may not be easily distinguishable. Researchers may immediately apply a critical framework which means that the interpretations and insights do 'immediately' express critique. We believe that there are some advantages in postponing the element of critique: interpretive work becomes more systematic and the steps may be thought through more clearly, more aspects may be explicitly considered before moving further with the critical project and the reader may follow the logic more clearly.

7

Developing critical sensitivity
in management research

Many people study the negative by-products of modern organizational activities. They study, for example, environmental pollution, corporate crimes, sexual harassment, racial discrimination, experiences of the unemployed, effects of manipulation of customers and other obvious illegitimate effects. Of most significance for these research projects is persistence in finding sources and providing empirical documentation. Most versions of critical research, however, are oriented towards investigating themes that are more hidden, that do not materialize so easily, or that are not fully registered or experienced by the subjects involved. A high degree of theoretical sophistication must inform critical sensitivity in management research in order to study cultural 'depth structures', how common-sense categories and dominating vocabularies carry hidden meanings that pre-structure and constrain choices and space for action. We do not say more about the theory we find most useful in this chapter since we covered this theme sufficiently in Chapters 2 and 3. However, we do address how we can work with the concepts of de-familiarization and productive dissensus as sensitizing devices. We also discuss a real danger in critical research: a too strong or biased sensitivity for power, domination and social imperfections may lead to negativity and hyper-critique. Related is the problem of the marginalization and perceived irrelevance of critical research in management. As a partial 'solution' to this problem a broadening of the capacity for making interpretations may be suggested. We here talk about the interpretative repertoire as indicating the spectrum of aspects that can be taken seriously. A well-formed repertoire may handle the problem of hyper-critique as well as develop the capacity for a sound, imaginative critical sensitivity.

De-familiarization: turning the well-known into the exotic

A particularly important element in critical research is to avoid seeing the corporate world as self-evident and familiar, and rather to conceptualize it as a strange place. Research then becomes a matter of de-familiarization, of observing and interpreting social phenomena in novel ways compared to culturally dominant categories and distinctions. De-familiarization means that we see things not as natural or rational but as exotic and arbitrary, as an expression of action and thinking within frozen, conformist patterns (Alvesson, 1993a; Ehn and Löfgren, 1982; Marcus and Fischer, 1986).

This is indeed a difficult enterprise. Researchers, like other members of a society, are trapped by cultural ethnocentrism and parochialism – meaning that the cultural phenomena they encounter are not recognized as such but are seen as natural, as part of the world order, and not bound to national or late capitalist/ post-industrial society and business culture. Parochialism is common in management and organization behaviour research, especially in the US (Boyacigillar and Adler, 1991). Organizational culture research does not, on the whole, perform much better on this dimension than organization theory in general. This is ironic, since the proponents of this approach have sometimes claimed that their aim is to understand certain basic premises which are taken for granted by the people living in a culture.

Many agree that the essence of culture lies in the unstated premises or ethos which are taken for granted and so are largely implicit (Trice and Beyer, 1984: 664). However, most basic premisses tend to be taken for granted by most organizational culture authors (Alvesson, 1993a). Furthermore, the problem of cultural ethnocentrism and parochialism is seldom addressed by organization researchers. Gregory, an anthropologist working in the organizational culture area, is exceptional when she remarks that the literature often says 'more about the culture of the researchers than the researched' (1983: 359). This kind of research problem is more generally recognized by anthropologists (Marcus and Fischer, 1986). Going even a bit further, some proponents warn against the study of one's own society. Leach, for example, writes that:

> fieldwork in a cultural context of which you already have intimate first-hand experience seems to be much more difficult than fieldwork which is approached from the naive viewpoint of a total stranger. When anthropologists study facets of their own society their vision seems to become distorted by prejudices which derive from private rather than public experience. (1982: 124)

An interesting illustration of cultural blindness is the fact that hardly any organizational culture researchers have observed that the preoccupation with 'managing', 'organizing' and making life as 'efficient' as possible, is a key feature of Western culture and of business organizations in particular. This has, however, been noted by Smircich (1985) who speculates that anthropologists a thousand years from now will pass the following judgement on our present societal and organizational culture:

> These people were crazy for organization. They valued discipline, order, regulation, and obedience much more than independence, expressiveness, and creativity. They were always looking for efficiency. They wanted to control everything. They had a fetish for 'managing'. They managed stress, time, relationships, emotions, but mostly they managed their careers. (1985: 56)

On a fairly general level, the problem can be formulated as a lack of distance – or a great similarity – between organizational researchers and managerial/business culture. This makes it difficult to look upon phenomena and practices that are well known and natural to 'the natives' with fresh eyes. As an investigator, this requires one to ask oneself constantly, 'What do they think they are up to?' when witnessing the customs and symbolism of managers and employees, producers and their customers. This ability is partly a matter of creativity (which will not be treated here as such) and partly a matter of socialization (lack of a sufficiently helpful) and intellectual training. Scholarly socialization, which clearly differs from the kind that leads to full acceptance and internalization of general managerial culture, could be regarded as a prerequisite for the adoption of a critical–cultural approach to organizations. The extent to which a normal academic setting concerned with management research/teaching leads to such socialization may be open to question. The main purpose of educating people for managerial positions appears to be to create a close relationship between them and the values and goals of the business community and to harmonize the cultures of most corporations with the values and understandings of most management researchers. This can be seen as a source of both benefits and problems. Of course, it facilitates the understanding of, and interaction with, representatives of the corporate world. However, in the context of culture studies in general, and in de-familiarization oriented critical research in particular, it is clearly a weakness in certain respects. Here a cultural difference between the researcher's and the research object's frameworks is vital.

In ethnographic work within anthropology, the initial difference between the traditions involved (the researcher's and the object of study's) produces breakdowns in understanding: 'A breakdown is a lack of fit between one's encounter with a tradition and the schema-guided expectations by which one organizes experience' (Agar, 1986: 21). The researcher resolves this problem by trying to understand the cultural elements that are causing the breakdown, and then adjusting the research schema. Breakdowns continue to appear until the researcher fully understands the studied culture. This means that ethnography can be described 'as a process of coherently resolving breakdowns' (Agar, 1986: 39).

When studying relatively familiar phenomena like the organizations and management of one's own country, the problem is not only or even primarily to *resolve* breakdowns but to *create* them. In foreign cultures breakdowns occur automatically, but in one's own they are mostly marginal. The trick then is to locate one's framework (cultural understanding) away from the cultural terrain being studied, so that significant material to 'resolve' emerges. The problem – and rationale – for organizational culture studies is to be able to avoid being trapped by the well known and self-evident, and to turn it into something exotic and explicit, to raise and answer the question: 'What does it mean (apart from the obvious)?' (see Asplund, 1970). This is, of course, to a large extent a matter of creativity but it is also a matter of wanting to achieve 'anthropological' rather than familiar or 'technical-pragmatic' results. To some degree it is a matter of using the 'critical strategy of de-familiarization': 'Disruption of common sense, doing the unexpected, placing familiar subjects in unfamiliar, even shocking, context are the aims of this strategy to make the reader conscious of difference' (Marcus and Fischer, 1986: 137).

Modes of accomplishing de-familiarization
De-familiarization calls for creativity and imagination. There are no cookbook recipes for how to accomplish this. One may, however, point at systematically creating cultural distance to what is to be studied and working with negations as possible research principles. The open-minded, self-reflective employment of a helpful framework offering a systematic counter-point is, of course, the most effective device, but it may work together with distanciation and negations.

Creating distance   Many students of management and organization could benefit by viewing their objects of study with fresh eyes. A very simple idea, but a possibly fruitful one would be to let people who are not business or organization researchers carry out or – perhaps even better – participate in the research. Management and organization researchers 'know' what business and organizations are about; they have specific ideas about what to look for and are, consequently, unlikely to discover anything new in an anthropological sense. Their tradition overlaps that of organizations too much. These people cannot be expected to adopt the 'naïve' and questioning perspective of a person unfamiliar with a particular culture or to avoid falling into unquestioning assumptions about the culture concerned. Better candidates could be people who are 'foreign' to the research objects, like artists or theologians, or why not people with a background in social or behavioural science from another culture (hopefully not overly influenced by Western ideas). But using people as researchers who lack any background knowledge of the object of study also creates problems. Ignorance is not simply an advantage. Distance is not the sole issue for cultural research – empathy and understanding of what is on the natives' mind are also crucial and this is greatly facilitated by knowledge and insight about the setting. A possible solution may be to employ such outsiders as co-researchers in management and organization theory research. Another possibility is, of course, for researchers to try to get experience from different (national) cultures (Boyacigillar and Adler, 1991). This may reduce parochialism and make researchers more sensitive to broader cultural variations than organization-specific ones.

Some of the advantages of having lived and worked in different countries – with different national cultures – are illustrated in a study of Polish, US and Swedish organizations by Czarniawska-Joerges (1988). The idiosyncracies of each national culture can be perceived much more clearly. Czarniawska-Joerges's interpretations show the variety of cultural patterns on productive breakdowns. But quite a lot of dominant cultural patterns and discourses transcend specific 'subgroups' – the ideology of consumerism dominates across classes, genders, ethnic groups and nations – so one should not rely too heavily on the mentioned distinctions. Critical research is quite different from cross-cultural comparisons, but experiences from, and comparisons with, other contexts than the one being studied may be a valuable resource in the former. Critical research has broader concerns than cultural studies which focuses on individual organizations within a given societal cultural framework. Ouchi's (1981) study also includes interesting insights through comparisons between US and Japanese management, thereby raising some questions about the self-evident rationality of the former at the same time. The Ouchi study, however, is hardly an example of critical research. Besides living in different countries, other examples of cross-cultural experiences (that is, crossing experiences of subcultural borders) include academics with working-class backgrounds studying senior executives or expensive consumption or females studying male-dominated work organizations.

Countertext: working with negations   An important principle, if interesting interpretations are to be produced, is to think in a dialectic way. It is in the state of tension between different realized ideas and practices on the one hand, and alternatives to these on the other, that it becomes possible to avoid getting caught by established ideas and institutions (Adorno and Horkheimer, 1979 [1947]; Marcuse, 1964). By negating the existing order, it becomes possible to see it in a different and meaningful way.

By consistently seeking counter-images – not with a view to suggesting ideals but to provide meaningful contrasts – it is possible to produce interpretations in which empirical phenomena are elucidated in a state of tension between the established order and the transcendental. It is important to stress that it is not necessarily a question of contrasting the existing order with some sort of Utopia. Rather, it is about the way the empirical phenomena are conceptualized and interpreted in terms of the natural or the exotic, the neutral or the political, the unproblematic or the irrational. It is about making the familiar foreign (*Entfremdung*, defamiliarization), about problematizing the self-evident and pointing out that future realities need not be a reproduction of what currently exists. A touch of imagination is required. Of course the risk of ending up with a Utopia anyway is always there. While Utopian conceptions may arise, the goal is to strive towards better social forms of work and production than providing a specific blueprint for an ideal future.

One way of reducing the risk of cultural parochialism is to widen the range of the frame of reference that guides thinking and research attention. Instead of reading exclusively (mainstream) management and organization theory or even exclusively 'antimanagement' texts, the researcher could get more from studying anthropological and historical texts which illuminate the relativity of present Western society and its business culture. Fiction may also provide a valuable source of inspiration. This literature – academic and fictional – might serve as inspiration for reworking one's own framework and for 'moving it away' from too much overlap with business culture.

The use of particular frames of reference that provide powerful counterpoints to conventional views could, therefore, be a method. This approach might be called 'negative dialectics', a concept employed by the proponents of critical theory (for example, Marcuse, 1968) but used rather freely here in relation to this tradition. This would mean that existent phenomena, that is the prevailing empirical reality, should not be studied solely as given and inevitable facts, but rather as elements of a limited phase in the history of mankind. Normally, were we to study empirical phenomena only, our understanding of existent reality would become a prisoner of that socially constructed reality. Conditions would be taken for granted and no interesting understanding of culture would be produced. By negating existent reality and confronting various phenomena with the idea of very different social forms, events and conditions, fruitful insights can be achieved. This means that we are not only preoccupied with actuality, but also consider potentiality when we reflect upon social phenomena. The point is that reality becomes illuminated in a very different way when the negation of reality or some aspect of it is taken into consideration.

Drawing on theory and provocative metaphors   Especially important here are, of course, creative social scientists who have managed to perceive society in a radically new light (see Chapter 3). The 'anti-management' orientation characterizing these kinds of authors is important, because working with an opinion antithetical to the common one is an important starting point for the kind of project advocated in this book. Breakdowns will then emerge.

Negation may refer either to empirically non-existent (or at least infrequently accomplished) but imaginable social conditions or to phenomena actually existing in the real world (in other cultures than the focal one or in particular spheres of the society addressed). An example of the former could be the study of organizations in terms of communicative distortions (Habermas, 1970, 1984), where the ideal speech situation is one in which all discourses are allowed to be expressed and questioned without any (or at least not too much) repression or inequalities among the participants (for example, Forester, 1983). The idea of this negation – that is to say the 'free', undistorted discourse – is that a number of aspects of communication that are normally taken for granted become visible and can be recognized as phenomena worthy of investigation. Hierarchical relationships, norms for interaction and communication which stop people from saying what they feel is important, asymmetries among organizational groups in terms of deciding upon legitimate and illegitimate discourses – all of these can be seen as communicative distortions to be investigated in detail. The tacit and not the espoused are then seen as themes of study. Similar examples of negations used to confront prevalent social conditions could involve looking at present-day capitalist, hierarchical organizations from the viewpoint of anti-hierarchical, bottom-up controlled organization forms (for example, Clegg and Dunkerley, 1980), or setting the dominating technological-instrumental rationality against a humanistic, anti-repressive form of reason (for example, Alvesson, 1987).

As a basis for reducing ethnocentricity and increasing the opportunities for less 'prejudiced' cultural analysis, a dialectical approach to management and organization may also proceed from less abstract and more empirically grounded types of negation. One example could be the gender issue. Here we can point out several cases where males and females have (more or less) equal positions (for example, Billing and Alvesson, 1994; Blomqvist, 1994). We can also see how the gender division of labour and the ascribing of masculinity (or femininity) to certain jobs or tasks are arbitrary, and vary across cultural contexts (Leidner, 1991). Instead of taking for granted the reproduction of gender differences in organizations, we could proceed from the regulative ideal of equality and abolished gender division of labour and then see all deviations as phenomena calling for investigation. Rather than taking for granted that executives are men and secretaries women, this gender division of labour may be zoomed in on for exploration. In order first to show variety in the social world 'out there', and secondly (and more significantly in the context of critical research) to encourage more imaginative interpretations, variations in empirical material may be sought for. The point here is not that all this variation must be studied in detail; simply encountering it may encourage a more open orientation.

The analytical principle of negation of existent conditions has important implications as to how the analysis and presentation of cultural conditions are conducted. Without the idea of negation (as for example sexual equality/inequality, exploitation/environmental protection), the very fact that sexual discrimination or exploitation of nature takes place would not have been recognized. Division of labour between the sexes would not be considered worth mentioning in organization research if the possibility of negation (non-gendered division of labour or even the absence of division of labour in its extended form) were not recognized. It is perhaps the presence of a rather large number of examples of gender equality that accounts for all the focus on gender inequality in current society: these examples make us aware of the arbitrary and cultural nature of gender differences. When gender oppression dominates, no one will notice as it is seen as completely 'natural'.

Addressing gender inequality in terms of access to various positions on the career ladder only points at a relatively limited aspect of the parochialism problem (Alvesson and Billing, 1997). The ideal of careerism and the more basic form of inequality associated with hierarchical organizational forms and labour markets sometimes tend to be taken for granted in our culture. A narrow form of gender analysis mainly interested in equal access to given career opportunities might express elements of a parochial attitude in a society in which upward mobility is a central value.

Thus far we have looked at drawing upon certain empirical examples or principles and ideals compared to which social phenomena studied may appear as less natural, self-evident or unproblematic than they may seem for those that have got used to 'how things are' due to the constraints of their lived experiences. But imaginative metaphors may also be invoked. Morgan (1986) has done much to advocate the idea of multiple readings. This ideal in itself goes somewhat along the way of critical research, especially such of a postmodernist bend. Of more interest than pluralism in interpretations are, however, the nature and quality of these. Morgan's psychic prison and domination metaphors are of relevance for critical research, but the former is too psychological and the latter is too objectivistic to be really helpful in the critical research context advocated here. In Alvesson and Willmott (1996) some alternative metaphors are suggested: management as distorted communication/the instrumentalization of reason; management as mystification, that is the selective construction and confusion of needs and understandings; management as cultural doping, that is the corporation as a socialization agency, and management as colonizing power, the erosion of the lifeworld. The advantage of a metaphor is that it captures the imagination and provides a coherent image that one may stick to. This is important in qualitative empirical work, where it is easy to get lost in complexities and details of the empirical world, and one gets dragged into socially dominating categories, distinctions and ideas embraced by the field, thereby seriously weakening critical sensitivity in producing empirical material.

Some illustrations of de-familiarization
We briefly illustrate these interrelated points about creating distance, working with negations and using critical theories and metaphors by way of three rather different examples: marketing of professional services, racial division of labour, and management control.

Networking in accounting firms   One example is the significance and meaning of contacts and networks in many business contexts. Grey (1994) has studied this in a large accounting firm and observes that as employees rise up the professional hierarchy to manager and partner levels, it becomes increasingly important to maintain and develop contacts that transcend the private and professional sectors of life. Here networks of contacts represent selling opportunities. Much selling of professional services occurs in 'social' or 'non-business' settings. As one manager states:

> If you're going to have a career here beyond manager, you've got to use every opportunity to make contacts, so you're never really away from the job in that sense. ...It is the only way to get on because you'll only make partner by bringing in the jobs. (Cited in Grey, 1994: 492)

While contacts, networking and professionalism are words that for most people sound positive, normal, natural and functional, one may turn the understanding into a more de-familiarizing tone. Grey notes that 'friends become transformed into "contacts" and social activity becomes "networking"' and interprets this as the transformation of the non-work sphere into a specific aspect of professional career development. To use a metaphor mentioned above, the corporate world then works as a 'colonizing power' as it erodes the lifeworld. All relations are, potentially, instrumentalized. Career also becomes a defining feature of marriage. As one of Grey's interviewees says, 'it is important to have a well-packaged wife'. Marriage thus becomes, at least in part, an adjunct to career.

An example of de-familiarization language would be to conceptualize the spouse as a 'career-adjunct'. Labels of this kind notwithstanding, turning the understanding from a marketing and promotion of professional service context, and its rationality, and conceptualizing it as an instrumentalization of all social relations shows how de-familiarization may work. In Grey's case, inspiration came partly from Foucault, although other critical theories may also have been helpful. The contrast between a business-marketing instrumental rationality and a Habermasian notion of the colonization of the lifeworld would have been productive and carried the study further. A similar notion seems, however, to have guided the author in his negation of the dominant logic of the case company (and this kind of industry in general).

Racial division of labour in a company office   A second example concerns division of labour along the lines of skin colour and ethnic heritage. In a study of female clerical work, one author reports:

> Racism is ... clearly visible to anyone who walks through a big company office. Pretty young white women work as private secretaries. ... Black clericals are mainly reserved for the key-punching room, the typing pool, or the data processing centre – the routine, pressurised low-paid jobs. (Tepperman, 1976: 49)

It is worth noting that the great majority of organizational culture researchers seem hardly to recognize this type of phenomenon as an expression of the cultures they are investigating. Either they find the phenomena irrelevant to an understanding of the cultures of the organizations, or they are not surprised by it and consequently do not observe it. Just producing this simple description shows how the well known may easily strike the reader as something strange. In this case little theoretical sophistication is called for as the example is so obvious. Nevertheless, the implicit regulatory ideal of non-racial division of labour informs the account. Without it, the observation would be pointless.

Management control in ITT   A third example is from accounting: to be more precise, management control at ITT under its president during the 1960s, Harold Geneen, often referred to as the 'super accountant'. In their study, Hopper and Macintosh (1993) draw upon Geneen's own book as well as other books on ITT. Geneen was famous for his sophisticated financial control systems and heavy reliance on detailed quantitative information. He and a large staff carefully monitored all subsidiaries in the quickly expanding conglomerate. A cadre of technical staff and product managers was set up in the headquarters. They were free to go to any location without an invitation to investigate anything within their area of expertise. At large monthly meetings with 150 European general managers and 40 headquarters staff the situation of the subsidiaries was carefully scrutinized.

> We sat around a large U-shaped table, covered in green felt, facing one another, and I asked questions based upon the notes I had made on their monthly operating reports. Why were the sales down? Was he sure of the reasons? Had he checked it out? How? What was he doing about it? What did he expect in the month or two ahead? Did he need help? How did he plan to meet or outdistance the competition? (Geneen, cited by Hopper and Macintosh, 1993: 198)

Geneen and his support staff came armed with a series of 'red-ink queries'. On a large screen everybody could see what performances, according to reported numbers, looked like compared to budget commitments.

Hierarchy, logic and order, measurement in detail, ratings and rankings, careful scrutiny of profit centres, close monitoring of all deviations from budget commitments, Geneen himself spending 12–16 hours a day, 7 days per week (working partly to be able to do all the homework in terms of reading reports and knowing all the numbers, partly to set the work norm of self-discipline for the rest of the company) – all of this may seem to be a masterpiece of management rationality.

A counter-picture emerges, however, if the whole corporation is seen from a Foucauldian perspective. Here, the metaphor of

Panopticon proves useful. The Panopticon was a model for a prison architecturally designed so that all the isolated inmates in their cells could become visible from the central tower, in which the chief guardian himself remained invisible for most of the time. The inmates, thus, rarely if ever knew when they were being watched, assuring normalization and obedience.

From the central headquarters office, the accounting system cast its constant normalizing gaze into every responsibility centre throughout the organization. At a glance it could monitor any part of ITT. It effected a continual flow of both formal and informal information into Geneen's office. Individual managers, however, never knew at any particular moment whether Geneen was 'gazing' directly at them through the windows of the numbers, or if not him personally, then some other member of the anonymous headquarters' staff. Within this accounting and control Panopticon, the line organization anxiously conformed to the 'prescribed normalization of the numbers' (Hopper and Macintosh, 1993: 208).

In this case Foucault's framework acts as a counter-text to conventional understandings. Foucault, proceeding from studies of prisons and how disciplinary power was developed in these in the eighteenth century and then distributed to schools, hospitals and factories, utilizes a long-term perspective in order to create distance and apply it to well-known, naturalized corporate practices. As mentioned in Chapter 3, Foucault's work has been productively used in several studies on accounting. The Panoptican metaphor is effectively used as a means of de-familiarization by Hopper and Macintosh.

Summing up

Creating cultural/framework distance, working with negations and drawing upon critical theories and metaphors are, of course, not separate means for de-familiarization. Even though they strongly overlap, they also include different elements and may to some extent contradict each other. Being strongly inspired by a particular critical theory may reduce the chance of producing interesting breakdowns: at worst a particular theory may lead to the routine and predictable slotting in of findings in this theory and the sense-making machinery it may function as. Technocratic consciousness (Habermas) or prison-like organizational arrangements (Foucault) may be the interpretation searching for empirical material to respond to. Theory should be used in a self-critical way, providing space also for de-familiarizations in other terms than those of the favoured vocabulary. There is a risk that, over time, a favoured theoretical vocabulary might domesticate the empirical material one encounters and make it 'familiar'. Creativity, imagination and a flexible mind are necessary in order to learn from empirical studies.

By combining elements of distance creation, working with negations, and reflectively working with theoretical frameworks and metaphors (and doing so under the guideline of critical imagination), empirical accounts, interpretations and critical/transformative 'results' may involve de-familiarization as a key methodological principle as well as an outcome of the study ('results', reader effect).

Dissensus: breaking up meanings and discursive closure

In general we understand the issues of domination when raised by strategy, manipulation and instrumental uses of communication, even though such issues are not always taken seriously and the effort to overcome them may be great. The more serious issues posed by modern analyses are the invisible constraints that are disguised as neutral and self-evident. In a general way these can be described as discursive closures and systematically distorted communication. Both concepts become central when we turn to look at the processes of domination in development decisions and consider alternative communicative practices. The outcome of discursive closures and systematically distorted communication is the appearance of a well-formed consensus that is flawed or premature in some way. Here the researcher attempts to find suppressed conflicts and differences hidden by the apparent consensus, to create dissensus and the need for discussion and redetermination where none appears necessary. This is the construction of anti-positive knowledge (Knights, 1992).

Forester (1989) has been very helpful in the planning literature in describing the various common forms of domination and closure. Some limitations are inevitable, but there are clear differences between those which are random and particularistic and those which are systematic and structural. Discursive closure exists whenever potential conflict is suppressed. This may derive from several processes, many of which have been described (see Deetz, 1992). One of the most common is the disqualification of certain groups or participants. Disqualification can occur through the denial of the right of expression, the denial of access to speaking forums, the assertion of the need for certain expertise in order to speak, or through rendering the other unable to speak adequately, including processes of de-skilling. Closure is also possible through the privileging of certain discourses and the marginalization of others. For example, Habermas and other critical theorists have extensively detailed the domination of technical-instrumental reasoning over other forms of reasoning in the Western world. Foucault in his many works has shown how certain discourses historically arise as normal and preferred. Organizational studies clearly show how managerial groups and technical reasoning become privileged (Mumby, 1987, 1988). Further, closure is present in each move to determine origins and demonstrate unity. In each case the multiple motived and conflict-filled nature of experience becomes suppressed by a dominant aspect. This has most clearly been developed in narrative theory (for example, Jameson, 1981). With unity, the continued production of experience is constrained since the tension of difference is lost.

Systematically distorted communication is itself both evidence for and productive of discursive closure, but the concept provides a slightly different focus for the analysis. Habermas presented the concept based on a psychoanalytical analogue as descriptive of those times when an interactant is self-deceived. The most obvious case of this is when a certain experience is repressed, and consequently the psychological experience and the expression of it become displaced or projected. In this sense an individual is out of touch with self-interests, needs and feelings, and may well substitute other socially derived experiences and expression for his or her own – an ideological expression or false consciousness. In the extreme model only though a 'talking cure' may the code be broken so that the disguised expression of the repressed state can be read and the individual may become reconnected with self-experience. In this view, society and organizations can be seen as filled with 'social neurosis'. This particular version is not of much interest here. The role of social therapist is elitist and filled with contradictions. The searching for real motives, needs and interests can certainly structure another privileged discourse (Clegg, 1989). And the implicit assumption that linguistic expression should represent a fixed, knowable interior provides a weak understanding of language and experience. But we can learn from this analysis.

Intuitively we know that we respond to unknown elements of experience. We see people unwittingly act in opposition to their own values and needs. And we hear and participate in discourses that feel restrictive – like trying to express a sunset on canvas when you do not know how to paint. These are significant to the communication process. Here systematic distortion is not based on a simple mismatch of a fixed interest with a fixed expression but an interactionally determined reduction of certain experiences to other ones. In each case potential conflict and dissensus remain invisible.

Methodologically the reclaiming of dissensus requires historical insight into the discussion that the consensus ended and the processes by which the consensus was produced; it also requires creativity in outlining the discussions that may have happened. Premature or flawed consensus potentially exists anywhere in organizational life.

Every named identity, for example, 'worker' or 'manager', supresses potential alternative ways people could be divided up or categorized and the complex array of identities that make up a full human being. Every organizational routine suppresses a discussion of alternative activities. Occasionally dissensus arises in particular arenas as organizational practices change. For example, the maintenance of a 'managerial' prerogative and highly differential pay is difficult as team processes develop, with many traditional managerial functions being performed by workers in teams. The easily reproduced and seemingly natural distinction is now opened to redetermination.

The presence of 'information' in organizational life often hides the knowledge formation process and/or accounting practices that produce it. As people accept or use information they unwittingly assume a consensus on these productive activities. A discussion that might very well be had – or should be had – regarding these activities is precluded. Work like that of Harding (1991) showing a male bias in social science knowledge production can be applied to show what is potentially conflictual in organization knowledge production as well. Domesticated spaces return to contested terrain.

The research seeks to re-problematize aspects of organizational life by displaying the dissent that would be present if the flawed consensus was removed. The activity is to find the conversations that did not happen or were cut off.

An illustration

Deetz (1997, 1998) showed how a business concept or mission statement can function to produce both discursive closure and systematically distorted communication. In his case study, members of a division of a major international telecommunications company organized themselves around a conception of 'providing integrated computer solutions offered through an internal consulting firm'. The apparent consensus on both the 'integrated solutions' conception and 'consultant' model blocked discussion of alternatives – even as the group was struggling and finally failed financially.

For example, 'integrated solutions' led to a preference for big projects that took months to acquire and over a year to complete. And, if a contract was cancelled, a major financial instability was created. In the short term, at least, the unit needed smaller projects to keep it afloat. Unfortunately the consensus on the positive term, 'integrated solutions', had already established a negative conceptual opposite, 'smokestack services'; these were 'piecemeal' programmes, usually preformed by women for specific clients. The descriptive term itself (evoking a less than modern, industrial belt image) partly accomplished the disregard of potential conflict and supported the consensus. No matter how valuable 'smoke-stack' projects were, or even if people liked doing them, participating in them made an individual a less valued employee. To advocate such activities was nearly impossible within the discursive set-up.

Exploring dissensus requires investigating the wider discourses and structural arrangement in which the consensus arose and was sustained, analysing the relative power of members and the advantages accruing to different groups given the conception, and the detailing of the actual discursive processes by which alternative discussions were foreclosed or distorted. Deetz showed the relationship of the 'integrated services' conception to technological ideology and relative technological expertise, and how these were connected to male members and the particular individuals who initially championed the development of the unit. Further the 'consultant' model fulfilled a marketplace ideology and the preference for economic over political decision-making processes. In addition, and importantly, it supported the development of unobtrusive control processes whereby individual members' autonomy was used to control their work processes and their own responses in ways which were much more stringent and complete than any management could have accomplished.

The study could reclaim unarticulated competing positions held by members that were neither thought nor expressed in routine organizational life. With such alternatives in place the culture could be seen as much more differentiated and fragmented, and the control systems much more coercive than initially thought by either members or the researcher. Not only was the suppression of alternative conceptions clear at the end, but many routine activities in the organization – such as taking cold medication or sleeping on folding beds in remote sites – which were used to increase productivity became seen as oppressive when renamed in the context of structural and unobtrusive control processes.

Hyper-critique: negativity and one-dimensionality in critical research

Developing critical sensitivity is hardly accomplished without losses and sacrifices. It may mean that a fine-tuned feeling for the operations of power and ideology is developed at the expense of the capacity to appreciate the positive or not-so-bad features of management and corporate life. A strong belief in the importance of questioning conventional beliefs and assumptions – a major task of academic knowledge and seriously under-represented in the majority of management studies – does not prevent us from recognizing a tendency to one-sidedness in many critical projects (including some of our own works). This one-sidedness parallels, in some respects, the one-dimensional technicism that dominates conventional management theory (Alvesson and Willmott, 1992, 1996). The negativity of much critical research creates problems, both in terms of how the objects and subjects of critique are represented, and in terms of demonstrating the relevance of its concerns (Hardy and Clegg, 1997). Critical research must, therefore, be careful about the fallacy of hyper-critique, that is a one-sided and intolerant approach, in which only what is seen as the imperfections of the corporate world are highlighted. There is sometimes a narrow interest in issues of domination over workers, while critical research does not seriously address the tasks of management to use resources effectively to produce goods and services to be purchased by customers. Critical research portrays corporations as sites of relations of power and domination, while the productive outcomes of corporations – to some extent facilitated by pressure for productivity and quality – receive little if any attention.

Tendencies to hyper-critique may account for its very marginal presence within, and impact upon, management and organization studies. Although this position is largely attributable to the dominance of values that are antithetical to those of critical research, antagonism is fueled by blanket dismissals of the preoccupations of practitioners, and of management theory and education, as well as the inaccessibility of the language employed within critical research. The critical approach is effectively marginalized and 'silenced' (Calás and Smircich, 1987). Critical theory in management then hardly reaches a position from which 'resistance', even less so 'opposition', to mainstream management and organization theory can be exercised. It is important to ensure that critical research is not perceived as negative and un-constructive. Critical research must include elements of self-critique and reflection.

The very task of critical management research is to be sensitive to how meanings may carry privileged interests (Deetz, 1992). This task may be combined with a somewhat broader appreciation of meaning and interests. A challenge for the researcher is, simultaneously: (a) to concentrate on local actors' meanings, symbols and values; (b) to place these within a wider political, economic and historic framework; and (c) to avoid such a framework pressing the material into a particular theory and language (a dominating voice), thus obscuring the ambiguities and variations of the empirical situation and the multiple ways in which it can be accounted for. The trick is to be sensitive to all these three elements, and avoid ignorance as well as hypersensitivity to either, to keep to the critical project as the primary one while avoiding tunnel vision.

Creating space also for 'non-critical' aspects can be suggested as a part of a less heady emancipatory project. Depth interviews are more likely to provide insights into how organizational members can hold both affirmative and critical opinions about a particular organization and how it is managed. The researcher's role is then one of 'uncovering, reading, and making visible to others the critical perspectives and possibilities for alternatives that exist in the lives of his subjects' (Marcus and Fischer, 1986: 133).

One possibility is to undertake studies that combine 'critical' and 'non-critical' perspectives (for example managerial, 'non-critical' subordinate), paying attention to the needs for liberation as well as the value of the efficient management of concrete organizational problems under contemporary conditions and restrictions. By treating conflicts and contradictions as well as consensual matters, such an approach would be even more novel, minimize the risk of hyper-critique and open up a possibility for reducing the gap between critical and conventional management studies. We will come back to how this may be done in research practice in Chapter 8, and devote the next section to how to work with a framework which creates a balance between critical sensitivity and hyper-critique.

Interpretive repertoire

In critical research the theoretical frame of reference possesses a special importance. The theoretical frame can counterbalance any tendency on the part of the researcher to become trapped by the complexities of the empirical material, to become swamped by observations, interview statements and other accessible material that seldom lends itself to direct or simple interpretation on a basis of an emancipatory cognitive interest. Almost by definition it is impossible for an interviewee to talk about communicative distortions, for instance, or about how one constructs one's own psychic or cultural prisons. Interviewees can hardly inform researchers about how they are constituted within specific discourses. A well-developed theoretical frame of reference is absolutely necessary in order to make good interpretations, something which requires particular attention in critical theory as the idea is to go beyond surface meanings. What is needed in order to avoid hyper-critique and make critical research more relevant for practioners and mainstream management – at least the 'thoughtful', non-technocratic part of the mainstream – is a broader base for interpretations.

To some extent common sense, life experiences, general education and intellectual skills, including the kind of critical thinking (in the sense of error-detecting) that academic socialization facilitates, means a slightly broader base for seeing other aspects than one favoured by a specific theory. This is, however, often insufficient, as saying something of real interest from a non-critical perspective also normally calls for considerable theoretical support. Doing sophisticated critical research and combining it with common-sense observations and comments hardly balances the project in the sense that readers outside the critical or critique-receptive camps may also find something valuable in the research results.

What is needed, we believe, is a combination of theoretical knowledge that allows the researcher to see a multitude of different aspects and facilitates the development of results that may be the product of more than one point of departure and a single knowledge-constitutive interest. We refer to the full set of aspects and themes that a researcher masters to a sufficient degree to make a knowledge contribution as an *interpretive repertoire*. Such a repertoire includes the paradigmatic, theoretical and methodological qualifications and restrictions that guide and constrain research work. The interpretive repertoire is made up of theories, basic assumptions, commitments, metaphors, vocabularies and knowledge. It indicates the 'academic' part of the researcher's pre-structured understanding and the whole spectrum of theoretical resources that may be put into use in confrontations with empirical material. It marks the limits of what a researcher can do in terms of making something out of a particular piece of empirical material – material that is itself produced on the basis of the interpretive inclinations of the researcher.

The interpretive repertoire is made of elements of relative degrees of depth and superficiality. At one extreme there are theories and discourses of which the researcher has an excellent grasp and great skills in putting into use; at the other end of the spectrum there are theories and vocabularies which are familiar to the researcher, but can only be applied in a crude and uncertain manner. We can refer to these end points as professional and amateurish elements in the repertoire. The professional elements are intensive and central in the interpretive repertoire whereas amateurish elements may be described as the shallow in terms of mastery and peripheral with regard to interest and awareness. The former typically means a strong tendency to use the element, great skill in doing so and a likelihood that they will lead to results, although sometimes in a rather predictable way. The amateurish elements in the interpretive repertoire are only activated in research work if the empirical material may be easily read in line with these elements. This typically indicates that the empirical material is seen as important or interesting when framed in this way. The researcher has three alternatives when he or she thinks that the empirical material triggers thinking activating the shallow or peripheral elements in the interpretive repertoire: to drop the theme; to refer to it briefly or mainly in empirical/low-abstract terms; or to develop the relevant parts of the interpretive repertoire and then do a more advanced investigation of the phenomena. The third alternative means that the shallow part of the repertoire is more centre stage and the researcher develops her or his skills in using it. Much reading is necessary. In such a case, empirical material typically has the chance to make a real impact on the research outcome.

The interpretive repertoire – empirical material interaction

Let us explore how the interpretive repertoire may work in an empirical research context. We can start from the data-constructing level, where researchers make observations, talk to people, create images of empirical phenomena, make preliminary interpretations, etc., and where the degree of interpretation is relatively low or somewhat unclear to the researchers themselves. (Sometimes objectivist researchers misleadingly describe this as 'collecting data', see Alvesson and Sköldberg, 2000.) We could speak of first-hand interpretations or of interpretations close to what goes on 'out there' or at a low level of abstraction. The interpretive repertoire guides the work: choices of empirical site(s), the interview questions asked and followed up, what elements of lived experience in observational situations receive attention, etc. The produced empirical material (interview transcripts and field notes) is then subject to further interpretation of a more or less systematic kind, guided by ideas which can be related to academic theories (scientific paradigms) or to other frames of reference (cultural ideas or taken-for-granted assumptions, implicit personal theories, etc.). Ideally, the researcher allows the empirical material to inspire, develop and reshape theoretical ideas. It is thus not so much that objective data talk to the theory (data are after all constructions and dependent on perspective); it is rather that the interpretive repertoire allows the consideration of different meanings in empirical material. The repertoire means that certain lines of interpretation are given priority, that others are possible but are not so readily emphasized, while yet others never even appear possible. A very narrow repertoire gives very limited possibilities. An economist who has learnt that self-interest lies behind everything is hardly likely to notice any empirical indications of altruism. The suggestion of any such thing either fails to be noted or is simply explained away. A highly committed Foucauldian is inclined to see prison-like arrangements, operations of power and disciplinary power everywhere – everything is, if not inherently bad, at least dangerous. A person ignorant about gender theory will fail to see any subtle sign of gender repression. However, the possibility of reciprocity between the researcher (the theory) and what is being studied should be emphasized in the interpreter's construction of data. Unruly, ambivalent or unexpected empirical material (interview statements, incidents observed) can affect the interpretive repertoire so that peripheral elements in it may also be developed. At the level close to the data, reflection is a question of reinforcing such reciprocity by influencing the interpretive repertoire (Alvesson and Sköldberg, 2000).

The particular interpretive options that are open to the researcher are crucial in this context. Four aspects appear to be of central importance:

- creativity in the sense of ability to see various aspects;
- theoretical sophistication;
- theoretical breadth and variation;
- ability to reflect at the metatheoretical level.

The first point is to some extent a consequence of the other three, but over and above these are individual capacity, the research milieu, the researcher's network, etc., which all play an important part.

Optimally the interpretive repertoire assists the researcher in critical studies to develop critical imagination and avoid hypercritique. Here the powerful ideas and concepts of critical theory, Foucault and others are used sensitively, for example they guide interpretations but are open to the empirical material. Such openness, and a willingness and capacity also to develop interesting 'non-critical' (which is not the same as uncritical) ideas, calls for other theories – metaphors other than those of the core critical camp which are a relatively well-developed part of the interpretive repertoire.

One condition for reflection on the interplay between empirical material and interpretations is thus the breadth and variation of the interpretive repertoire. This will prevent a specific theory (metaphor, expectation) from dominating seeing. If the researcher has at least some knowledge of two or more theories, and feels positive towards them, then interpretations will be more open. Empirical material can then generate the consideration of some fairly disparate interpretations (or perhaps several interpretations). Alternatively we could say that the construction of the data is undertaken with due thought, and that the 'data' – at least for a while – remain more open. (Ultimately, however, the researcher is compelled to exclude certain possibilities and to reduce the multiplicity of meanings.) The possibility of multiple interpretations enhances reflection (and vice versa). The formula for this, to put it rather mechanistically, is thus: rich data (multiplicity of meanings) + breadth and variation in the interpretive repertoire improves the chances for 'empirically grounded imagination' (Norén, 1990). We argued in Chapters 2 and 3 for the use of both critical theory and Foucauldian ideas in management critical research, partly in order to have a critical framework which encourages consciousness about the dilemmas and strong/weak points in doing specific forms of critical enquiry. This would mean some breadth in the interpretive repertoire, but will not solve the problems of hyper-critique and lack of contact with management practitioners and 'conventional' students of management. For this reason we think that the repertoire should also include a fair dose of theoretical knowledge of a more pro-managerial or 'managerial-neutral' nature. A good critical management research project should thus be based on – or during the time of the project develop – a capacity to develop knowledge of interest from different points of view, for example emancipation/resistance as well as corporate performance. Doing multiple readings based on the different paradigms may, from a postmodern perspective, be seen as optimal; but there are some problems.

Problems with multiple interpretations
One ideal, then, would be to have researchers who are 'multilingual' – researchers who could move across orientations with grace and ease, doing qualified critical research but also having something important to say to mainstream management theory and to practitioners engaged in struggles to sell their products, to

improve quality and productivity, and generally to use their human 'resources' more effectively. Morgan (1986) has been very influential in suggesting research and analysis based on the mastery and use of a variety of metaphors for organizations: machine, organism, brain, culture, psychic prison, etc. In practice, however, this type of teflon-coated multi-perspectival cosmopolitan envisioned by Morgan, and researchers inspired by him (for example, Hassard, 1991) is often both illusionary and weak (see Parker and McHugh, 1991). Good scholars have deep commitments. Multi-perspectivalism often leads to shallow readings and uses of alternative orientations since unexamined basic assumptions have unexpected hidden qualities. Some scholars are more multilingual than others, but doing good work within an orientation still must be prized first. A tenuous balance between tentativeness and commitment is probably a sign of maturity in any scholar. Struggling with understandings and having arguments across programmes of work are important, but it is tricky to bring about an outcome that is well conceived in either synthetic (integrative) or additive (pluralistic, supplementary) terms. Complementarity of forms of research questions and procedures is probably better (see Apel, 1979; Albert et al., 1986).

Complementing critical research: maintaining bilinguality
A realistic ideal for a critical management research – that is research that takes seriously the problems of its own blinkers, the risk of hyper-critique, and that the goal has to be seen as relevant by the large majority of management students and practitioners – is to give priority to good analysis encouraging emancipation and/or resistance, but to work with a less practitioner-unfriendly theme as a secondary theme or interest. Even if full multilinguality is not possible to achieve, a certain level of bilinguality may be possible. By bilinguality and multilinguality we refer not just to the mastery of similar dialects – to master two or more similar languages is not that difficult – but paradigmatically different ones.

Being bilingual in management research is thus not necessarily that hard to accomplish; and such a capacity should not always be utilized. Sometimes – given certain research tasks or field experiences – it is better to use one language than another. In order to develop bilinguality or, given high competence, extend beyond it, intellectual curiosity and the desire to develop the capacity for multiple readings, the metaphor of nomadic theorizing may be fruitful here:

> Theorizing that is nomadic, that ranges across territories of intellectual life is, we believe, more valuable and more interesting than theory that

sticks to its own knitting, secure within its conventions and boundaries. Better boundary-spanning and extension than boundary-maintenance. (Hardy and Clegg, 1997: 14)

Aspirations in this direction must be guided by careful monitoring of the problems and one's own weaknesses: the risk of getting lost is significant. Similar to most societies, marginalized research groups have had to learn two paradigmatic-theoretical systems – their own and the dominant one – and dominant groups only one (Collins, 1988). This means that critical researchers typically have a relatively high degree of bilinguality. Often there is a dismissal and contempt of the socially dominant, normally the first learned language, as critical theories often execrate in the demonstration of the inadequacies of dominant frameworks: functionalism, positivism, managerialism. (Some of our own work may very well be read in this way.) There is a strong tendency that not only any research group dominating over time, but also critical camps, become inward looking, isolated from the problems of the larger society, and filled with blind spots and trained incapacities. Its acts of perpetuation exceed its attempts at social service, its prophets become priests. While this is probably more true for dominant orientations than critical ones, efforts to maintain or restore bilinguality are certainly possible as well as potentially productive for critical management people. To accomplish this calls not solely for theoretical-cognitive efforts, but also for the clarification and working through of emotional commitments and research identities.

An illustration
A brief example may illustrate how interpretive repertoire and empirical material may interact. In a study of an advertising agency, originally guided by an interpretive/cultural theory framework without any specific gender theory development ambitions, it turned out that the gender division of labour was highly salient – and much more so than one would expect in this kind of industry. In the agency there were 11 males, all but one in 'professional' jobs (project manager, art director and copy writer) and 10 females, on average 10 years younger than the males, in jobs as assistants. In addition, all the women were attractive and seemed to care about their appearance. Interestingly, the professionals described themselves, their work and their organization in a vocabulary that matched what are typically described as feminine terms: the advertising professionals are, according to themselves, intuitive, emotional, non-rational; they are very sensitive to personal relations and work environment; they do not like structure,

administration and hierarchy, etc. Their view (or at least account) of the organization resembles many feminist descriptions of feminist organizations and work principles. This was seen as an interesting phenomenon, worthy of further investigation. To note this called for some familiarity with the gender literature, including some understanding of concepts such as cultural masculinity and femininity. But in order to do something more qualified out of this material – as well as produce additional material to the first round of more general observations and interviews – much reading was required to expand and deepen knowledge of gender theory in order to understand the subtle gender dynamics and the paradox of extreme gender of labour, with men in all senior positions in combination with highly 'non-masculine' work and organizational conditions (Alvesson, 1998).

This deepening of some parts of the interpretive repertoire was done during and after fieldwork. The original intention was to develop critical knowledge of the ethical aspects of advertising work – there is much to be said about its consequences on consciousness, self-esteem, pollution, worshipping of youth, impoverishment of language, etc. (Lasch, 1978; Pollay, 1986). This intention, however, was not fulfilled for three reasons:

- the members of the agency refused to discuss ethical issues (explained them away, changed subject);
- the particular site of study turned out to work with business-to-business communication, which tends to be more informative than advertising promoting consumer goods;
- other interesting aspects (such as gender and identity) attained interest.

See Alvesson, 1994, 1998; Alvesson and Köping, 1993.

Summary

To sum up this chapter, we think that critical management research, like all research, needs some mastery of different theories and aspects in order to facilitate openness in relation to empirical material. Critical management research must address sensitivity in two vital respects. One is the making of sophisticated interpretations of empirical material where it is 'depth structures' rather than surface manifestations that are of interest. Two interpretive strategies in critical research are helpful here: de-familiarization and dissensus reading. De-familiarization aims to turn the well known into something strange, thus making it less self-evident, natural and unavoidable. Dissensus readings break up established meanings and closure in how we reason through exploring language. A rich interpretive repertoire is particularly significant in order not to become swamped by conventional understandings of empirical material but to be able to produce de-familiarization and dissensus as significant ingredients in, and outcomes of, the critical research process.

Sensitivity must, however, also guide critical management research so that it is not caught in its scepticism and perpetual critique. We think that the problem of 'hyper-critique', involving unfair descriptions and other problems associated with a biased negativity, must be taken seriously. The chapter discusses the possibilities of making critical research less anti-management and more relevant for organizational practitioners.

Working solely with critical theory gives direction, commitment and sharpness, but may lead to a somewhat closed attitude to empirical material, an inclination to hyper-critique and a marginalization in relation to groups not primarily interested in critical understandings. Combining insights from different schools may solve some of these problems, but broadening the interpretive repertoire also to incorporate knowledge which gives a fair chance of seeing aspects in empirical material that may be productively used also for other purposes than emancipation-stimulation, may have several advantages. It may bring about richer, and more varied and carefully considered interpretations as more meanings may be detected and different languages can be used, thus facilitating critical as well as 'non-critical' interpretations and results. More significantly, it makes the critical project less bounded by its reliance on detecting indications on domination, repression and closure, and facilitates bridging to other streams and concerns.

Interpretative repertoires are to a very large degree an outcome of the researcher's life history, and before and during a specific project it may be difficult radically to develop or expand it, but there are always some possibilities in moderately modifying it. Over a longer time span, and during specific phases with limited time pressure, radical expansions and/or shifts in emphasis may be possible. Encounters with rich empirical material may here have triggering effects – and hopefully in the future more so than is currently common in empirical critical management research.

8

On the practice of critical management research

Critical researchers, like most qualitative researchers, conduct case studies. Qualitative case studies, whether critical or not, rely mainly on interviews and observation of real settings for getting empirical material. In addition, archival material (texts of various kinds) and secondary sources, for example biographies by executives and other people, may be useful. The methods available for the qualitative researcher working in a particular site is 'asking questions', 'hanging out' or 'reading texts' (Dingwall, 1997). Of course, all kinds of quantitative material may also be utilized in mainly qualitative research: statistics, questionnaires, counting of occurrences, content analysis, tests, and so on. We will here restrict ourselves to discuss four issues of specific interest for critical management research: the problem of access; interviews; ethnographies; and finally, in particular, a version of ethnography which we label a partial ethnography.

Access

All management researchers encounter problems with access. Ideally, the researcher may wish to choose the site for her or his study without constraint: picking the ideal case company and the parts of it that appear of most interest and relevance, being entirely free to talk to any person about any issue, and having no restrictions in terms of participating and observing everyday work life as well as important situations. Of course, in practice there are all sorts of problems. A company may not want to let a researcher in for various reasons. Introducing and guiding a researcher takes some time and energy; participating in interviews takes even more. As Easterby-Smith et al. (1991) point out, one of the characteristics of senior managers, compared to many other people, is that they tend to be heavily occupied; this makes interviewing difficult.

Further, critical research may be especially problematic in terms of getting access. Projected research results may not be perceived as very useful for those allowing access, and may even be seen as directly negative for them and the company. From some perspectives critical empirical research may be seen as impossible, if carried out honestly and explicitly. Why should corporate managers allow a valuable corporate resource – time – to be used against their own and maybe the company's interest? While there is no necessary contradiction between the type of open participatory organization we hope to promote and making a reasonable profit, the perception may easily be otherwise. The question of access is similar in some respects and yet different in others from other types of organizational research. These complexities require attention.

Of course, options exist even when conventional access is difficult. In some cases, one may rely on secondary sources or approach individuals without getting the approval of the corporate management. One may interview people who have left the organization being studied, an issue we take up later. In some special cases one may take a job at the workplace and take notes based on informal interaction and observation. Under such circumstances one takes on special ethical responsibilities. Since organizational members cannot give informed consent, the research text must be somewhat more general and completely anonymous.

If we take a more typical situation of a researcher wanting to make a case study of a company that will entail interviews and participant observation, the research project needs to be approved by the appropriate senior managers. Even if critical issues are to be pursued, the researcher can argue for the openness of the approach and suggest a non-offensive description for the overall project. One of us has good experience with the phrase 'corporate culture in knowledge-intensive companies'. This sounds good and relevant without dishonesty, and has the advantage of eliminating very little in terms of possible foci for the study. Jackall (1988), in contrast, tried 'ethics in managerial work', which proved to make access very difficult in US companies.

Critical research takes on a special responsibility to produce something that is experienced as relevant for those being studied. This does not have to be a typical managerial issue, but may relate to gender, stress or other work experiences. One may consider producing different versions of the research report: one for internal use and one, where the corporate identity is disguised, for the public. A broad interpretative repertoire, making the researcher capable of interacting with and producing something of value for practitioners, is of course of great value here.

One may distinguish between surface access and depth access. One may get approval for interviewing people and doing some observations, for example of public or other open events (corridor behaviour, public speeches), but this does not qualify as depth access. It may still be hard to get interviews fixed and interviewees may be restrictive in their accounts. Depth access means that one can arrange the interviews one wants to do, get interviewees to produce rich accounts, and have considerable access also to 'non-public' or internal settings for making observations, for example the 'real' leadership or decision-making situations. We develop a few ideas on the subject of how to get beyond surface access in the following section on interviews.

Interviews

Undoubtedly the most common qualitative method is the loosely structured interview. Much has been written on it and we have no intention to cover the literature or even to do a quick review of types of interviews, purposes of these or traps and techniques worth considering (see for example, Easterby-Smith et al., 1991; Fontana and Frey, 1994; Kvale, 1996).

Most see the interview as a difficult but highly useful method for getting valuable information and viewpoints from people living in the reality one is interested in. As many researchers define qualitative research as dealing with meaningful phenomena (meanings, not frequencies is sometimes used as a catchword), interviews become indispensable. It is difficult – or at least more time-consuming – to appreciate the meanings, ideas and understandings of a group of people if one has not talked with them. There are, however, as we saw in Chapter 4, increasing doubts as to whether interviews can be used for adequately tapping into subjects' experiences, feelings, observations and values (Hollway, 1989; Potter and Wetherell, 1987; Silverman, 1993). The big question is whether accounts in interviews refer to something external to the interview situation and the language use – either what goes on in people's heads and hearts or a social reality 'out there' – or are a reflection of the interview situation as a complex social setting, and all the norms and scripts for expression which guide verbal behaviour in such settings (for the latter view, see Dingwall, 1997; Silverman, 1993 and, for a defence against the critique, see Miller and Glassner, 1997).

Our response is that one has to manoeuvre between two unhelpful positions. The first is the naïve humanism assuming that there is a pre-fabricated set of feelings, experiences and knowledges that the qualified researcher, through interactive skills, can truthfully capture on the tape recorder. The second is the hyperscepticism and too narrow micro-focus which assumes that human beings are necessarily tightly restricted by rules for language use, and conformist adaptation to scripts and norms for how one expresses oneself in a particular situation. Social context – for example the interview situation – matters for the accounts produced by an interviewee. And language does not simply mirror people's minds or social reality. Both are complications that need to be taken seriously when appreciating interview accounts, but interviews may still give rich, imaginative indications of how a person may feel, think, reflect and tell an interviewer something valuable about what goes in the organization.

All interview material, therefore, calls for careful critical reflection. It must be interpreted in terms of possible qualities going beyond script-following accounts and impression management. The material is seldom innocent or can just be processed, it is never pure data (except as empirical material indicating how a specific interviewee talked in an interviewed situation). Interview data can be used to show interesting features of corporate reality beyond the artefacts of the micro-setting of the interview situation. The researcher should reach such a judgement only after careful evaluation and the researcher should present good reasons why he or she takes interview accounts as valid and reliable indications of social reality.

One cannot get around the context-dependency of the interview statements – one cannot neglect that they are produced in a specific social situation and that language games are important. The metaphorical, constitutive, and performance-oriented aspects of talk cannot be disregarded. However, one may still think through and reduce some of the more obvious problems, including those salient to a critical management research project. One such problem concerns self-censorship and caution in interviews related to corporate and organizational issues. These are highly politicized; being perceived as unreliable is extremely dangerous for managers (Jackall, 1988). One should, therefore, be prepared not to see interviewees as truth-tellers but as politically conscious actors. Such actors may, however, produce informative accounts.

Easterby-Smith et al. (1991) present several examples of how managers seem to respond more openly and freely when interviewed outside their offices on more neutral ground, for example in a restaurant or in a first-class compartment on a train. There are, of course, other tricks: matching interviewer and interviewee in terms of gender, age, ethnicity, educational background; being there for some time, developing closer relations with interviewees, perhaps doing repeat interviews. Apart from being more innovative in interviewing than just meeting people at their offices with one's tape recorder ready and perhaps avoiding too much social distance, other means to get people to talk about more politically and personally sensitive experiences and observations may be considered.

Reassuring interviewees about anonymity is, of course, trivial and yet vital. One may do so several times and stress the reasons for why the interviewees should believe the research interviewer, for example, the independence of the researcher, research ethics, his or her self-interest (that is, their research career is dependent upon being perceived as absolutely trustworthy in this respect). Tapes may be a source of worry. If the researcher uses a tape recorder, he or she may offer to switch it off during specific parts of the interview. He or she may also offer to refrain from directly using certain pieces of information, assuming that this may encourage the interviewee to talk more openly. The researcher may then not cite it, even anonymously, but simply refer to a phenomenon without the support of a direct quote. This may be frustrating, but it is clearly better to listen to accounts about sensitive materials within such constraints than to be ignorant about them altogether.

Interviewing should not be restricted to the people currently working at a company. People who have left – changed employer, retired, are on maternity leave – are often better informants, as they may have some distance from the company and, therefore, a clearer perspective on it, and they probably feel much freer in terms of what they can and will say. Of course, a drawback may be that their experiences are a little out of date. We have ourselves in some projects contacted former employees and got very valuable accounts from them, of specific relevance for critical work. Of course, there may be a negative bias among some people who have left, but it is probably less strong and much less problematic than the positive one of people who are still in the company, and who are normally under considerable normative pressure to appear positive, committed and loyal. Also the need to rationalize one's employment in a specific organization may lead to positive story-telling. In an article on ITT, *Business Week* addresses the big meetings reviewing subsidiary monthly performances (see Chapter 7):

> Some former employees complain that the big meetings reek of Kafkanesque courts, of volleys of verbal invective fired at under-achievers. 'Many of us have frankly left the organization for having been spit upon publicly', says a former European unit manager. Geneen, by contrast, views the meetings as open, business-like forums at which

participants try to help each other. (*Business Week* 3 Nov., 1973, cited in Hopper and Macintosh, 1993: 207)

Of course, the former employees may have been more sensitive to these meetings than others or may be inclined to rationalize their departure from ITT and present employment, but nevertheless still reveal interesting aspects compared to what people still in the company may be inclined to do.

Perhaps more important and perhaps less self-evidently is to use the method of what may be labelled 'drilling'. This means that the researcher in the research process learns more and more about the case study object and that this learning may facilitate the transcendence of norms and scripts that otherwise may guide interview statements. When getting some interview accounts that highlight sensitive or problematic issues, the researcher may use this material in subsequent interviews. Through demonstrating knowledge about these sensitive issues the researcher shows that he or she is trusted by other informants and is transcending the dividing line between outsider and insider. The researcher also shows that other people talk about certain kinds of issues. One may be explicit about this: 'other interviewees have mentioned that ...'. In this way the norm held by others – they talk about these things – is shown. The researcher also shows that he or she does not reveal the identity of informants: of course the researcher must not say who has told what (and should be careful about not revealing viewpoints that an insider may track to a specific person). Gradually, more and more inside and sensitive issues can thus be put on the agenda in interviews and interviewees are likely to fuel this process. Through drilling one may gradually explore the 'deeper' aspects of those phenomena one wants to investigate. Developing trust and getting more knowledge is essential to all organizational research. But in the context of critical research and the political nature of management phenomena, this also means struggling with norms and normalization that emphasize reliability and giving a good impression of oneself and the organization – and the adherence to established rules and scripts for how one talks about (or avoids talking about) particular issues. Drilling may, therefore, be seen as a process where the norms for interview talk are redefined and some of the 'research-inhibiting' disciplinary effects of organizational loyalty, impression management and risk avoidance may be reduced.

Drilling is a means of working one's way towards depth access in the research process. The process may be facilitated by referring to experiences from other organizations, published research and theories that 'normalize' the addressing of certain issues. One may, for example, say: 'in other companies I have encountered, women have had difficulties …' or 'according to the literature, politics and conflicts are very much a part of corporate life …'. There is, of course, a risk that the researcher too persuasively leads the interviewee into saying certain things, but the risk of very open questions fueling uncertainty and leading to the reproduction of official stories is probably often more profound. Perhaps the best option is to bear in mind that 'normalizing' describing organizations also in non-formal, non-rational terms (politics, male domination) may encourage the production of particular kinds of accounts and it is advisable to use it as a vehicle only if and when one gets stuck in cautious interviews.

The purpose of drilling is not necessarily to come close to the genuine feelings, thoughts, values and experiences of people or to get them, objectively and accurately, to report about things 'out there' ('the truth behind the appearances'). Although we do not want to dismiss this possibility, as explained in Chapter 4 there are problems with holding such expectations of interviewees and interview material (and other kinds of empirical material as well). Still, accounts of corporate life may point at hidden and not so nice aspects, thus contributing to critical imagination and the chances of offering ideas on how we can understand forms of domination.

Another, perhaps more general problem in terms of using interview material in addition to and beyond the interview setting relates to the multitude of identities and subjectivities that can be constituted in interactive situations such as interviews. As briefly discussed in Chapter 4, an interviewee can be interpellated (approached in terms of) and respond from a variety of subject positions, meaning that quite diverse accounts may be expected. What subject positions become actualized is partly dependent on how the researcher relates to the interviewee (frames the situation, for example in terms of his or her own background, interest, purpose in conducting the interview and the research project), and what specific questions and vocabularies are used. But there is no simple mechanics here as how the interviewee him- or herself frames (reframes) the situation and associates with the interviewer and her or his own talk cannot be controlled by the researcher. The researcher cannot anticipate, for example, how the interviewee may react to words like 'gender' and 'equality' in interviews or to a particular self-presentation (such as, 'I am a Ph.D. student in management and am doing research on corporate ethics').

What can be done is that before and during the interview the kinds of identities and subject positions that are possible and that seem to be experienced can be considered and the identity interpellations varied so that different kinds of responses are produced. One can address a person not only as a female manager, but also as a woman, as a manager, an engineer, a subordinate, a person having been in the company for two years, etc. Varied responses, then, may provide rich empirical material, less useful for discovering one overall, coherent, summarizing meaning (what the respondent 'really means') than a variety of somewhat inconsistent meanings. Of these some may be particularly informative in terms of pointing at repressed conflicts, contradictions and other aspects of interest for critical research.

Much more, of course, can be said about interviewing, but we rest our case with these comments on a few points that we think are of general relevance for qualitative work, but especially so for critical management research.

Ethnography

As discussed in Chapter 4, ethnography has aroused increased interest, perhaps partly as a consequence of increasing awareness of problems with interviews. Its reliance on first-hand experiences and combination of participant observation and interviews allows the researcher to go beyond relying solely on interview accounts. When carried out in the context of an ethnography, interviews are also likely to be more revealing. The researcher can use his or her first-hand impressions and ask more informed questions; additionally, his or her long-term presence means that interviewees feel more open and relaxed in interview situations.

In Chapter 4 we pointed out a number of problems with ethnography. In the context of critical research, the risk of being swamped by all the impressions and the enormous job of sorting out all empirical material may mean that the critical analysis is lost or at least weakened, or that a researcher holds rigidly to a particular theory. It is very difficult to work with a lot of empirical material and carefully interpret its multiple meanings at the same time, even in the same project.

Thomas (1993) cites the following points in connection with critically–oriented research projects: ontology, choice of subject, method, analysis and interpretation of data, discourse, and reflection upon the whole research process. Thomas follows much the same model as that used by practitioners of more traditional, inductive ethnography but adds a highly significant element of a critical character. Critical ethnography, according to Thomas:

1 views cultural phenomena in more critical terms (accentuating the repressive and circumscribing aspects of culture);

2 chooses its subject matter (focus) in terms of injustices, control, etc.;
3 is more inclined to scepticism with regard to data and information;
4 adopts a de-familiarizing mode in its interpretations (tries to avoid established ways of thinking and emphasizes whatever is non-natural in the phenomenon under study);
5 considers language in terms of power;
6 reflects upon the research process itself – how has the researcher's involvement affected the data;
7 asks about the broader relevance of the research, that is how do we answer the question 'so what'?

Thomas contended that in such a form critical ethnography can counteract the focus on professional technique and authority that characterizes most empirical studies in the social sciences. Of course, this makes the research more difficult to conduct. If a researcher should carry out all this in a sophisticated manner and do perhaps a year-long fieldwork study, the work of an average ethnographer is far exceeded both in terms of the amount of work (readings, interpretations) and the intellectual challenge involved.

The fieldwork ambitions may need to be cut somewhat in order to do qualified interpretations, raise critique, point at possibilities of transformative re-definitions, and thus accomplish de-familiarization and dissensus readings. Of course, there are a variety of forms of ethnographies, both in terms of their purpose and focus (Baszanger and Dodier, 1997) and the amount of empirical work, but we feel that 'having been there' for some time is important. Having a certain depth understanding of the local context as well as a general understanding of cultural context is essential in order to qualify for the label ethnography. One does not, however, have to stick to the old anthropological norm of being at least one year in the field, but can limit and concentrate the efforts. Some weeks of participant observation is, according to our experience, sometimes sufficient. In studying organizations, the problem is not only or primarily one of getting close to the 'natives' and understanding the unfamiliar, it is – as pointed out in Chapter 7 – one of achieving distance and critical perspective on things that too easily are seen as normal, natural and rational. Critical ethnography then may reduce the period in the field and expand the time for doing something critically imaginative with the material. Our ideas on case studies outlined above may facilitate such a move. Nevertheless, the very idea of an ethnography is still rather time-consuming in terms of fieldwork. As an alternative, therefore, we suggest that a partial ethnography be considered.

A partial ethnography: a situational focus

What may be referred to as a situational approach is highly consistent with and helpful in accomplishing some of the ideals discussed above. A situational focus means that a particular situation – a meeting, a job interview, a spontaneous encounter, an event, a decision process, a problem or a task delimited in time and space – rather than stable behaviour patterns, attitudes or traits is the focus of study. It is empirically studied as a core phenomenon, that is 'leadership action' or a 'service encounter' rather than talk about it or square-ticking behaviour on questionnaires is studied. In a situational focus, actors as well as the institutional context are present. Compared to an ethnography it covers far less empirical ground. The focus makes it easier than with most other methods to describe the empirical material so that it is open for other interpretations. Given the problems of elitism in social research – including much critical research – this strikes us as an advantage.

Process in an institutional context

With a situational focus the individual actors, as well as the institutional context in which they live, find clear expression. The social context is manifestly linked to the individuals who act within it and to the actions performed (Collins, 1981; Johansson, 1990; Knorr-Cetina, 1981). By focusing on a particular event, the organizational process is placed firmly in the centre. By adopting this focus we move the spotlight away from any assumptions about the consistent and unambiguous nature (or the opposite) of the people involved. Interest can turn on the multiple and indeterminate aspects of social processes and relations and the actions of subjects. Of course, it is also possible with a situational focus to emphasize the actor as central or to see what is happening as an expression of structural properties, that is downplaying the importance of the individuals concerned. But the general idea is to avoid such reductionism and take into account several aspects without giving priority to any of them. In the vocabulary of Kenneth Burke (1969), the act (what took place?), the agent(s) (who performed the act), the scene (what is the context in which it occurred?), the purpose (why was it done?) and agency (how was it done?) are considered. Even though one may – indeed sometimes must – give these different elements various weights and degrees of attention in specific cases, any specific element should not be viewed in isolation from the others and allowed to completely dominate the description and analysis. The agent should, for example, be seen as partly formed by the scene (context) in which he or she acts, while the scene (for instance the organization or its environment) is affected by the agent(s) involved and their acts.

Providing an account that is open for various interpretations
The delimited empirical phenomena may be described 'thickly' (that is, a rather rich and detailed account) so that it may be interpreted, without too much constraint, from different angles of approach than the one favoured by the researcher offering the account (Alvesson, 1996). Since the empirical material is restricted but fairly completely presented, the reader can evaluate and reconsider the interpretations and conclusions of the researcher. Fewer of the data are hidden by coding and, since the researcher's ethnographic authority is somewhat less, the engagement of the reader is more invited. Restricting the empirical phenomena under scrutiny makes the description less strongly coloured by the researcher's framework and the use of empirical material as rhetorical support less salient than if one presents (highly) selected extracts from, say 30 open interviews or a year-long ethnography. In saying this we do not mean to understate the problem of reproducing the empirical material in the text – representation is always problematic – but simply to point out that it is less evident than with many other approaches. The extensive material collected in a full ethnography is always collected, constructed, and (selectively) presented along the lines of a theoretical framework (possibly in the sense of a set of taken-for-granted ideas). This presentation will reflect the norms of (part of) the research community that the researcher identifies with, the idiosyncrasies of the researcher and, in the case of interviews, the interaction dynamics constructing the interview situation, whether the researcher wants it or not (Alvesson and Sköldberg, 2000). Such a construction process is less active and salient in the approach suggested here, as data are not constructed in interviews or surveys where the researcher must actively produce responses for something to happen. Arguably, the 'bias' (closure of interpretive possibilities) in describing the event or process with a situational focus may be relatively weak, compared to other approaches.

The work methodology
The situational study includes a certain amount of ethnographic work in order, first, to get local knowledge of the work organization and, second, to get access to a number of situations in order to find one (or more) to concentrate on. This may take some weeks of intensive study. The researched situation is then described in detail, either in terms of transcribed tape recordings – if it is a highly delimited situation such as a short meeting or a section of

an interaction – or in terms of relatively detailed notes if the situation is somewhat more extended in time and space, thus calling for summaries in the description. Different criteria may be used for the choice of situation. It may be relatively typical or everyday; it may be atypical but perceived as significant, for example a meeting prior to a major corporate change; or it may be seen as simply interesting because it breaks with established norms and taken-for-granted assumptions. It may exhibit strong domination, that is a manager talking down to his or her group, or be more symmetrical in interaction. It may be useful for the exploration of various leadership themes, for example socialization, punishment, social integration, initiating structure, or the generation of new ideas. The researcher may use different types of situations for different purposes. Most important is that they function in an inspiring way for him or her, and that he or she is explicit and reflective about the use.

What about generalization from the situation? The situation should be seen as saying something interesting about what goes on in the specific situation but also be revealing in terms of understanding some other situations. For example, if a situational study allows the illumination of some aspects of male domination, this does not mean that such domination forms the average pattern in the (type of) organization that is 'hosting' the focused situation. Still, it may be informative in grasping certain aspects of such domination, irrespective of when and where a version of this domination materializes in social interaction. A balance between going beyond the specific case and avoiding generalizing consistency in human behaviour (also in the case of one organization or the people figuring in the situation) should be aspired to (Alvesson, 1996). Thus theoretical rather than empirical generalization is aimed for. The idea of qualitative research is, as remarked above, to explore the meaning of social phenomena, including forms of repression, not to count instances and make claims about frequencies.

Interviews with the people involved should be conducted, if the researcher is not certain that he or she can make interesting observations directly based on local knowledge achieved through ethnographic work and his or her own analysis. Interviews normally complement the description of what happened in the situation through giving some clues (though these remain uncertain) about the participant's meanings, intentions and interpretations of what took place. The situational focus – including the knowledge the researcher has of it – may restrict the tendency of interviewees to provide abstract answers with limited anchorage in 'real' events, that is counteract what may be referred to as 'moral storytelling' in interviews. The combination of various pieces of empirical material – direct observation and interviewees' accounts – gives a broad and rich picture of the situation concerned. For examples of this kind of approach in critical management and organization studies, see Alvesson (1996), Forester (1992), Knights and Willmott (1987, 1992), Kunda (1992), Rosen (1985) and Smircich (1983). That so much of the critical work in management has adapted an approach at least akin to what we here refer to as a partial ethnography indicates its usefulness for this kind of research – even though, of course, it can also be used for other research purposes.

The situational focus differs from ethnography in three ways. First, the purpose is to explore and learn from a situation and not an entire cultural system. The knowledge gained during a shorter time of informal talk and observation is used primarily in order to identify a good situation and achieve background knowledge – it is thus not, as in an ethnography, used mainly for detailed analysis and description. Secondly, the limited focus of the situational study makes it possible to describe the empirical material in some detail. Finally, the concentration of this type of study makes more intensive interpretations possible. The empirical material gathered and/ or constructed during an ethnography (often a year long) normally calls for extensive work with data production, systematization, analysis and presentation. The time and energy left for depth interpretation is reduced. The ethnography-based text is typically more independent of the organizational processes and relations it studies than the impression that the research text suggests. The writer is usually forced to be highly selective in the presentation of the story. Even the most complete ethnography still has a fictional character, see Clifford, 1986; Van Maanen, 1988; Watson, forthcoming). Of course, an ethnography may include or lead to one or several situational studies (for example, Rosen, 1985), so the distinction is far from always razor sharp.

Advantages and disadvantages of a situational focus
The drawback of this focus on a particular event is that such events are limited in time, space and representativeness. One risks giving a somewhat selective impression of the management–organization context of the phenomenon under study. A certain amount of contextual knowledge is needed, but the suggested focus implies that such knowledge is primarily limited to enabling an understanding of events but should not be used for far-reaching generalizations inside or outside the organization. The particular event under scrutiny can hardly be used as the only springboard for an account of the whole history of the particular group or event in an

organizational setting studied. Nor does it particularly tell us a great deal about outcomes or causalities, apart from temporary ones. Moreover, this focus means that the insights and ideas of the research subjects are not directly exploited to the same extent as a stronger actor-and-meanings orientation, typically associated with an interview study.

These problems should not be exaggerated. Far-reaching generalizations may also be a problematic ideal at the level of a single organization, as organizations and management are perhaps equally well – or better – thought about in terms of ambiguity, variation, multiple orderings and fragmentation than order, patterns and averages (Alvesson, 1993a; Law, 1994; Martin, 1992). The part of the study aiming to get a sufficient understanding of contextual matters should allow the researcher to say something with a somewhat broader empirical bearing than solely on the situation targeted. Accounts in interviews that interact productively with the observations of the situation – the accounts may offer interesting pieces to the puzzle – may be fully utilized as long as they are not taken for granted and draw attention away from the situation focused upon.

On the other hand, the approach has some advantages. Interpreting a particular event means acquiring a limited but, one may hope, profound and enlightening insight into certain aspects of the social relations and processes in companies. Importantly, the emphasis is placed on the processual aspects. As several authors have suggested, there is a need for a sociology and an organization theory of verbs and to study modes of ordering rather than social order (for example, Hosking, 1988; Law, 1994). Here the strongest methodological advantages of the approach suggested are that it allows for the detailed description of naturally occurring events. As stated above, a lot of empirical work is, in various ways, artificial and too remote from 'core empirical phenomena' and may, therefore, tell us rather little of what actually goes on in acts of (or possibly interpreted in terms of) management. The type of study advocated here has a depth and precision in terms of the quality of the empirical material which are radically different from those typical in most other kinds of studies. The democratic value in presenting a description that readers themselves can make their own interpretations of, carefully evaluating the claims of the author, is an advantage compared to work where selective empirical material, normally supporting the author's claims, is included in the text.

Finally, it should be emphasized that the situational focus means that more time and energy is left for interpretive and reflexive work: the mechanics of data 'collection' are subordinated to creative sense-making and intensive interpretation of the material. Given the difficulties of working with empirical material in a sophisticated way, this is perhaps the single most crucial advantage.

A brief illustration

We shall briefly illustrate the situational approach through an extract from a study one of us did focusing on an 'information meeting' about the reorganization of a Swedish industrial company (Alvesson, 1996). Present during this two-hour long meeting were 100 employees who were low and middle-level managers. The interpretation of the first utterance of the top manager is several pages long, but for reasons of space only the first part of it will be presented here.

> The top manager, the head of the business sector, begins the meeting by saying: 'Why are you here? That is because you are managers at IndCo.' He seems to be keen to emphasize that those present are 'managers'. This is why they have been invited. No doubt they understood this anyway, but a reminder of this aspect of their status does no harm. Arguably, the idea is to reinforce the sense of responsibility associated with the role and perhaps to give them some small confirmation of their identities. The opportunity to participate in the meeting – to 'meet' (listen to and observe) the head of their sector – could also be seen as a kind of symbolic reward. Those present belong to 'the chosen few'. They are being informed about the change one day before the rest of the personnel. But the agenda and the content were roughly the same on both occasions.
>
> Referring to a specific group of people as 'managers' is not always obvious. Appointing somebody to a particular formal position is not becoming a manager fully since the identity and the ideology (discourse) which characterize the person in question are also crucial factors. It is not obvious that people who are given such positions regard themselves primarily as managers (even at second or third hand), or that they are regarded as managers by their environment. The crucial factor, in this context, is the capacity in which they have been interpelled, 'called' – we have only to think of all the possible identities and ideologies which are available (cf. Deetz, 1992; Therborn, 1980). For example, a person with the title of 'department manager' is (or may be viewed as) a manager, a professional (for example an engineer or a marketer), a subordinate and a colleague – as well as a friend, a member of a family, a female, middle-aged, perhaps a 'green', a union member, and so on. People are subject to a variety of other people's expectations and efforts to put them into categories and a variety of self-constructs.
>
> The meanings of and membership within the categories of discursive practice will be constant sites of struggle over power, as identity is posited, resisted and fought over in its attachment to the subjectivity by which individuality is constructed (Clegg, 1989: 151). In the United

States, for example, university organizations have struggled over the appropriate name for the 'administrative head' of an academic department. Are they to be 'Chairs', 'Heads', or 'Departmental Executive Officers'? Each is a very different kind of 'manager', and has different implied relationships to other department members and 'higher' administration. Are these 'managers' performing intellectual leadership, a service function, or authority and control? Implicit in these distinctions are views of the university as a whole and the relation of professionals (faculty in this case) to administration. Could all administration be out-sourced as a peripheral service function or are faculty simply employees providing one of many university products?

Corporate management competes with other groups and categories for the individual's time, self-perception, attention and loyalty. Ideally, from top management's point of view, 'managers' should regard themselves primarily as company people. It is therefore important to maintain and reinforce this identity of theirs. Appealing to them as 'managers' also means that certain ideas and values about the job are being accentuated: it is a question of responsibility, loyalty, work morale, result orientation, etc. Thus, it is an important task for top management continually to constitute people who take 'managership' very seriously, and who give priority to values, ideas, feelings and actions associated with being a 'manager'. At the present meeting this is what is taking place (on a small scale). The basic idea of the meeting could be to remind people that they should perceive the reorganization through pro-managerial spectacles. (From Alvesson, 1996: ch. 3.)

One can, of course – based on this interpretation – raise more general ideas about leadership as a process in which the interpellation of identities is an important element. Leadership is then viewed as working through the regulation of identities; social expectations and self-images are invoked which contribute to the leader being able to frame issues and control meaning. The more or less conscious and instrumental, explicit or implicit switching and de-switching of diverse identities is then viewed as salient in leadership work.

It is not our purpose here to develop this idea or situate it in relationship to earlier work. It just illustrates how links between the detailed study of an empirical material and wider theoretical concerns can be made.

Final thoughts and conclusions

Critical management research may, of course, be conducted in a multitude of ways. There are many sources of theoretical inspiration – of which we have only addressed Frankfurt School critical theory and some versions of postmodernism – and many ways of engaging in research practices. Common for all critical research is the ambition to stir things up, to challenge the ongoing reproduction of modes of social ordering evaluated to constrain human possibilities. Critical management research aims to reduce the pre-structured limitations of thinking, feeling and relating to established values, practices and institutions. Ideals such as *de-familiarization* – making the well known, natural and self-evident into something strange, arbitrary and possible to redo or undo – and *dissensus* – disruptions of consensus and seemingly harmonious, robust meanings – may then work as overall methodological guidelines. Each of these ideals may be connected to either critical theory's more optimistic goals of facilitating emancipation – for example, through less distorted communicative action – or Foucault's more 'defensive' project of temporarily weakening power through acts of resistance.

All research can be seen as a struggle between closeness and distance, between being familiar with the site under study and being able not to be caught by this familiarity. In qualitative research getting close to the people we try to understand, getting a feeling for their meanings, ideas, consciousness, wants, practices and constraints is always important. The other side of the coin, creating intellectual distance so that we can see things in novel light and opening up new intellectual worlds, is also important. The problem with most neo-positivistic work is that it accomplishes neither. Questionnaires and laboratory studies typically mean a poor understanding of context and meaning; these values are typically sacrificed for the purpose of abstractions and finding law-like patterns. In most conventional qualitative work closeness is privileged. Existing orders are taken for granted and privileged. In most qualitative research there is tendency to give priority to distance (cf. the debate between interpretivists and critical theories in Putnam et al., 1993).

Emphasizing distance is certainly a productive research strategy in many areas, for example when macro issues such as the nature of late capitalist society (Adorno and Horkheimer, 1979 [1947]), McDonaldization (Ritzer, 1996), or the impact of mass media (Boorstin, 1961) are addressed. In critical management research the situation is typically a bit different. Here research should, according to our opinion, have things to say to actors – managers and (other) employees – that is of relevance for their situation. This calls for appreciation of constraints and contingencies of work practices. A primary task of companies and other organizations is the production of goods and services (even though this is not the only thing of interest and one may well argue for a downplaying of ideals of productivity in what Carter and Jackson [1987] refer to as post-affluent society). Organizational life can never, or at least not within the foreseeable future, be the ultimate site for emancipation from every form of domination or resistance to every form of disciplinary power. The struggle for emancipation may nevertheless reduce socially unnecessary forms of constraints and suffering, and loosen the grip of the net of techniques for disciplinary power. This struggle should be informed by careful consideration of the forms and degrees of management control and, in particular, coordination deemed relevant and legitimate in specific sites under study. This calls for a fair amount of sensitive listening to and consideration of the local situation, including taking managerial viewpoints seriously. The balance between closeness and distance thus calls for several considerations. Closeness is vital in order, first, to study how consciousness and subjectivity bear the imprint of ideological domination and disciplinary power and, secondly, to understand business, practical considerations and requirements for productive work. Distance is necessary so that it is possible: to see how ideologies, cultural conventions, capitalist regimes and institutionalized orders operate behind the backs of people under study; to evaluate how business and management tasks may be perspectivated and reformed in order to reduce the contradiction between emancipatory and coercive-instrumental values; and to be able to interpret established social reality in a genuinely novel light (de-familiarization).

We live in a time partly ruled by ideologies and practices of managerialism (Deetz, 1992). We can rightly talk about the managerialization of the world. In this light, critical management research is very important as an antidote. The challenge is to develop such research so that it is not too easily dismissed as unfair and irrelevant. This calls for a much stronger interest in empirical work than has characterized critical scholars in management so far, although the situation is improving. Critical theory and Foucault's ideas offer extremely powerful and inspiring stimuli for rethinking contemporary society and its institutions, including management. The shortage of empirical projects is only to a minor extent a consequence of the lack of methodologies for critical management research. Critical scholars have chosen to give priority to conceptual work. There are also problems in accomplishing a nice interaction between critical ideas and inspiration from field experiences. Nevertheless, it is our hope that this book offers methodological help and encouragement for more empirically sensitive critical research projects as well as a more critical and reflexive redirection of management and organization research methods. Both are much needed.

References

Abercrombie, N., Hill, S. and Turner, B.S. (1980) *The Dominant Ideology Thesis*. London: Allen and Unwin.

Acker, J., Barry, K. and Esseveld, J. (1991) 'Objectivity and truth: problems in doing feminist research', in M. Fonow and J. Cook (eds), *Beyond Methodology: Feminist Scholarship as Lived Research*. Bloomington, IN: Indiana University Press.

Adorno, T. and Horkheimer, M. (1979 [1947]) *The Dialectics of Enlightenment*. New York: Verso.

Agar, M.H. (1986) *Speaking of Ethnography*. Beverly Hills, CA: Sage.

Albert, M., Cagan, L., Chomsky, N., Hahnel, R., King, M., Sargent, L. and Sklar, H. (eds) (1986) *Liberating Theory*. Boston, MA: South End Press.

Alvesson, M. (1987) *Organization Theory and Technocratic Consciousness: Rationality, Ideology, and Quality of Work*. Berlin/New York: de Gruyter.

Alvesson, M. (1990) 'Organization: from substance to image?', *Organization Studies*, 11: 373–94.

Alvesson, M. (1993a) *Cultural Perspectives on Organizations*. Cambridge: Cambridge University Press.

Alvesson, M. (1993b) 'The play of metaphors', in J. Hassard and M. Parker (eds), *Postmodernism and Organizations*. London: Sage.

Alvesson, M. (1994) 'Talking in organizations. Managing identity and impressions in an advertising agency', *Organization Studies*, 15: 535–63.

Alvesson, M. (1995) 'The meaning and meaninglessness of postmodernism: some ironic remarks', *Organization Studies*, 15: 1047–75.

Alvesson, M. (1996) *Communication, Power and Organization*. Berlin/New York: de Gruyter.

Alvesson, M. (1998) 'Gender relations and identity at work: a case study of masculinities and femininities in an advertising agency', *Human Relations*, 51 (8): 969–1005.

Alvesson, M. and Björkman, I. (1992) *Organisationsidentitet och organisationsbyggande. En studie av ett industriföretag*. Lund: Studentlitteratur.

Alvesson, M. and Billing, Y.D. (1997) *Understanding Gender and Organization*. London: Sage.

Alvesson, M. and Kärreman, D. (2000) 'Taking the linguistic turn'. *Journal of Applied Behavioural Science* (in press).

Alvesson, M. and Köping, A.-S. (1993) *Med känslan som ledstjärna. En studie av reklamarbetare och reklambyråer*. Lund: Studentlitteratur.

Alvesson, M. and Sköldberg, K. (1999) *Reflexive Methodology*. London: Sage.

Alvesson, M. and Willmott, H. (eds) (1992) *Critical Management Studies*. London: Sage.

Alvesson, M. and Willmott, H. (1995) 'Strategic management as domination and emancipation: from planning and process to communication and praxis', in C. Stubbart and P. Shrivastava (eds), *Advances in Strategic Management*. Vol. 11. Greenwich, CT: JAI Press.

Alvesson, M. and Willmott, H. (1996) *Making Sense of Management. A Critical introduction*. London: Sage.

Andriessen, E. and Drenth, P. (1984) 'Leadership: theories and models', in P. Drenth, H. Thierry, P.J. Willems and C.J. de Wolff (eds), *Handbook of Work and Organizational Psychology*. Vol. 1. Chichester: Wiley.

Angus, I. (1992) 'The politics of common sense: articulation theory and critical communication studies', in S. Deetz (ed.), *Communication Yearbook 15*. Newbury Park, CA: Sage.

Apel, K-O. (1979) *Toward a Transformation of Philosophy*. London: Routledge and Kegan Paul.

Asplund, J. (1970) *Om undran inför samhället*. Lund: Argos.

Astley, G. (1985) 'Administrative science as socially constructed truth', *Administrative Science Quarterly*, 30: 497–513.

Atkinson, P. and Hammersley, M. (1994) 'Ethnography and participant observation', in N. Denzin and Y. Lincoln (eds), *Handbook of Qualitative Research*. Thousand Oaks, CA: Sage.

Austin, J. (1961) *Philosophical papers*. (eds Urmson and Warnock) Oxford: Clarendon Press.

Barker, J. (1993) 'Tightening the iron cage: concertive control in self-managing teams', *Administrative Science Quarterly*, 38: 408–37.

Barley, S., Meyer, G.W. and Gash, D.C. (1988) 'Cultures of culture: academics, practitioners and the pragmatics of normative control', *Administrative Science Quarterly*, 22 (1): 24–60.

Baudrillard, J. (1975) *The Mirror of Production*. St. Louis, MO: Telos Press.

Baudrillard, J. (1983) *Simulations*. New York: Semiotext(e).

Baudrillard, J. (1988) 'Simulacra and simulations', in M. Poster (ed.), *Jean Baudrillard: Selected Writings*. Stanford, CA: Stanford University Press.

Baszanger, I. and Dodier, N. (1997) 'Ethnography: relating the part to the whole', in D. Silverman (ed.), *Qualitative Research*. London: Sage.

Benson, J.K. (1977) 'Organizations: a dialectical view', *Administrative Science Quarterly*, 22: 1–21.

Berg, P.O. (1989) 'Postmodern management? From facts to fiction in theory and practice', *Scandinavian Journal of Management*, 5: 201–17.

Berger, P., Berger, B. and Kellner, H. (1973) *The Homeless Mind: Modernization and Consciousness*. New York: Random House.

Bergquist, W. (1993) *The Postmodern Organization: Mastering the Art of Irreversible Change*. San Francisco, CA: Jossey-Bass.

Bernstein, R. (1984) *Beyond Objectivism and Relativism*. Philadelphia, PA: University of Pennsylvania Press.

Bernstein, R.J. (1983) *Beyond Objectivism and Relativism*. Oxford: Basil Blackwell.

Billing, Y.D. and Alvesson, M. (1994) *Gender, Managers and Organizations*. Berlin/New York: de Gruyter.

Blomqvist, M. (1994) *Könshierarkier i gungning. Kvinnor i kunskapsföretag*. Uppsala: Acta Universitatis Upsaliensis. Studia Sociologica Upsaliensia 39.

Boland, R. (1987) 'The in-formation of information systems', in R. Boland and R. Hirschheim (eds), *Critical Issues in Information Systems Research*. New York: Wiley.

Boorstin, D. (1961) *The Image*. New York: Atheneum.

Borgert, L. (1994) 'Contrasting images. An essay on the search for reflexivity in organizing and organization studies'. Unpublished paper. University College of Falun/Borlänge, Sweden.

Bourdieu, P. (1979) *Outline of a Theory of Practice*. Cambridge: Cambridge University Press.

Bourdieu, P. (1984) *Distinctions: A Social Critique of the Judgement of Taste*. Cambridge: Cambridge University Press.

Bourdieu, P. (1991) *Language and Symbolic Power*. Cambridge, MA: Harvard University Press.

Boyacigillar, N. and Adler, N. (1991) 'The parochial dinosaur: the organizational sciences in a global context', *Academy of Management Review*, 16: 262–90.

Braverman, H. (1974) *Labor and Monopoly Capital*. New York: Monthly Review Press.

Brown, R.H. (1977) *A Poetic for Sociology*. Chicago, IL: University of Chicago Press.

Brown, R.H. (1990) 'Rhetoric, textuality, and the postmodern turn in sociological theory', *Sociological Theory*, 8: 188–97.

Brown, R.H. (1994) 'Reconstructing social theory after the postmodern critique', in H. Simons and M. Billig (eds), *After Postmodernism. Reconstructing Ideology Critique*. London: Sage.

Bryman, A. (1996) 'Leadership in organizations', in S. Clegg, C. Hardy and W. Nord (eds), *Handbook of Organization Studies*. London: Sage.

Bryman, A. et al. (1988) 'Qualitative research and the study of leadership', *Human Relations*, 41 (1): 13–30.

Burawoy, M. (1979) *Manufacturing Consent*. Chicago, IL: University of Chicago Press.

Burawoy, M. (1985) *The Politics of Production: Factory Regimes under Capitalism and Socialism*. London: Verso.

Burke, K. (1969) *A Rhetoric of Motives*. Berkeley, CA: University of California Press.

Burrell, G. (1988) 'Modernism, postmodernism and organizational analysis 2: the contribution of Michel Foucault', *Organization Studies*, 9 (2): 221–35.

Burrell, G. (1994) 'Modernism, postmodernism and organizational analysis 4: the contribution of Jürgen Habermas', *Organization Studies*, 15: 1–19.

Burrell, G. and Morgan, G. (1979) *Sociological Paradigms and Organizational Analysis*. Aldershot: Gower.

Calás, M. and Smircich, L. (1987) 'Post-culture: is the organizational culture literature dominant but dead?' Paper presented at the 3rd International Conference on Organizational Symbolism and Corporate Culture, Milan, June 1987.

Calás, M. and Smircich, L. (1988) 'Reading leadership as a form of cultural analysis', in J.G. Hunt et al. (eds), *Emerging Leadership Vistas*. Lexington, MA: Lexington Books.

Calás, M. and Smircich, L. (1991) 'Voicing seduction to silence leadership', *Organization Studies*, 12: 567–602.

Calás, M. and Smircich, L. (1992a) 'Feminist theories and the social consequences of organizational research', in A. Mills and P. Tancred (eds), *Gendering Organizational Analysis*. London: Sage.

Calás, M. and Smircich, L. (1992b) 'Re-writing gender into organizational theorizing: directions from feminist perspectives', in M. Reed and M. Hughes (eds), *Re-thinking Organization: New Directions in Organizational Theory and Analysis*. London: Sage.

Carter, P. and Jackson, N. (1987) 'Management, myth, and metatheory – from scarcity to postscarcity', *International Studies of Management and Organization*, 17 (3): 64–89.

Castoriadis, C. (1992) 'Power, politics, autonomy', in A. Honneth et al. (eds), *Cultural–Political Interventions in the Unfinished Project of Enlightenment*. Cambridge, MA: MIT Press.

Chia, R. (1995) 'From modern to postmodern organizational analysis', *Organization Studies*, 16 (4): 579–604.

Clegg, S. (1989) *Frameworks of Power*. London: Sage.

Clegg, S. (1990) *Modern Organization. Organization Studies in the Postmodern World*. London: Sage.

Clegg, S. (1994) 'Weber and Foucault: social theory for the study of organizations', *Organization*, 1: 149–78.

Clegg, S. and Dunkerley, D. (1980) *Organization, Class and Control*. London: Routledge and Kegan Paul.

Clifford, J. (1986) 'Introduction: partial truths', in J. Clifford and G. Marcus (eds), *Writing Culture. The Poetics and Politics of Ethnography*. Berkeley, CA: University of California Press.

Clifford, J. and Marcus, G.E. (eds) (1986) *Writing Culture*. Berkeley, CA: University of California Press.

Collins, R. (1981) 'Micro-translation as a theory-building strategy', in K. Knorr-Cetina and A. Cicourel (eds), *Advances in Social Theory and Methodology*. Boston: Routledge and Kegan Paul.

Collins, R. (1988) 'The micro contribution to macro sociology', *Sociological Theory*, 6 (2): 242–53.

Collinson, D. (1992) 'Researching recruitment: qualitative methods and sex discrimination', in R. Burgess (ed.), *Studies in Qualitative Methodology. Vol. 3*. Greenwich, CT: JAI Press.

Cooper, R. (1989) 'Modernism, postmodernism and organizational analysis 3: the contribution of Jacques Derrida', *Organization Studies*, 10: 479–502.

Cooper, R. and Burrell, G. (1988) 'Modernism, postmodernism and organizational analysis: an introduction', *Organization Studies*, 9: 91–112.

Culler, J. (1983) *On Deconstruction*. London: Routledge and Kegan Paul.

Czarniawska-Joerges, B. (1988) *Ideological Control in Nonideological Organizations*. New York: Praeger.

Dahrendorf, R. (1959) *Class and Class Conflict in Industrial Society*. Stanford, CA: Stanford University Press.

Deal, T. and Kennedy, A. (1982) *Corporate Cultures. The Rites and Rituals of Corporate Life*. Reading, MA: Addison-Wesley.

Deetz, S. (1973) 'An understanding of science and a hermeneutic science of understanding', *Journal of Communication*, 23: 139–59.

Deetz, S. (1982) Critical-interpretive research in organizational communication, *Western Journal of Speech Communication*, 46 (2): 131–49.

Deetz, S. (1985) 'Critical-cultural research. New sensibilities and old realities', *Journal of Management*, 11 (2): 121–36.

Deetz, S. (1992) *Democracy in the Age of Corporate Colonization: Developments in Communication and the Politics of Everyday Life*. Albany, NY: State University of New York Press.

Deetz, S. (1994a) 'The future of the discipline: the challenges, the research, and the social contribution', in S. Deetz (ed.), *Communication Yearbook 17*. Newbury Park, CA: Sage.

Deetz, S. (1994b) 'Representative practices and the political analysis of corporations', in B. Kovacic (ed.), *Organizational Communication: New Perspectives*. Albany, NY: State University of New York Press.

Deetz, S. (1994c) 'The micro-politics of identity formation in the workplace: the case of a knowledge intensive firm', *Human Studies*, 17: 23–44.

Deetz, S. (1994d) 'The new politics of the workplace: ideology and other unobtrusive controls', in H. Simons and M. Billing (eds), *After Postmodernism: Reconstructing Ideology Critique*. Newbury Park, CA: Sage.

Deetz, S. (1995a) *Transforming Communication, Transforming Business: Building Responsible and Responsive Workplaces*. Cresskill, NJ: Hampton Press.

Deetz, S. (1995b) 'Transforming communication, transforming business: stimulating value negotiation for more responsive and responsible workplaces', *International Journal of Value-Based Management*, 8: 255–78.

Deetz, S. (1996) 'Describing differences in approaches to organizational science: rethinking Burrell and Morgan and their legacy', *Organization Science*, 7: 191–207.

Deetz, S. (1997) 'The business concept, discursive power, and managerial control in a knowledge-intensive company: a case study', in B. Sypher (ed.), *Case Studies in Organizational Communication*. 2nd edn. New York: Guilford Press.

Deetz, S. (1998) 'Discursive formations, strategized subordination, and self-surveillance: an empirical case', in A. McKinlay and K. Starkey (eds), *Foucault, Management and Organizational Theory*. London: Sage.

Deetz, S. and Kersten, A. (1983) 'Critical models of interpretive research', in L. Putnam and M. Pacanowsky (eds), *Communication and Organizations*. Beverly Hills, CA: Sage.

Deetz, S. and Mumby, D. (1990) 'Power, discourse, and the workplace: reclaiming the critical tradition in communication studies in organizations', in J. Anderson (ed.), *Communication Yearbook 13*. Newbury Park, CA: Sage.

Denzin, N. (1994) 'The art and politics of interpretation', in N. Denzin and Y. Lincoln (eds), *Handbook of Qualitative Research*. Thousand Oaks, CA: Sage.

Denzin, N. (1997) *Interpretive Ethnography*. Thousand Oaks, CA: Sage.

Denzin, N. and Lincoln, Y. (1994) 'Introduction: entering the field of qualitative research', in N. Denzin and Y. Lincoln (eds), *Handbook of Qualitative Research*. Thousand Oaks, CA: Sage.

Dingwall, R. (1997) 'Accounts, interviews and observations', in G. Miller and R. Dingwall (eds), *Context and Method in Qualitative Research*. London, Sage.

Donaldson, L. (1985) *In Defence of Organization Theory*. Cambridge: Cambridge University Press.

Easterby-Smith, M., Thorpe, R. and Lowe, A. (1991) *Management Research: An Introduction*. London: Sage.

Edwards, R. (1979) *Contested Terrain: The Transformation of the Workplace in the Twentieth Century*. New York: Basic Books.

Ehn, B. and Löfgren, O. (1982) *Kulturanalys*. Lund: Liber.

Enz, C. (1992) 'The culture of social science research', in P. Frost and R. Stablein (eds), *Doing Exemplary Research*. Thousand Oaks, CA: Sage.

Epstein, C. (1988) *Deceptive Distinctions*. New Haven, CT: Yale University Press.

Featherstone, M. (ed.) (1988) *Postmodernism*. Newbury Park, CA: Sage.

Ferguson, K. (1984) *The Feminist Case Against Bureaucracy*. Philadelphia, PA: Temple University Press.

Fetterman, D.M. (1989) *Ethnography. Step by Step*. Newbury Park, CA: Sage.

Fischer, F. (1990) *Technocracy and the Politics of Expertise*. Newbury Park, CA: Sage.

Fischer, F. and Sirianni, C. (eds) (1984) *Critical Studies in Organization and Bureaucracy*. Philadelphia, PA: Temple University Press.

Flax, J. (1990) *Thinking Fragments: Psychoanalysis, Feminism and Postmodernism in the Contemporary West*. Berkeley, CA: University of California Press.

Fontana, A. and Frey, J. (1994) 'Interviewing: the art of science', in N. Denzin and Y. Lincoln (eds), *Handbook of Qualitative Research.* Thousand Oaks, CA: Sage.

Forester, J. (1983) 'Critical theory and organizational analysis', in G. Morgan (eds), *Beyond Method.* Beverly Hills, CA: Sage.

Forester, J. (ed.) (1985) *Critical Theory and Public Life.* Cambridge, MA: MIT Press.

Forester, J. (1989) *Planning in the Face of Power.* Berkeley, CA: University of California Press.

Forester, J. (1992) 'Critical ethnography: on fieldwork in a Habermasian way', in M. Alvesson and H. Willmott (eds), *Critical Management Studies.* London: Sage.

Forester, J. (1993) *Critical Theory, Public Policy, and Planning Practice.* Albany, NY: State University of New York Press.

Foster, H. (1983) *Postmodern Culture.* London: Pluto.

Foucault, M. (1970) *The Order of Things.* New York: Random House.

Foucault, M. (1972) *The Archaeology of Knowledge.* Tr. A.S. Smith. New York: Pantheon.

Foucault, M. (1977) *Discipline and Punish: The Birth of the Prison.* Tr. A.S. Smith. New York: Random House.

Foucault, M. (1980a) *The History of Sexuality.* New York: Random House.

Foucault, M. (1980b) *Power/Knowledge.* New York: Pantheon.

Foucault, M. (1982) 'The subject and power', *Critical Inquiry,* 8: 777–95.

Foucault, M. (1983) 'Structuralism and post-structuralism: an interview with Michel Foucault', by G. Raulet, *Telos,* 55: 195–211.

Foucault, M. (1988) 'Technologies of the self', in L. Martin, H. Gutman and P. Hutton (eds), *Technologies of the Self.* Amherst, MA: University of Massachusetts Press.

Frank, R., Gulovich, T. and Regan, T. (1993) 'Does studying economics inhibit cooperation?', *Journal of Economic Perspectives,* 7: 159–171.

Fraser, N. (1987) 'What's critical about critical theory? The case of Habermas and gender', in S. Benhabib and D. Cornell (eds), *Feminism as Critique.* Cambridge: Polity Press.

Fraser, N. and Nicholson, L. (1988) 'Social criticism without philosophy: an encounter between feminism and postmodernism', *Theory, Culture and Society,* 5: 373–94.

Freire, P. (1970) *Pedagogy of the Oppressed.* New York: Herder and Herder.

Frost, P.J. (1980) 'Toward a radical framework for practicing organizational science', *Academy of Management Review,* 5: 501–7.

Frost, P.J. (1987) 'Power, politics, and influence', in F. Jablin, L. Putnam, K. Roberts and L. Porter (eds), *Handbook of Organizational Communication.* Newbury Park, CA: Sage.

Frost, P., Moore, L., Louis, M., Lundberg, C. and Martin, J. (eds) (1985) *Organizational Culture.* Beverly Hills, CA: Sage.

Frost, P., Moore, L., Louis, M., Lundberg, C. and Martin, J. (eds) (1991) *Reframing Organizational Culture.* Newbury Park, CA: Sage.

Gadamer, H. (1975) *Truth and Method.* Tr. G. Barden and J. Cumming. New York: Seabury.

Galbraith, J.K. (1958) *The Affluent Society.* Harmondsworth: Penguin.

Geertz, C. (1973) *The Interpretation of Cultures.* New York: Basic Books.

Geertz, C. (1983) *Local Knowledge.* New York: Basic Books.

Geertz, C. (1988) *Work and Lives: The Anthropologist as Author.* Cambridge: Polity Press.

Gergen, K. (1978) 'Toward generative theory', *Journal of Personality and Social Psychology,* 31: 1344–60.

Gergen, K. (1982) *Towards Transformation in Social Knowledge*. New York: Springer-Venlag.

Gergen, K. (1991) *The Saturated Self: Dilemmas of Identity in Contemporary Life*. New York: Basic Books.

Gergen, K. (1992) 'Organization theory in the postmodern era', in M. Reed and M. Hughes (eds), *Rethinking Organizations*. London: Sage.

Gergen, K. and Gergen, M. (1991) 'Toward reflexive methodologies', in F. Steier (ed.), *Research and Reflexivity*. London: Sage.

Giddens, A. (1979) *Central Problems in Social Theory*. London: Macmillan.

Giddens, A. (1984) *The Constitution of Society. Outline of the Theory of Structuration*. Cambridge: Polity Press.

Giddens, A. (1991) *Modernity and Self-Identity*. Cambridge: Polity Press.

Glaser, B.G. and Strauss, A.L. (1967) *The Discovery of Grounded Theory*. Chicago, IL: Aldine.

Gramsci, A. (1971) *Selections from the Prison Notebooks*. New York: International.

Gregory, K.L. (1983) 'Native-view paradigms. Multiple cultures and culture conflicts in organizations', *Administrative Science Quarterly*, 28: 359–76.

Grey, C. (1994) 'Career as a project of the self and labour process discipline', *Sociology*, 28: 479–97.

Grossberg, L. (1987) 'Critical theory and the politics of empirical research', in M. Gurevitch and M. Levy (eds), *Mass Communication Review Yearbook, Vol. 6*. Newbury Park, CA: Sage.

Guba, E. and Lincoln, Y. (1994) 'Competing paradigms in qualitative research', in N.K. Denzin and Y.S. Lincoln (eds), *Handbook of Qualitative Research*. Thousand Oaks, CA: Sage.

Habermas, J. (1970) *Toward a Rational Society*. London: Heinemann.

Habermas, J. (1971) *Knowledge and Human Interests*. London: Heinemann.

Habermas, J. (1975) *Legitimation Crisis*. Boston, MA: Beacon Press.

Habermas, J. (1983) 'Modernity – an incomplete project', in H. Foster (ed.), *Postmodern Culture*. London: Pluto Press.

Habermas, J. (1984) *The Theory of Communicative Action, Vol. 1: Reason and the Rationalization of Society*. Boston, MA: Beacon.

Habermas, J. (1987) *The Theory of Communicative Action, Vol. 2: Lifeworld and System*. Boston, MA: Beacon Press.

Hammersley, M. (1990) 'What is wrong with ethnography? The myth of theoretical description', *Sociology*, 24: 597–615.

Hamnett, M., Porter, D., Singh, A. and Kumar K. (1984) *Ethics, Politics and International Social Science Research*. Honolulu, Hawaii: East–West Center and University of Hawaii Press.

Hanson, N. (1965) *Patterns of Discovery*. Cambridge: Cambridge University Press.

Harding, S. (1991) *Whose Science? Whose Knowledge?* Ithaca, NY: Cornell University Press.

Hardy, C. and Clegg, S. (1997) 'Relativity without relativism: reflexivity in post-paradigm organization studies', *British Journal of Management*, 8 (6): 5–17.

Hassard, J. (1991) 'Multiple paradigms and organizational analysis: a case study', *Organization Studies*, 12: 275–99.

Hassard, J. and Parker, M. (eds) (1993) *Postmodernism and Organizations*. London: Sage.

Hawes, L. (1991) 'Organizing narratives/codes/poetics', *Journal of Organizational Change Management*, 4: 45–51.

Hearn, J. and Parkin, W. (1987) *'Sex' at 'Work'. The Power and Paradox of Organization Sexuality*. Brighton: Wheatsheaf Books Ltd.

Heckscher, C. (1995) *White-Collar Blues: Management Loyalties in an Age of Corporate Restructuring*. New York: Basic Books.

Hodge, H., Kress, G. and Jones, G. (1979) 'The ideology of middle management', in R. Fowler, H. Hodge, G. Kress and T. Trew (eds), *Language and Control*. London: Routledge and Kegan Paul.

Hollway, W. (1984) 'Fitting work: psychological assessment in organizations', in J. Henriques, W. Hallway, C. Urwin, C. Venn and V. Walkerdine (eds), *Changing the Subject*. New York: Methuen.

Hollway, W. (1989) *Subjectivity and Method in Psychology*. London: Sage.

Hollway, W. (1991) *Work Psychology and Organizational Behavior*. London: Sage.

Hopper, T. and Macintosh, N. (1993) Management accounting as disciplinary practice: the case of ITT under Harold Geneen, *Management Accounting Research*, 4: 181–216.

Hopwood, A. (1987) 'The archaeology of accounting systems', *Accounting, Organizations and Society*, 12: 207–34.

Hosking, D.M. (1988) 'Organizing, leadership and skilful process', *Journal of Management Studies*, 25 (2): 147–66.

House, R. and Aditya, R. (1997) 'The social scientific study of leadership: quo vadis?', *Journal of Management*, 23 (3): 409–73.

Hoy, D. (ed.) (1986) *Foucault. A Critical Reader*. Oxford: Basil Blackwell.

Huberman, M. and Miles, M. (1994) 'Data management and analysis methods', in N. Denzin and Y. Lincoln (eds), *Handbook of Qualitative Research*. Thousand Oaks, CA: Sage.

Husserl, E. (1962) *Ideas: General Introduction to Phenomenology*. London: Collier-Macmillan.

Ingersoll, V. and Adams, G. (1986) 'Beyond organizational boundaries: exploring the managerial myth', *Administration and Society*, 18: 360–81.

Jackall, R. (1988) *Moral Mazes. The World of Corporate Managers*. Oxford: Oxford University Press.

Jackson, J. (1995) '"Déjà Entendu": the liminal qualities of anthropological field-notes', in J. Van Maanen (ed.), *Representation in Ethnography*. Thousand Oaks, CA: Sage.

Jaggar, A.M. (1989) 'Love and knowledge', *Inquiry*, 32: 51–176.

Jameson, F. (1981) *The Political Unconscious: Narrative as a Social Symbolic Act*. Ithaca, NY: Cornell University Press.

Jeffcutt, P. (1993) 'From interpretation to representation', in J. Hassard and M. Parker (eds), *Postmodernism and Organizations*. London: Sage.

Jehenson, R. (1984) 'Effectiveness, expertise and excellence as ideological fictions: a contribution to a critical phenomenology of the formal organization', *Human Studies*, 7: 3–21.

Jermier, J. (1985) '"When the sleeper wakes". A short story extending themes in radical organization theory', *Journal of Management*, 11 (2): 67–80.

Johansson, O.L. (1990) *Organisationsbegrepp och begreppsmedvetenhet*. Göteborg: BAS.

Kellner, D. (1988) 'Postmodernism as social theory: some challenges and problems', *Theory, Culture and Society*, 5 (2–3): 239–69.

Kelly, G. (1955) *Psychology of Personal Constructs*. New York: Norton.

Kilduff, M. (1993) 'Deconstructing organizations', *Academy of Management Review*, 18: 13–31.

Knights, D. (1992) 'Changing spaces: the disruptive impact of a new epistemological location for the study of management', *Academy of Management Review*, 17: 514–36.

Knights, D. and Morgan, G. (1991) 'Corporate strategy, organizations, and subjectivity: a critique', *Organization Studies*, 12: 251–73.

Knights, D. and Willmott, H. (1985) 'Power and identity in theory and practice', *The Sociological Review*, 33: 22–46.

Knights, D. and Willmott, H. (1987) 'Organisational culture as management strategy', *International Studies of Management and Organization*, 17 (3): 40–63.

Knights, D. and Willmott, H. (1989) 'Power and subjectivity at work: from degradation to subjugation in social relations', *Sociology*, 23: 535–58.

Knights, D. and Willmott, H. (1990) *Labour Process Theory*. London: Macmillan.

Knights, D. and Willmott, H. (1992) 'Conceptualizing leadership processes: a study of senior managers in a financial services company', *Journal of Management Studies*, 29: 761–82.

Knorr-Cetina, K. (1981) 'Introduction. The micro-sociological challenge of macro-sociology: towards a reconstruction of social theory and methodology', in K. Knorr-Cetina and A. Cicourel (eds), *Advances in Social Theory and Methodology*. Boston: Routledge and Kegan Paul.

Kunda, G. (1992) *Engineering Culture: Control and Commitment in a High-Tech Corporation*. Philadelphia, PA: Temple University Press.

Kvale, S. (1996) *Inter-viewing*. London: Sage.

Laclau, E. and Mouffe, C. (1985) *Hegemony and Socialist Strategy*. Tr. W. Moore and P. Cammack. London: Verso.

Lasch, C. (1978) *The Culture of Narcissism*. New York: Norton.

Lasch, C. (1984) *The Minimal Self*. London: Picador.

Laurent, A. (1978) 'Managerial subordinacy', *Academy of Management Review*, 3: 220–30.

Law, J. (1994) *Organizing Modernity*. Oxford: Basil Blackwell.

Lazega, E. (1992) *Micropolitics of Knowledge: Communication and Indirect Control in Workgroups*. New York: Aldine de Gruyter.

Lehman, T. and Young, T. (1974) 'From conflict theory and conflict methodology', *Sociological Inquiry*, 44: 15–28.

Leidner, R. (1991) 'Serving hamburgers and selling insurance: gender, work, and identity in interactive service jobs', *Gender & Society*. 5 (2): 154–77.

Lincoln, Y. and Denzin, N. (1994) 'The fifth moment', in N. Denzin and Y. Lincoln (eds), *Handbook of Qualitative Research*. Thousand Oaks, CA: Sage.

Linstead, S. (1993) 'Deconstruction in the study of organizations', in J. Hassard and M. Parker (eds), *Postmodernism and Organizations*. London: Sage.

Linstead, S. and Grafton-Small, R. (1990) 'Theory as artefact: artefact as theory', in P. Gagliardi (ed.), *Symbols and Artefacts: Views of the Corporate Landscape*. Berlin/New York: de Gruyter.

Linstead, S. and Grafton-Small, R. (1992) 'On reading organizational culture', *Organization Studies*, 13: 331–55.

Lipman-Blumen, J. (1992) 'Connective leadership: female leadership styles in the 21st-century workplace', *Sociological Perspectives*, 35 (1): 183–203.

Lukács, G. (1971) *History and Class Consciousness*. Tr. R. Livingstone. Cambridge, MA: MIT Press.

Lukes, S. (1974) *Power: A Radical View*. London: Macmillan.

Lukes, S. (1978) *Authority and Power*, in T. Bottomore and R. Nisbet (eds), *A History of Sociological Analysis*. London: Heinemann.

Lyotard, J.-F. (1984) *The Postmodern Condition: A Report on Knowledge*. Minneapolis, MN: University of Minnesota Press.

Lyytinen, K. and Hirschheim, R. (1988) 'Information systems as rational discourse: an application of Habermas's theory of communicative action', *Scandinavian Journal of Management*, 4: 19–30.

Marcus, G. and Fischer, M. (1986) *Anthropology as Cultural Critique*. Chicago, IL: University of Chicago Press.

Marcuse, H. (1964) *One-dimensional Man*. Boston: Beacon Press.

Marcuse, H. (1968) *Negations*. Harmondsworth: Penguin.

Margolis, S. (1989) 'Postscript on modernism and postmodernism. Both', *Theory, Culture & Society*, 6: 5–30.

Martin, J. (1990a) 'Breaking up the mono-method monopolies in organizational analysis', in J. Hassard and D. Pym (eds), *The Theory and Philosophy of Organizations*. London: Routledge.

Martin, J. (1990b) 'Deconstructing organizational taboos: the suppression of gender conflict in organizations', *Organization Science*, 11: 339–59.

Martin, J. (1992) *The Culture of Organizations. Three Perspectives*. New York: Oxford University Press.

Martin, J. (1994) 'Methodological essentialism, false difference, and other dangerous traps', *Signs*, 19: 630–57.

Martin, J. (1995) 'The organization of exclusion: the institutionalization of sex inequality, gendered faculty jobs, and gendered knowledge in organizational theory and research', *Organization*, 1: 401–31.

Martin, P.Y. and Turner, B. (1986) 'Grounded theory and organizational research', *The Journal of Applied Behavioural Science*, 22 (2): 141–57.

Marx, K. (1964 [1844]) *Economic and political manuscripts of 1844*. Tr. M. Miligan. New York: International.

Marx, K. (1967 [1867]) *Das Kapital. Bd 1*. Berlin: Dietz.

McGrath, J., Kelly, J. and Rhodes, J. (1993) 'A feminist perspective on research methodology: some metatheoretical issues, contrasts and choices', in S. Oskamp and M. Costanzo (eds), *Gender Issues in Contemporary Society*. Newbury Park, CA: Sage.

Mills, C.W. (1940) 'Situated actions and vocabularies of motives', *American Sociological Review*, 5: 904–13.

Miller, J. and Glassner, B. (1997) 'The "inside" and the "outside": finding realities in interviews', in D. Silverman (ed.), *Qualitative Research*. London: Sage.

Mintzberg, H. (1975) 'The manager's job: folklore and fact', *Harvard Business Review*, July–August: 49–61.

Montagna, P. (1986) 'Accounting rationality and financial legitimation', *Theory and Society*, 15: 103–38.

Morgan, G. (1980) 'Paradigms, metaphors and puzzle solving in organization theory', *Administrative Science Quarterly*, 25: 605–22.

Morgan, G. (1986) *Images of Organization*. Newbury Park, CA: Sage.

Morgan, G. and Smircich, L. (1980) 'The case for qualitative research', *Academy of Management Review*, 5: 491–500.

Morrow, R. (1994) *Critical Theory and Methodology*. Thousand Oaks, CA: Sage.

Mumby, D.K. (1987) 'The political function of narrative in organizations', *Communication Monographs*, 54: 113–27.

Mumby, D. (1988) *Communication and Power in Organizations: Discourse, Ideology, and Domination*. Norwood, NJ: Ablex.

Mumby, D. and Putnam, L. (1992) 'The politics of emotion: a feminist reading of bounded rationality', *Academy of Management Review*, 17: 465–86.

Natter, W., Schatzki, T. and Jones III, J.P. (1995) *Objectivity and its Other*. New York: Guilford Publications.

Norén, L. (1990) *Om fallstudiens trovärdighet. FE-rapport*. Företagsekonomiska inst: Göteborgs Universitet.

Offe, C. and Wiesenthal, H. (1980) 'Two logics of collective action: theoretical notes on social class and organizational form', in M. Zeitlin (ed.), *Political Power and Social Theory, Vol. 1*. Greenwich, CT: JAI Press.

Ouchi, W.G. (1981) *Theory Z*. Reading: Addison-Wesley.

Parker, I. (1992) *Discourse Dynamics*. London: Routledge.

Parker, M. (1992) 'Post-modern organizations or postmodern organization theory?', *Organization Studies*, 13: 1–17.

Parker, M. (1993) 'Life after Jean-François', in J. Hassard and M. Parker (eds), *Postmodernism and Organizations*. London: Sage.

Parker, M. and McHugh, G. (1991) 'Five texts in search of an author: a response to John Hassard's "Multiple paradigms and organizational analysis"', *Organization Studies*, 13: 451–56.

Peters, T. (1987) *Thriving on Chaos*. New York: Alfred A. Knopf.

Pettigrew, A. (1985) *The Awakening Giant. Continuity and Change in Imperial Chemical Industries*. Oxford: Basil Blackwell.

Pfeffer, J. (1981a) 'Management as symbolic action: the creation and maintenance of organizational paradigms', in L.L. Cummings and B.M. Staw (eds), *Research in Organizational Behavior, Vol. 3*. Greenwich, CT: JAI Press.

Pfeffer, J. (1981b) *Power in Organizations*. Boston, MA: Pitman.

Pollay, R.W. (1986) 'The distorted mirror: reflections on the unintended consequences of advertising', *Journal of Marketing*, 50 (4): 18–36.

Potter, J. and Wetherell, M. (1987) *Discourse and Social Psychology. Beyond Attitudes and Behaviour*. London: Sage.

Power, M. (1994) 'The audit society', in A. Hopwood and P. Miller (eds), *Accounting as Social and Institutional Practice*. Cambridge: Cambridge University Press.

Power, M. and Laughlin, R. (1992) 'Critical theory and accounting', in M. Alvesson and H. Willmott (eds), *Critical Management Studies*. London: Sage.

Prasad, P. (1997) 'Systems of meaning: ethnography as a methodology for the study of information technologies', in A. Lee et al. (eds), *Information Systems and Qualitative Research*. London: Chapman & Hall.

Pringle, R. (1988) *Secretaries Talk: Sexuality, Power and Work*. London: Verso.

Putnam, L., Bantz, C., Deetz, S., Mumby, D., and Van Maanen, J. (1993) Ethnography versus critical theory, *Journal of Management Inquiry*, 2: 221–35.

Reason, P. (1994) 'Three approaches to participative inquiry', in Y. Lincoln and N. Denzin (eds), *Handbook of Qualitative Research*. Thousand Oaks, CA: Sage.

Ritzer, G. (1996) *The McDonaldization of Society*. Thousand Oaks, CA: Sage.

Rorty, R. (1979) *Philosophy and the Mirror of Nature*. Princeton, NJ: Princeton University Press.

Rorty, R. (1981) 'Hermeneutics and the social sciences'. Paper presented at the annual conference of the Society for Phenomenology and Existential Philosophy.

Rorty, R. (1982) *Consequences of Pragmatism*. Minneapolis, MN: University of Minnesota Press.

Rorty, R. (1989) *Contingency, Irony and Solidarity*. Cambridge: Cambridge University Press.

Rose, D. (1990) *Living the Ethnographic Life*. Newbury Park, CA: Sage.

Rosen, M. (1985) 'Breakfirst at Spiro's: dramaturgy and dominance', *Journal of Management*, 11 (2): 31–48.

Rosen, M. (1988) 'You asked for it. Christmas at the bosses' expense', *Journal of Management Studies*, 25 (5): 463–80.

Rosen, M. (1991) 'Coming to terms with the field: understanding and doing organizational ethnography', *Journal of Management Studies*, 28: 1–24.

Salaman, G. (1981) *Class and the Corporation*. Glasgow: Fontana.

Sangren, S. (1992) 'Rhetoric and the authority of ethnography', *Current Anthropology* (Supplement), 33: 277–96.

Sarup, M. (1988) *An Introductory Guide to Post-structuralism and Post-modernism*. Hemel Hempstead: Harvester Wheatsheaf.

Schaffer, S. (1989) 'Realities in the eighteenth century: nature's representatives and their cultural resources'. Paper presented at the Realism and Representation Conference, Rutgers University.

Schein, E. (1992) *Organizational Culture and Leadership*. 2nd edn. San Francisco, CA: Jossey-Bass.

Schwartzman, H. (1993) *Ethnography in Organizations*. Newbury Park, CA: Sage.

Scott, J. (1991) 'Deconstructing equality-versus-difference: or, the uses of poststructuralist theory for feminism', in M. Hirsch and E.F. Keller (eds), *Conflicts in Feminism*. New York: Routledge.

Seltzer, J. and Bass, B. (1990) 'Transformational leadership: beyond initiation and consideration', *Journal of Management*, 16: 693–703.

Shamir, B. (1991) 'Meaning, self and motivation in organizations', *Organization Studies*, 12: 405–24.

Shotter, J. (1993) *Conversational Realities: The Construction of Life through Language*. Newbury Park, CA: Sage.

Shotter, J. and Gergen, K. (eds) (1989) *Texts of Identity*. London: Sage.

Shotter, J. and Gergen, K. (1994) 'Social construction: knowledge, self, others, and continuing the conversation', in S. Deetz (ed.), *Communication Yearbook 17*. Newbury Park, CA: Sage.

Shrivastava, P. (1986) 'Is strategic management ideological?', *Journal of Management*, 12: 118–37.

Shrivastava, P. (1995) *Eco-centric Management*. Working paper: Bucknell University.

Sievers, B. (1986) 'Beyond the surrogate of motivation', *Organization Studies*, 7: 335–52.

Silverman, D. (1985) *Qualitative Methodology and Sociology*. Aldershot: Gower.

Silverman, D. (1989) 'Six rules of qualitative research: a post-romantic argument', *Symbolic Interaction*, 12 (2): 25–40.

Silverman, D. (1993) *Interpreting Qualitative Data*. London: Sage.

Silverman, D. (1994) 'On throwing away ladders: rewriting the theory of organisations', in J. Hassard and M. Parker (eds), *Toward a New Theory of Organizations*. London: Routledge.

Silverman, D. (1997) 'The logics of qualitative research', in G. Miller and R. Dingwall (eds), *Methods and Context in Qualitative Research*. London: Sage.

Simonds, A. (1989) 'Ideological domination and the political information market', *Theory and Society*, 18: 181–211.

Simons, H. (ed.) (1989) *Rhetoric in the Human Sciences*. London: Sage.

Sless, D. (1988) 'Forms of control', *Australian Journal of Communication*, 14: 57–69.

Smart, B. (1986) 'The politics of truth and the problem of hegemony', in D. Hoy (ed.), *Foucault: A Critical Reader*. Oxford: Basil Blackwell.

Smircich, L. (1983) 'Concepts of culture and organizational analysis', *Administrative Science Quarterly*, 28 (3): 339–58.

Smircich, L. (1985) 'Is organizational culture a paradigm for understanding organizations and ourselves?', in P.J. Frost et al. (eds), *Organizational Culture*. Beverly Hills, CA: Sage.

Smircich, L. and Calás, M. (1987) 'Organizational culture: a critical assessment', in F. Jablin, L. Putnam, K. Roberts and L. Porter (eds), *Handbook of Organizational Communication*. Newbury Park, CA: Sage.

Smircich, L. and Morgan, G. (1982) 'Leadership: the management of meaning', *The Journal of Applied Behavioural Science*, 18 (3): 257–73.

Stablein, R. and Nord, W. (1985) 'Practical and emancipatory interests in organizational symbolism', *Journal of Management*, 11 (2): 13–28.

Stead, W.E. and Stead, J.G. (1992) *Management for a Small Planet*. Newbury Park, CA: Sage.

Steffy, B. and Grimes, A. (1992) 'Personnel/organizational psychology: a critique of the discipline', in M. Alvesson and H. Willmott (eds), *Critical Management Studies*. London: Sage.

Steier, F. (1991) 'Reflexivity and methodology: an ecological constructionism', in F. Steier (ed.), *Research and Reflexivity*. London: Sage.

Storey, J. (1983) *Managerial Prerogative and the Question of Control*. London: Routledge & Kegan Paul.

Strauss, A. and Corbin, J. (1990) *Basics of Qualitative Research*. Newbury Park, CA: Sage.

Strauss, A. and Corbin, J. (1994) 'Grounded theory methodology: an overview', in N. Denzin and Y. Lincoln (eds), *Handbook of Qualitative Research*. Thousand Oaks, CA: Sage.

Tepperman, S. (1976) 'Organizing office workers', *Radical America*, 10 (1).

Therborn, G. (1980) *The Ideology of Power and the Power of Ideology*. London: New Left Books.

Thomas, J. (1993) *Doing Critical Ethnography*. Newbury Park, CA: Sage.

Thompson, J. (1984) *Studies in the Theory of Ideology*. Berkeley, CA: University of California Press.

Thompson, P. (1993) 'Post-modernism: fatal distraction', in J. Hassard and M. Parker (eds), *Postmodernism and Organizations*. London: Sage.

Thompson, J.B. and Held, D. (eds) (1982) *Habermas. Critical Debates*. London: Macmillan.

Tompkins, P. and Cheney, G. (1985) 'Communication and unobtrusive control in contemporary organizations', in R. McPhee and P. Tompkins (eds), *Organizational Communication: Traditional Themes and New Directions*. Newbury Park, CA: Sage.

Townley, B. (1993) 'Foucault, power/knowledge, and its relevance for human resource management', *Academy of Management Review*, 18: 518–45.

Trice, H.M. and Beyer, J.M. (1984) 'Studying organizational cultures through rites and ceremonies', *Academy of Management Review*, 9: 653–69.

Tunstall, J. (1964) *The Advertising Man in London Advertising Agencies*. London: Chapman & Hall.

Tyler, S. (1988) *The Unspeakable: Discourse, Dialogue, and Rhetoric in the Postmodern World*. Madison, WI: University of Wisconsin Press.

Vallas, S. (1993) *Power in the Workplace: The Politics of Production at AT&T*. Albany, NY: State University of New York Press.

Van Maanen, J. (1988) *Tales of the Field. On Writing Ethnography*. Chicago, IL: University of Chicago Press.

Van Maanen, J. (ed.) (1995) *Representation in Ethnography*. Thousand Oaks, CA: Sage.

Van Maanen, J. and Barley, S.R. (1985) 'Cultural organization. Fragments of a theory', in P.J. Frost et al. (eds), *Organizational Culture*. Beverly Hills, CA: Sage.

Vattimo, G. (1992) *The Transparent Society*. Baltimore, MD: Johns Hopkins University Press.

Veen, P. (1984) 'Characteristics of organizations', in P. Drenth et al. (eds), *Handbook of Work and Organizational Psychology*. Vol. 2. Chichester: Wiley.

Waltzer, M. (1986) 'The politics of Foucault', in D. Hoy (ed.), *Foucault: A Reader*. Oxford: Basil Blackwell.

Wagner, J. III. and Gooding, R. (1987) 'Effects of societal trends on participation research', *Administrative Science Quarterly*, 32: 241–62.

Watson, T. (1994) *In Search of Management*. London: Routledge.

Watson, T. (1995) 'Rhetoric, discourse and argument in organizational sense making: a reflexive tale', *Organization Studies*, 16: 805–21.

Watson, T. (forthcoming) 'Ethnographic fiction science', *Organization*.

Weedon, C. (1987) *Feminist Practice and Poststructuralist Theory*. Oxford: Basil Blackwell.

Weick, K.E. (1979) *The Social Psychology of Organizing*. 2nd edn. Reading, MA: Addison-Wesley.

Weick, K.E. (1985) The significance of corporate culture, in P. Frost et al. (eds), *Organizational Culture*. Beverly Hills: Sage.

Whyte, W. (ed.) (1991) *Participatory Action Research*. Thousand Oaks, CA: Sage.

Willmott, H. (1983) 'Paradigms for accounting research', *Accounting, Organizations and Society*, 8: 389–405.

Willmott, H. (1987) 'Studying managerial work: a critique and a proposal', *Journal of Management Studies*, 24: 248–70.

Willmott, H. (1990) 'Subjectivity and the dialectic of praxis: opening up the core of labour process analysis', in D. Knights and H. Willmott (eds), *Labour Process Theory*. London: Macmillan.

Willmott, H. (1993) 'Strength is ignorance; slavery is freedom: managing culture in modern organizations', *Journal of Management Studies*, 30 (4): 515–52.

Willmott, H. (1994) 'Bringing agency (back) into organizational analysis: responding to the crises of (post)modernity', in J. Hassard and M. Parker (eds), *Towards a New Theory of Organizations*. London: Routledge.

Willmott, H. and Knights, D. (1982) 'The problem of freedom. Fromm's contribution to a critical theory of work organization', *Praxis International*, 2: 204–25.

Wolcott, H. (1995) 'Making a study "more ethnographic"', in J. Van Maanen (ed.), *Representation in Ethnography*. Thousand Oaks, CA: Sage.

Yukl, G. (1989) 'Managerial leadership: a review of theory and research', *Journal of Management*, 15: 251–89.

Index